Start Your Own

RESTAURANT AND MORE

Additional titles in *Entrepreneur's* Startup Series

Start Your Own

Entrepreneur
MAGAZINE'S

start*up*

4TH EDITION

Start Your Own

RESTAURANT AND MORE

Pizzeria ◆ Coffeehouse
Deli ◆ Bakery
Catering Business

Entrepreneur Press and Jacquelyn Lynn

EP
Entrepreneur
PRESS®

Entrepreneur Press, Publisher
Cover Design: Beth Hansen-Winter
Production and Composition: Eliot House Productions

This publication is designed to provide accurate and authoritative information in regard
to the subject matter covered. It is sold with the understanding that the publisher is not
engaged in rendering legal, accounting or other professional services. If legal advice or
other expert assistance is required, the services of a competent professional person should
be sought.

Library of Congress Cataloging-in-Publication Data
Lynn, Jacquelyn.
    Start your own restaurant and more: pizzeria-coffeehouse-deli-bakery-catering
business/by Entrepreneur Press and Jacquelyn Lynn.—4th ed.
        p.   cm.
    Includes index.
    ISBN-13: 978-1-59918-443-2 (alk. paper)
    ISBN-10: 1-59918-443-5 (alk. paper)
        1. Restaurant management. 2. Food service management. 3. New business
enterprises. I. Entrepreneur Media, Inc. II. Title.
TX911.3.M27L9776 2012
647.95068—dc23   2012006075

Printed in the United States of America

16 15 14 13 12   10 9 8 7 6 5 4 3 2 1

Contents

Chapter 11
Inventory: Buying, Storing, and Tracking Supplies 153

Chapter 12
Structuring Your Business 163

Chapter 13
Locating and Setting Up Your Business 173

▲

Preface

Food is a basic need. Though tastes and trends change, technology advances and demographics shift, people always need to eat.

Now that doesn't mean that starting and running a profitable food-service business will be a proverbial piece of cake. Quite the contrary: This will probably be the hardest work you've ever done. But it has the potential to be tremendously rewarding, both financially and emotionally—and it can be lots of fun.

There are many ways you can enter the food-service industry, from buying a small coffee cart to building a high-end restaurant from the ground up. In this book, we examine six basic food-service businesses: a restaurant, a pizzeria, a sandwich shop/delicatessen, a coffeehouse, a bakery, and a catering business. It's important to remember that these aren't mutually exclusive businesses; they can be customized and combined to create the specific business you have in mind.

Perhaps you know exactly what type of food-service business you want to start, or perhaps you haven't made a final decision yet. Either way, it's a good idea to read all the chapters in this book—even those that pertain to businesses you think you aren't interested in. If you read with an open mind, you may get ideas from one type of operation that you can apply to another.

This book will give you the basic information you need to start a food-service business. You'll learn how to develop a business plan; what the day-to-day operation is like; how to set up your kitchen and dining area; how to buy and maintain equipment and inventory; how to deal with administrative, financial, personnel, and regulatory issues; and how to market your venture.

Because the best information about business comes from the people who are already in the trenches, we interviewed successful food-service business owners who were happy to share their stories. Their experiences span all types of food-service operations, and several of them are illustrating in practice that you can successfully blend more than one type of operation. Throughout the book, you'll read about what works—and doesn't—for these folks and how you can use their techniques in your own business.

You'll also learn what the food-service business is really like. The hours can be flexible, but they're usually long. The profit margins are good, but only if you're paying attention to detail. The market is tremendous, but you'll have a substantial amount of competition, which means you'll need a plan to set yourself apart. The opportunity to express yourself creatively is virtually limitless, but sometimes you'll have to do what the market demands—even if it's not your preference.

Like anything else, there's no magic formula, no quick path to success. Thriving in the food-service business takes hard work, dedication, and commitment. But it can be well worth the investment of your time, energy, and resources. After all, everybody's got to eat—including you.

Introduction to the Food-Service Business

As increasing numbers of consumers want to dine out or take prepared food home, the number of food-service operations in the United States has skyrocketed from 155,000 about 40 years ago to nearly 960,000 today. But there's still room in the market for your food-service business.

Shifting demographics and changing lifestyles are driving the surge in food-service businesses. Busy consumers don't have the time or inclination to cook. They want the flavor of fresh bread without the hassle of baking. They want tasty, nutritious meals without dishes to wash. In fact, the rise in popularity of to-go operations underscores clear trends in the food-service industry. More singles, working parents, dual-career families, and elderly people are demanding greater convenience when it comes to buying their meals.

Beware!
The three primary reasons why food-service businesses fail:

1. undercapitalization
2. poor inventory control
3. poor payroll management

Although the future looks bright for the food-service industry overall, there are no guarantees in this business. Even the most successful operators will tell you this isn't a "get rich quick" industry. It's more like a "work hard and make a living" industry. Paul Mangiamele, president and CEO of Bennigan's, says, "Although we all love it, this business is very difficult. It's a wonderful business, a great business, a satisfying business. It's a lucrative business. But there are a thousand moving parts, and you need to be knowledgeable of all of them."

A hard reality is that many restaurants fail during their first year, frequently due to a lack of planning. But that doesn't mean your food-service business has to be an extremely complex operation. In fact, the more streamlined you can make it, the better your chances for success. One restaurateur observed, "The restaurant business is a simple business that people make complicated." A basic formula for success is quality food, good service, and great people—an approach that's worked for all the restaurant owners you'll hear from in this book.

Who Are the Diners?

No single food-service operation has universal appeal. This is a fact that many newer entrepreneurs have trouble accepting, but the reality is that you will never capture 100 percent of the market. When you try to please everyone, you end up pleasing no one. So focus on the 5 or 10 percent of the market that you can get, and forget about the rest.

That said, who's eating at restaurants? Let's take a look at the main market categories of food-service business customers.

Generation Y

This generation, also tagged the "millennial generation," the "echo," or the "boomlet" generation, and sometimes called "Generation We," includes those born between 1980 and 2000. At least 75 million strong, Generation Y is the most ethnically diverse generation yet and is more than three times the size of Generation X. Gen Y teenagers have an average of $118 per week of disposable income, and 40 percent of them hold at least a part-time job. In terms of living arrangements, one in four lives in a single-parent household, and three out of four have working mothers. They're forming dining habits that will last a lifetime, and they're a prime market for food-service businesses. In fact, more than any other generation, they view prepared food as a staple, not a luxury. Even so, compared with older generations, they don't have as much money to spend on eating out. When choosing a restaurant, the top factors for Gen Y are low prices, great services, and proximity to home or job. They look for discounts and coupons.

Members of Generation Y go for fast-food and quick-service items. About 25 percent of their restaurant visits are to burger franchises, followed by pizza restaurants at 12 percent. In many ways, this group's food consumption behavior isn't significantly different than previous generations at the same age, but they do tend to be more experimental and open to extreme flavors. Another clear difference about them is that they love places where they can be wired in so they can go online, check email and social media, and play games while they eat. They also like restaurants where they feel they are welcome to stay as long as they like. They have a low threshold for boredom. They also like gadgets that will save them time and they're comfortable with technology, such as self-serve terminals for placing food orders. So if you're looking to attract Gen Y patrons, make your operation low cost and high interest.

Generation X

Generation X is a label applied to those who were born between 1965 and 1979. This group is known for strong family values. While earlier generations strove to do better financially than their parents, Gen Xers are more likely to focus on their relationship with their children. They are concerned with value, and they favor quick-service restaurants and midscale operations that offer all-you-can-eat salad bars and buffets. To appeal to this group, offer a comfortable atmosphere that focuses on value and ambience.

Baby Boomers

Born between 1946 and 1964, baby boomers make up the largest segment of the U.S. population. Prominent in this generation are affluent professionals who can afford to visit upscale restaurants and spend money freely. During the 1980s, they were the main consumer group for upscale, trendy restaurants. In the 1990s, many baby boomer families were two-income households with children. Today, those on the leading edge of the boomer

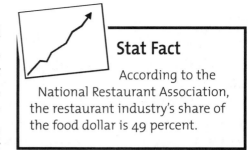

Stat Fact

According to the National Restaurant Association, the restaurant industry's share of the food dollar is 49 percent.

generation are becoming grandparents, making them a target of both restaurants that offer a family-friendly atmosphere and those that provide an upscale, formal dining experience. Many have become empty nesters—but others who thought they would be empty nesters at this point in their lives have seen their adult children return home to live and are caring for grandchildren. This is a tremendous demographic group that can't be reached with a one-size-fits-all product or marketing approach.

Empty Nesters

This group consists of people in the age range between the high end of the baby boomers and seniors (people in their early 50s to about age 64). Empty nesters typically have grown children who no longer live at home, and their ranks will continue to increase as the baby boomers grow older and their children leave home. With the most discretionary income and the highest per-capita income of all the generations, this group typically visits upscale restaurants. They're less concerned with price and are focused on excellent service and outstanding food. Appeal to this group with elegant surroundings and a sophisticated ambience.

Seniors

The senior market covers the large age group of those who are 65 and older. Generally, the majority of seniors are on fixed incomes and may not be able to afford upscale restaurants often, so they tend to visit family-style restaurants that offer good service and reasonable prices. "Younger" seniors are likely to be more active and have more disposable income than "older" seniors, whose health may be declining. Seniors typically appreciate restaurants that offer early-bird specials and senior menus with lower prices and smaller portions, since their appetites tend to be less hearty than those of younger people.

Stat Fact

Restaurants provide more than 70 billion meal and snack occasions each year.

Industry Trends

In the 1980s—by many accounts the decade of greed—new restaurants were typically upscale establishments that centered on unique and creative dishes by famous chefs. Young, professional baby boomers, often with liberal expense accounts, supported these concepts. The 1990s brought a trend to the restaurant industry that's continuing into the 21st century: an appreciation of value. There's no question that family-minded Generation Xers and baby boomers are concentrating on stretching their dollars.

Some other industry trends include:

- *Food trucks, carts, and kiosks.* Eating establishments no longer require customers to come to them. In many cases, the restaurant goes to the customer in the form of a food truck, cart, or kiosk. Many limited-service mobile facilities are operating at locations that attract large numbers of people, such as malls, universities, airports, sports stadiums, and arenas. These restaurants typically offer limited menus but attract customers with their recognizable names.

- *Co-branded operations.* Especially popular in the fast-food market, "co-branding," or "dual-branding," is when two or more well-known restaurants combine their menus in one location to offer customers a wider selection of items. The concept of co-branding began in the 1990s and continues to be a strong trend.

Behind the Angel-Hair Curtain

The typical American food-service business owner began his or her career in an entry-level position such as a busperson, dishwasher, or cook; works long hours; is energetic and entrepreneurial; and is usually more involved in charitable, civic, and political activities than the average American.

Although these traits are characteristic of restaurateurs, they're not required attributes. For example, some food-service business owners have entered their fields without any previous experience. They hire employees who have the experience they lack and who can help guide their operation to success. There is, however, no substitute for energy and a desire to succeed. Successful restaurateurs know they've chosen an industry where hard work is the norm, and they're willing to do what it takes to turn their dreams into reality.

- *Nutrition-conscious customers.* Restaurant-goers are showing a heightened interest in health and nutrition. Many are looking for low-fat dishes and fresh, locally sourced foods.

- *Popular menu items.* Barbecued foods and appetizers remain two of the most popular menu groups. Barbecue appears to satisfy customers seeking spicy foods and regional cuisines. Appetizer orders are increasing, thanks to customers who omit entrées and choose starters instead. Snack foods are growing in popularity. Customers are also increasingly looking for menu items that are compatible with weight-loss trends such as the low-carb, high-protein diets and Weight Watchers®. Another ingredient concern stems from food safety and ecological issues, and restaurants have responded with more natural and organic menu items, more local ingredients, and more sourcing information on the menu.

> ## Stat Fact
> More than 65 percent of restaurant customers agree that food served at their favorite restaurant provides flavor and taste sensations they cannot easily duplicate at home.
>
> An estimated 75 percent of restaurant-goers ask for alternative preparation methods, off-the-menu orders, and substitutions.

- *A focus on children.* Because many baby boomers still have children living at home and an increasing number of them are dining out with grandchildren, the majority of their restaurant experiences are family-oriented. Food-service operations wanting to reach this market are offering children's menus and children's value meals with smaller portions. Some offer child-friendly environments with booster seats, toys, balloons, crayons, menus featuring games on them, and even free table-side entertainment in the form of magicians and clowns.

- *Expanding the bar.* Restaurants want their guests to hang around, so they're offering more flavorful cocktails and savory appetizers, often available in bar areas designed for comfort and lingering. Classic, glamorous, old-fashioned cocktails have returned to popularity. And "mocktails"—nonalcoholic drinks with the same sophisticated flavors as the cocktail menu—are an attractive alternative for nondrinkers and designated drivers.

Menu Trends

As you put together a plan for your food-service business, be aware of some of the trends in terms of menu content and design. These factors could—and, in fact, should—influence the type of food-service business you open.

Restaurant operators report that vegetarian items, tortillas, locally grown produce, organic items, fusion dishes (combining two or more ethnic cuisines in one dish or on one plate), and microbrewed or local beers continue to be popular. Pita dishes and wraps are also in high demand as an easy-to-consume alternative to sandwiches. You'll also see a strong demand for bagels, espresso, and specialty coffees, as well as "real meals," which are typically an entrée with a side order. Other top menu trends include locally sourced meats and seafood, locally grown produce and co-op food sources, sustainability as a culinary theme, nutritious kids' dishes, hyper-local items, children's nutrition as a culinary theme, sustainable seafood, gluten-free and food allergy-conscious items, back-to-basics cuisine, and farm-branded ingredients.

Customers also are demanding "comfort food": the dishes that take them back to their childhoods, when mothers baked from scratch, and meat and potatoes were at the center of each plate. Creative chefs are looking for ways to redefine and reinvigorate comfort food favorites. Instead of the traditional version of shepherd's pie, for example, you might see one made with mushrooms, spinach, carrots, and lobster sauce.

Menus are also showing a number of ethnic dishes and spice-infused offerings. It's not surprising to find Thai, Vietnamese, Creole, Tuscan, and even classic French cuisines on the same menu and even on the same plate.

At the same time, be sure to keep the kids in mind as you plan your selections. If families are a key part of your target market, you'll want to offer a range of four or five items in smaller portions that youngsters will enjoy, such as a half-portion of pasta or small hamburger. If you serve snack items as well as entrées, note that kids are choosing healthier snacks more often than they did a few years ago, thanks to concerned parents. For example, while both sweet and salty snacks remain popular, the top snack foods consumed by kids between ages 2 and 17 are: yogurt; potato chips; fresh fruit; string cheese, prepackaged cheese cubes, cheese shapes; hard candy; ice, fudge, and cream pops; chewy candy; corn chips; doughnuts; snack pies and pastries. About 40 percent of snacks are eaten with or instead of main meals. While most restaurants still offer fixed kids' meals, you might consider allowing your young diners to choose among a selection of nutritious options.

Though menu variety has increased over the years, menus themselves are growing shorter. Busy consumers don't want to

Bright Idea

Combine two or more types of food-service businesses for maximum profitability. For example, Cuisine Unlimited caterer Maxine Turner's Salt Lake City operation, is a combination upscale catering business and delicatessen. The businesses complement each other; deli customers often use the catering service, and catering customers visit the deli.

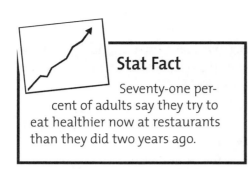

Stat Fact

Seventy-one percent of adults say they try to eat healthier now at restaurants than they did two years ago.

read a lengthy menu before dinner; dining out is a recreational activity, so they're in the restaurant to relax. Keep the number of items you offer in check, and keep menu descriptions simple and straightforward, providing customers with a variety of choices in a concise format. However, even as you keep your food offerings concise, consider the growing trend of storytelling on menus—information about the history of the restaurant as well as details on food preparation, origin, and health benefits.

Your menu should indicate whether dishes can be prepared to meet special dietary requirements. Items low in fat, sodium, and cholesterol should also be marked as such.

Most large chains do a significant amount of market research before adding new items to their menus. Occasional visits to popular chain outlets (or just paying attention to their ads or visiting their websites) can help you benefit from their investment. For example, Applebee's has teamed up with Weight Watchers International to develop menu items for diners who are counting "points." A number of restaurants offer low-carb items for customers on programs such as Atkins and South Beach. Seasons 52, which changes its menu every week, offers nutritionally balanced, lower-calorie items and desserts in bite-size portions. This follows the growing trend of seasonal menus and smaller portions, including "mini food," such as small sandwiches and desserts that are just a few bites. These items are often served on smaller plates to enhance the presentation. When P.F. Chang's China Bistro sponsored a marathon, it also created special high-carb, high-protein entrées for participating athletes. Even the fast-food outlets, which aren't known for nutritious fare, are offering healthier options.

Another trend growing in popularity is the offering of sharable items, such as appetizers that can be shared by the entire party and half portions of entrée items. We're also seeing increased flexibility in restaurant dayparts; the traditional set times for breakfast, lunch, and dinner are a thing of the past in our 24/7 world. In particular, offering breakfast any time of the day is rapidly becoming the new standard. Pay attention to these trends, and adjust your own menu when the market demands it.

Even as you consider trends, create your own signature dishes to distinguish your operation. Stefano LaCommare, owner of Stefano's Trattoria in Winter Springs, Florida, uses family recipes, dishes he remembers from when he was growing up in Italy. He'll sometimes change them slightly, resulting in a meal that no one else can offer, and that keeps his customers coming back.

Understanding Takeout Customers

Research conducted by the National Restaurant Association indicates off-premises consumption of restaurant food is on the rise. Of respondents to a survey conducted by the organization, 21 percent who use off-premises restaurant services purchase one or more such meals a day; 26 percent purchase off-premises meals every other day; 22 percent purchase them about twice a week; and 31 percent buy them less than once a week.

Stat Fact
The most popular items on children's menus are:

1. Chicken nuggets or strips
2. French fries
3. Hamburgers
4. Pasta
5. Grilled cheese sandwiches
6. Hot dogs
7. Pizza
8. Fish sticks
9. Cookies
10. Shrimp
11. Pancakes
12. Milkshakes

Fast-food restaurants (operations that prepare food quickly) represent the largest share of off-premises dining, followed by carryout restaurants (operations that target the off-premises diner either in part or exclusively). However, full-service establishments are increasing their takeout services. A growing number are allowing diners to call in their order and a description of their car and then delivering the food to them in a designated parking area. What motivates consumers to buy prepared food to consume elsewhere? Mainly, they're in a hurry and want easy access, fast service, and reasonable prices. Another reason is that they're just too tired to shop for and prepare food themselves. Often, consumers looking for a special treat are inclined to buy takeout food, particularly ice cream, snacks, and gourmet coffees. Another strong motivator of takeout customers is the desire to eat something that's good for them. These people tend to order takeout from full-service restaurants. They also get takeout items from grocery stores and cafeterias or buffets with tasty, fresh foods. Interestingly, studies show that takeout consumption increases during times of national crisis, when people are hungry for information and want to get home to their TVs as quickly as possible.

Where's the Competition?

Competition in the food-service industry is widespread, varied, and significant. When you open a restaurant, you'll be competing not only with other similarly themed restaurants but also with every restaurant in the area you serve. In addition, your customers themselves are a form of competition, because they can make their own meals at home if they choose. Let's take a closer look at the primary competition categories.

Chains

Chain restaurants may be the biggest threat to independent operators. Chains are growing as private companies and franchises take over a greater portion of the market. With well-known names and large advertising budgets, chains enjoy significant consumer recognition.

Dollar Stretcher

You don't have to prepare every item you serve from scratch. To increase productivity, more food-service businesses are offering menu items that are either fully or partially prepared off premises. Bread is the most commonly purchased prepared item, but a significant number of operators also purchase pre-portioned meats, prepared desserts, soups, and sauce bases. You can also purchase pre-chopped salads.

What these restaurants don't offer is the personalized attention that many small, independent operations provide—so this is where independent restaurants have an advantage. Many restaurateurs become acquainted with their regular customers and build relationships with them. This isn't to say that chains don't offer personalized service—indeed, many of them excel in this area. But there's a difference when customers know they're dealing directly with the owner.

Independent restaurants have several other competitive advantages over chains. For one thing, independently owned fine-dining establishments are often willing to take reservations, while chains usually aren't. Independents may also offer live music, experienced chefs (rather than just basic cooks), and creative foods and beverages. While chains have the advantage of a well-known name, many independents offer the atmosphere customers prefer.

Supermarkets and Convenience Stores

Supermarkets and convenience stores are fairly recent competitors for restaurants. These businesses offer customers food that's freshly prepared and ready to go—although not always healthy. Their menus typically include fried chicken, sandwiches, side dishes, salads, and desserts. The primary concern of customers who visit these establishments is convenience, so supermarkets and convenience stores offer serious competition to quick-service

Stat Fact

The restaurant industry's sales equal 4 percent of the U.S. gross domestic product.

restaurants that also compete on the basis of convenience and value. In fact, an increasing number of consumers are using convenience stores and quick-service restaurants interchangeably.

Eating at Home

Dining out isn't a necessity for most people. Restaurants, like other service businesses, sell convenience: They perform a task that consumers could otherwise handle themselves. Some consumers perceive dining out as something to do only on special occasions, which may be the attitude of a large portion of upscale restaurant customers. Quick-service and midscale restaurants must appeal to value- and time-conscious consumers. They must stress how eating out can save customers the time and trouble of cooking and how customers can relax while they eat and not worry about cleaning up afterward.

Restaurant Operations

Owning a food-service business may seem like an entrepreneurial dream come true. Even the smallest operations have an element of glamour: On the surface, it looks like the owners make their living greeting guests and serving meals while becoming recognizable figures in the community. And as more celebrities enter the food-service industry, they add to the restaurant business's image as an exciting, lucrative opportunity.

But dealing graciously with customers and playing the role of elegant host is only part of a restaurateur's many duties. Food-service business operators spend most of their time developing menus; ordering inventory and supplies; managing personnel; creating and implementing marketing campaigns; making sure their operation complies with a myriad of local, state, and federal regulations; completing lots of paperwork; and doing other administrative chores. Certainly the financial opportunities are there—as are the fun aspects of the business. But starting, running, and growing a food-service business is also hard work.

Regardless of the type of food-service business you intend to start, the best way to learn is to work for a similar operation for a while before striking out on your own. Doing so will give you significant insight into the realities and logistics of the business.

Jim Amaral, founder of Borealis Breads in Portland, Maine, started working in bakeries when he was 15. "I worked my way up from washing pots and pans to frying doughnuts to doing the basic retail bakery stuff," he recalls. Today, he owns a bakery that specializes in sourdough breads and brings in more than $10 million a year in both wholesale and retail business out of multiple locations in Maine.

Another restaurateur who started in the business at the age of 15 is Scott Redler. "As soon as I started working in a restaurant, I realized this was my passion," he says. "The energy level of a restaurant—there's nothing like it in the world. When you have a busy restaurant, and you're watching everything happen as it should, it's just a wonderful feeling of satisfaction. You're making people smile." After working in various restaurants for 11 years, he opened a Chinese fast-food place at the age of 26. That venture failed within eight months, then Redler went to work for a large restaurant company, where he eventually advanced to the position of senior vice president, overseeing 15 operations. But he still yearned for his own place, so he developed the concept that became Timberline Steakhouse & Grill in Kansas (which he sold in 2011). He recognized that the fast, casual segment was gaining momentum, so he created Freddy's Frozen Custard, which offers hot dogs, hamburgers, and (as you might expect) frozen custard. Freddy's Frozen Custard is now a franchise operation with 60 stores in nine states.

Ann Crane took a more direct path to restaurant entrepreneurship. For 15 years, she worked for Meyerhof's & Cuisine M, a catering business in Irvine, California. When the owner passed away, Crane bought the company from the heirs.

Stat Fact
Lunch is the most popular meal for people to eat away from home. Popular lunch items include hamburgers, wraps, salads, soups, and ethnic foods.

Originally from Marsala, Italy, Stefano LaCommare began his career cooking for the crew on his father's commercial fishing boat. He came to the United States in 1974 and opened his first restaurant in New York in 1982. He sold that restaurant and moved to Florida in 1989, where he went to work as the chef for a family-owned Italian restaurant. Wanting to be in business for himself, he offered to buy that restaurant. The family refused, so LaCommare resigned and opened the first Stefano's Trattoria in Winter Park, Florida, in 1994. He sold that restaurant, opened another under a different name (the original Stefano's was still operating under its new owner; it later went out of business, so he was able to use the name again), sold that one, and then opened his current Stefano's Trattoria in Winter Springs in 2006.

Closed for Business

If you have a retail food-service business, you may find you don't have time to spruce up your facility during the year. For this reason, many independent restaurants close for one to two weeks every year so the owners can look over their facilities and make necessary changes. They may add a fresh coat of paint, repair ripped upholstery, and inspect all the equipment. Since there are no customers or employees in the facility, repair people can work quickly and without interruption. This annual closing period also allows employees to take vacations.

To maintain good relations with your customers, give them advance notice of your upcoming closure. Post a sign on your door stating the dates during which you'll be closed and the date you'll reopen. The same information should be posted on your website and social media pages. If you maintain an email list, send an email blast notifying customers of the dates you'll be closed and another when you re-open. Record an outgoing message on your answering machine or voice mail with the same information. While you're closed, check your answering machine or voice mail regularly in case a supplier or anyone else needs to get in touch with you or someone on your staff.

Generally, restaurants close during the slowest time of the year, when the closing will have the least impact on revenue and customers. Of course, if you're a seasonal operation, you can take care of major maintenance and updates when you're closed during the off-season.

▲

Paul Mangiamele grew up in the restaurant business, working for quarters in his uncle's New York trattoria when he was a youngster. Through high school and college, he bussed tables, washed dishes, served, bartended, and learned the entire operation. After college, he worked for a number of large restaurant companies and owned his own franchised outlets. Today, he is the president and CEO of Bennigan's.

When Brian Neel was looking for work during his freshman year in college, he landed a job as a dishwasher at a Melting Pot Restaurant. He worked there all through college, moving from dishwasher to other kitchen work, serving, and eventually managing. After graduating college, he appraised real estate during the day and managed the restaurant at night. Two years later, he bought his first Melting Pot franchise and today he owns ten of them in five states.

Sam Mustafa's restaurant career began when he was 19, failing out of Southern Illinois University, and took a series of jobs at fast-food restaurants. He learned that he loved the business but didn't like working for someone else. His first restaurant was Sam's Café, located on the college's campus. After graduation, Mustafa opened a number of other restaurants around the SIU campus before moving to Charleston, South Carolina, in 2000. Today his company is Charleston Hospitality Group, LLC, which is the umbrella for four restaurants, a catering operation, a limousine company, and a bakery.

As you can see, there are several ways to get started in the food-service business. You can purchase a franchise, build an independent operation from the ground up, buy an existing operation, or lease space in an existing structure. Each approach has its advantages and disadvantages, which you need to consider carefully before making a final decision (Chapter 13 discusses these options in detail). But regardless of how you get started, there are some things you need to know about operations that are common to virtually all types of food-service businesses.

Setting Hours of Operation

Your hours of operation will vary depending on the particular type of food-service business you have. Ultimately, it's up to you to determine the hours for your business.

Most quick-service restaurants are open for lunch, dinner, and the post-dinner crowd. Typically, they open at 10:30 or 11 A.M. and close anywhere between 9 and 11 P.M. Some national fast-food franchises and chains also serve breakfast and open as early as 6 A.M. Others stay open until well past midnight on weekends, and some are open 24 hours a day.

The hours of midscale and upscale restaurants vary depending on the concept. A restaurant that offers only a buffet will most likely not serve breakfast and may only be open from 11 A.M. to 9 P.M. Many family-style restaurants, on the other hand, specialize in serving breakfast and typically open at 6 A.M. They continue serving meals until after dinnertime, closing around 9 P.M.

Casual-dining restaurants tend to cater to the lunch and dinner crowds. These establishments open around 11 A.M. and stay open late, especially on weekends, to appeal to the post-dinner crowd. During the week, they tend to close at 10 or 11 P.M. On Fridays and Saturdays, they may stay open until midnight or 1 A.M.

Often, upscale restaurants that only serve dinner are only open from 4:30 or 5 P.M. to 9 or 10 P.M. These businesses are able to survive on dinner sales alone because they have found a concept that works, and they're sticking with it. Most full-service restaurants, however, are open for both lunch and dinner, six or seven days a week. Those that are only open six days a week usually close on either Sunday or Monday.

Hours vary somewhat among full-service restaurants. If you open such a restaurant and don't plan to offer cocktail service, start off with a split-shift operation: Open for lunch from 11 A.M. to 2 P.M. and then open for dinner from 4:30 to 9 P.M. each day. If you decide to serve cocktails, you could keep the same dinner hours but serve appetizers and drinks at all hours, say from 11 A.M. to 11 P.M. If you have just a beer-and-wine bar, as opposed to a full bar, the split-shift system can work well.

Sandwich shops, delicatessens, and pizzerias are typically open for lunch and dinner six or seven days a week. Hours vary depending on location and market, but most open from 10 or 11 A.M. to 6 or 8 P.M. (for sandwich shops) or as late as 11 P.M. or midnight (for pizzerias and full-service delis).

Commercial bakeries begin baking the day's products as early as 2 or 3 A.M.; some even operate 24 hours a day. Retail bakeries and coffeehouses tend to open early enough to capture the breakfast crowd.

Caterers typically have an office staffed during normal business hours, perhaps 8 or 9 A.M. to 5 P.M. The actual hours people work depend, of course, on their particular jobs and span all hours of the day and all days of the week.

Scheduling Employees

When you'll need employees to report to work depends a great deal on the type of food-service business you have. As a general guide for restaurants, the first person to arrive in the morning should be your head cook or chef—the person responsible for the kitchen. He or she should arrive a few hours before the restaurant opens to begin preparing the side dishes that you will serve throughout the day. These items can include soups, vegetables, sauces, homemade breads or biscuits, rice, and generally anything else you might serve in large quantities over a span of several hours. The preparation of side dishes should be completed 30 minutes before the doors open for business.

The head chef or cook might also be responsible for accepting and inspecting deliveries, or, if you prefer, your manager or assistant manager can arrive at the same time to take care of paperwork and deliveries. If

Smart Tip

Be around and visible. Of course, large chain restaurants are run by managers, and you may want to hire managers to help you run your operation. But most successful independent food-service operations have an owner who works in the business every day. They're in touch with their customers and their employees, they know what's going on in the day-to-day operation, and they're available to make decisions as needed.

your head cook comes in before opening, he or she should be able to leave after the lunch or dinner crowd has been served, with the second cook carrying on until closing. The second cook will be responsible for cleaning the kitchen so it's ready for the next morning.

Your dining room manager, maitre d', or chief host or hostess should arrive 30 minutes to an hour before opening to make sure that everything in the front of the house is in order. This will allow time for him or her to check the dining room table settings, napkins, salt and pepper shakers, and any other elements that will make the front room more presentable to the public.

The person in charge of these front-of-the-house pre-opening chores can work through the lunch hour and dinner hour, if you serve both meals, or from the dinner hour through closing if you only serve dinner. This employee can also close out the cash register.

The bar manager should also come in 30 minutes before the restaurant opens for business. He or she will be responsible for the appearance of the lounge area, stocking the bar and keeping track of liquor inventory, making sure free bar snacks are out, and preparing to open the bar.

The bar manager will also likely be your chief bartender. This person will continue working through the early-evening shift, and your second bartender will usually handle the late-evening crowds. Because weekend evenings are the busiest for both bars and restaurants, schedule your bar manager to work Tuesday through Saturday to cover the most hectic times. In addition to the bar manager, one or two part-time bartenders can assist with the weekend crowd.

Service Procedures

Regardless of how formal or casual your operation is, your goal should be to treat customers like royalty, and you can meet this goal by providing strong, professional service from the moment your customers walk in the door. Because your team of employees will be responsible for how well your customers are treated, they should reflect the policies you've established as the owner.

Uniforms will help develop a sense of identity and pride among your staff, as well as project a professional image. All employees who work at the same level should wear an identical uniform. For example, all buspersons should wear the same uniform, and everyone on your waitstaff should wear the same uniform.

Set standards for your business's appearance. Everything from the restrooms to your plates and utensils should receive the same careful consideration. If you find spots on your glassware or plates, then you've failed to meet high standards. If toilet tissue and towels are strewn about the restrooms, then you've failed to meet high standards. If you want to create a dining experience that people will remember, make it a good one.

The actual service should range from polite to ingratiating. The host or hostess should greet customers with a cheerful hello and ask how many people are in the party and whether they prefer smoking or nonsmoking (unless you're located in an area that prohibits smoking in restaurants). If a line forms, or if all the tables are full, the host or hostess should take customers' names and let them know how long they should expect to wait. Unless you take reservations, customers should be seated on a first-come, first-served basis. If you have a bar, give customers the option of waiting there. Make menus available to people who are waiting so they can be thinking about what they'd like to order.

Once customers are seated, promptly present them with a menu and inform them that their server will be with them in a moment. The busperson should fill their water glasses immediately (unless you're in an area with water restrictions). When the server arrives, the first thing he or she should do is inquire if the customers would like anything before ordering their meals, such as a beverage or an appetizer.

After giving customers time to review the menu, the server should come back to answer questions and take meal orders. The server should be thoroughly familiar

Smart Tip

Tip...

To build a profitable food-service business, you need systems. Approach your operation with the understanding that regardless of how creative or fun it might be, it's a business, and successful businesses are built on systems that produce consistent, reliable results.

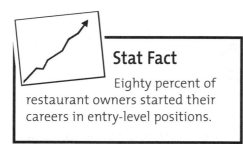

Stat Fact

Eighty percent of restaurant owners started their careers in entry-level positions.

with the menu and any specials. All orders should be recorded on a check and should be repeated back to customers to make sure they're correct.

Servers should remove food from the left and beverages from the right and should never reach in front of a customer to serve or remove anything.

The waitstaff and buspersons should always be in their stations checking to make sure customers have everything they need for a satisfying meal. They should refill water glasses regularly, supply the necessary condiments, and ask if the food is satisfactory after customers have had time to start eating. After the guests have finished their entrées, servers should ask if they would like dessert or coffee. When the server is sure the customer is finished with the meal, the check should be presented. However, a number of casual dining restaurants will leave the check shortly after serving the entrée, assuring the customers that they are not being rushed and returning to the table regularly to fill any additional requests.

If there has been a service failure of any sort, even an unavoidable one, do your best to make amends, perhaps with a free dessert or after-dinner drink. If a customer complains about a particular dish, offer to replace the item at no charge. Above all, never argue with a customer. When you do, even if you win, you lose, because chances are that customer will never return, and you will have created negative word-of-mouth advertising that might prevent other customers from visiting your establishment.

When They Don't Come In

Many restaurants offer drive-thru service. Lunch is the most frequently purchased meal in the drive-thru lane, and 53 percent of meals purchased at drive-thru windows are typically eaten at home, not in the car. Households with children typically use drive-thrus more than those without.

There's more to creating an efficient drive-thru than just setting up a window in your building and a lane in your parking lot. Consider this: For every 10 seconds saved serving drive-thru customers, you can add $1,000 in incremental sales.

To keep the line moving quickly, have a clear, easy-to-read menu board positioned before the ordering station. Assure accuracy by having employees confirm each order before the customer proceeds to the payment/pickup window. To speed up payment, have the customer's change ready before he or she gets to the payment window.

Some municipalities restrict drive-thrus due to environmental concerns. Before you plan for a drive-thru, check with the local planning and zoning board to be sure it will be allowed.

Cleaning Your Facility

At the end of every business day, you must clean your facility. You can either have your staff or an outside commercial cleaning service handle this task. Your cooks can clean the grill and mop the floor after closing. The waitstaff and buspersons can refill condiments and clean the tables, booths, and floors in the dining area. The dishwasher should finish the day's dishes and restock dishes for the cooks and waitstaff.

If you can't afford to pay your employees to complete all these duties or would simply prefer not to, a commercial cleaning service can take care of them. For a set fee, a cleaning service will visit your restaurant every night after the employees have left. They can clean the entire restaurant, including the kitchen, wait stations, dining area, and restrooms. If you decide to use a cleaning service, ask for references and check out the company before making a final decision. It's also a good idea to find out what cleaning products they use. You wouldn't want someone to clean the grills with the same product they use to clean the restrooms. A growing number of janitorial and commercial cleaning services are expanding to target the restaurant market. Ask other restaurant owners for recommendations, or check your telephone directory for companies.

Details on operational issues relating to specific types of food-service businesses are explained in later chapters.

Developing Your Business Plan

Whether you've got years of food-service experience behind you or you're a novice in the industry, you need a plan for your business—and you need to have it in place before you buy the first spoon or crack the first egg. This chapter will focus on a few issues pertaining to food-service businesses, but they are by no means all you need to consider when writing your business plan.

Many entrepreneurs view writing a business plan with even less enthusiasm than they had for homework when they were in school. But if you're excited about your business, creating a business plan should be an exciting process. It will help you define and evaluate the overall feasibility of your concept, clarify your goals, and determine what you'll need for startup and long-term operations.

This is a living, breathing document that will provide you with a road map for your company. You'll use it as a guide, referring to it regularly as you work through the startup process and then during operation of your business. And if you're going to be seeking outside financing, either in the form of loans or investors, your business plan will be the tool that convinces funding sources of the worthiness of your venture.

Putting together a business plan is not a linear process, although looking at the final product may make it seem that way. As you work through it, you'll likely find yourself jumping from menu development to cash flow forecasts to staffing, then back to cash flow, on to marketing, and back to menu development. Take your time developing your plan. Whether you want to start a coffee-and-snack cart or a gourmet restaurant, you're making a serious commitment, and you shouldn't rush into it.

Carving Your Niche

Before you can begin serious business planning, you must first decide what specific segment of the food-service industry you want to enter. While there are many commonalities among the variety of food-service businesses, there are also many differences. And while there is much overlap in the knowledge and skills necessary to be successful, your own personality and preferences will dictate whether you choose to open a commercial bakery, a coffee cart, a fine-dining restaurant, or another type of operation. Then, once you've decided what business best suits you, you must figure out what niche you'll occupy in the marketplace.

Chances are you already have a pretty good idea of the type of food-service business that appeals to you. Before you take the actual plunge, read through the chapters that describe the various operations and see if they suit your particular working style.

> **Beware!**
> When you make a change to one part of your business plan, be sure you think through how that change will affect the rest of your operation. For example, if you decide to add more items to your menu, do you need to change your kitchen setup to accommodate them? Or if your original plan was to offer limited service where customers ordered and picked up their food at a counter, but you have now decided to take the food to the tables, how will that affect your staffing plans?

For example, are you an early riser, or do you prefer to stay up late and sleep late? If you like—or at least don't mind—getting up before dawn, your niche may be a bakery or a casual breakfast-and-lunch operation. Night owls are going to be drawn to the hours required for bar-and-grill types of restaurants, fine-dining establishments, and even pizzerias.

Do you like dealing with the public, or are you happier in the kitchen? If you're a people person, choose a food-service business that gives you plenty of opportunity to connect with your customers. If you're not especially gregarious, you'll probably lean more toward a commercial type of business, perhaps a bakery or even a catering service, where you can deal more with operational issues than with people.

Some other types of questions to ask yourself include: Do you have a passion for a particular type of cuisine? Do you enjoy a predictable routine, or do you prefer something different every day? Are you willing to deal with the responsibilities and liabilities that come with serving alcoholic beverages?

As you do this self-analysis, think about your ideal day. If you could be doing exactly what you wanted to do, what would it be? Now compare your preferences with the requirements of each type of food-service business (described in Chapters 5 through 10) and come up with the best match for yourself.

Once you've decided on the right niche for you as an individual, it's time to determine if you can develop a niche in the market for your food-service business.

Researching Your Market

You must do an in-depth examination of your market. Market research will provide you with data that allows you to identify and reach particular market segments and to solve or avoid marketing problems. A thorough market survey forms the foundation of any successful business. Without market research, it would be impossible to develop marketing strategies or an effective product line. The point of doing market research is to identify your market, find out where that market is, and develop a strategy to communicate with prospective customers in a way that will convince them to patronize your business.

Market research will give you important information about your competitors. You'll need to find out what they're doing and how that approach meets—or doesn't meet—the needs of the market.

One of the most basic elements of effective marketing is differentiating your business from the competition. One marketing consultant calls it "eliminating the competition," because if you set yourself apart by doing something no one else does, then you essentially have no competition. However, before you can differentiate

▲

Bright Idea

Your business plan should include worst-case scenarios, both for your own benefit and for your funding sources. You'll benefit from thinking ahead about what you'll do if things don't go as you want them to. You'll also increase the comfort level of your lenders/investors by demonstrating your ability to deal with unexpected and potentially negative situations.

yourself, you need to understand who your competitors are and why your customers might patronize their businesses.

Are You on a Mission?

Your mission statement is the foundation of your business plan. Most food-service business owners have a reasonably clear understanding of the mission of their company. They know what they're doing, how and where it's being done, and who their customers are. Problems can arise, however, when that mission is not clearly articulated in a statement, written down, and communicated to others.

A mission statement defines what an organization is and its reason for being. Writing down your mission and communicating it to others creates a sense of commonality and a more coherent approach to what you're trying to do.

Even in a very small company, a written mission statement helps everyone involved see the big picture and keeps them focused on the goals of the business. At a minimum, your mission statement should define who your primary customers are, identify the products and services you offer, and describe the geographical location in which you operate. For example, a caterer's mission statement might read, "Our mission is to provide businesses and individuals in the Raleigh area with delicious food delivered to their location and set up and served according to their instructions." A coffeehouse's mission statement might read, "Our mission is to serve the downtown business community by providing the highest-quality coffees, espresso, baked goods, and sandwiches in an atmosphere that meets the needs of customers in a hurry as well as those who want a place to relax and enjoy their beverages and food."

A mission statement should be short—usually just one sentence and certainly no more than two. A good idea is to cap it at 100 words. Anything longer than that isn't a mission statement and will probably confuse your employees.

Bright Idea

Update your business plan every year. Choose an annual date when you sit down with your plan, compare how closely your actual operation and results followed your forecasts, and decide if your plans for the coming year need adjusting. You'll also need to extend your financial forecasts for another year, based on current and expected market conditions.

Once you've articulated your message, communicate it as often as possible to everyone in the company, along with customers. Post it on the wall, hold meetings to talk about it, and include a reminder of the statement in employee correspondence. You should also communicate it to your suppliers. If they understand what you're all about, it will help them serve you better. It's more important to adequately communicate the mission statement to employees than to customers. It's not uncommon for an organization to use a mission statement for promotion by including it in brochures and on invoices, but the most effective mission statements are developed strictly for internal communication and discussion. Your mission statement doesn't have to be clever or catchy—just motivating and accurate.

Smart Tip

Tip...

When you think your business plan is complete, look at it with fresh eyes. Is it a true and honest representation of the facts? Is it realistic? Does it consider all the possible variables that could affect your operation? After you're satisfied, show the plan to two or three associates whose input you value and trust. Ask them to be brutally honest with their evaluation; you need to know now if there are any glaring problems with your plan so you can correct them before they cost you time and money.

Although your mission statement may never win an advertising or creativity award, it can still be an effective customer-relations tool. For instance, you could print your mission statement on a poster-size panel, have every employee sign it, and hang it in a prominent place so customers can see it.

A critical part of your plan to open a food-service establishment will involve setting up your facility. In the next chapter, we'll take a look at the fundamentals of setting up a kitchen and dining area.

Kitchen and Dining Room Basics

The two key parts of your facility are the production area, where the food is prepared, and the public area, where your customers either dine or make their carryout purchases. How you design and equip these areas depends, of course, on the particular type of operation you want to have. This chapter will take a look at the basics that apply to most operations, and the following six chapters will go into more detail regarding specific types of food-service businesses. You'll find a "Furniture and Fixtures Checklist" on page 35 to help you plan for what you need.

As you begin planning your facility, consider hiring an experienced, reputable consultant to assist with the layout of your dining and production areas. Consultants can also help you link all the elements—menu content and design, pricing, décor, kitchen layout, staffing, training, and other support services. To find a good consultant, network with restaurateurs who have businesses similar to the one you want to open, read trade publications, talk with equipment dealers, and perhaps even ask restaurant brokers for referrals.

The information about setting up your facility applies whether you are starting from scratch with bare walls or refurbishing an existing restaurant. If you choose to open in a location that has previously housed an eatery or if you decide to purchase an operating restaurant (see Chapter 13 for more on "Locating and Setting Up Your Business"), it may include furnishings, fixtures, and equipment that you can use. While this could reduce your initial startup costs, you should take care that your décor reflects your concept and does not look used or shabby. If the concept of the previous restaurant and yours are similar, be sure you change enough of the interior so that it is clear this is a new operation.

The Dining Room and Waiting Area

Much of your dining room design will depend on your concept. It might help you to know that studies indicate that 40 to 50 percent of all sit-down customers arrive in pairs, 30 percent come alone or in parties of three, and 20 percent come in groups of four or more.

To accommodate various party sizes, use tables for two that can be pushed together in areas where there is ample floor space. This gives you flexibility in accommodating both small and large parties. Place booths for four to six people along the walls.

Develop a uniform decorating concept that will establish a single atmosphere throughout your restaurant. That means whatever décor or theme you choose for the dining area it should be reflected in the waiting area. Also, be sure your waiting area is welcoming and comfortable. Whether your customers are seated immediately or have to wait awhile for their tables, they will gain their first impression of your operation from the waiting area, and you want that impression to be positive.

Regardless of the type of operation you choose, the quality of your chairs is critical. Chairs are expensive, and how comfortable they are—or aren't—is the second most common source of environmental complaints in restaurants (the first is noise). But while your seats should be comfortable, they shouldn't be too soft, either—you don't want customers falling asleep. They should also allow for ease of movement. Diners should be able to get up and down easily and slide across seating surfaces without tearing clothing or hosiery. And they need to be sturdy. When an overweight customer sits down or even tips a chair back on one or two legs, the chair shouldn't break. Also, the appearance of your seating—including chairs, benches, stools, and sofas—should match your overall ambience. Choose materials that can tolerate abrasive cleaning products as well as the abuse of being stacked and unstacked.

High-Tech Needs High-Touch

Will your customers be able to call a server or place an order simply by touching a few buttons on their table? Use touch screens to play games or flirt with someone at a nearby table?

Table-top technology will become increasingly common as more consumers see it as a normal part of communication. Even better, many of the systems are affordable and improve productivity. However, glitzy devices will never be a replacement for genuine service. Human interaction will always be a critical element of successful food-service operations.

> **Smart Tip** *Tip...*
>
> All restrooms should be supplied with hand soap, paper towels or a hand-drying device, toilet tissue, and easily cleanable waste receptacles.

Production Area

Generally, you'll need to allow approximately 35 percent of your total space for your production area. Include space for food preparation, cooking, dishwashing, trash disposal, receiving, inventory storage, employee facilities, and an area for a small office where daily management duties can be performed.

Allow about 12 percent of your total space for food preparation and cooking areas. If you want to entertain your customers with "exhibition cooking," design a protective barrier that allows the cooking to be seen but limits physical access by customers.

Stefano LaCommare designed the kitchen at Stefano's Trattoria himself—it's compact, efficient, and creative. Prep tables are close to cooking surfaces. Refrigerator drawers are located under the stovetops for easy access to ingredients. Nonfood prep areas (such as dishwashing and supply storage) are distinctly separate to maintain health and sanitation standards.

To make your production area as efficient as possible, keep the following tips in mind:

▲

- Plan the shortest route from entrance to exit for ingredients and baked goods.
- Minimize handling by having as many duties as possible performed at each stop—that is, at each point the item or dish stops in the production process.

> **Bright Idea**
>
> Produce a concise paper version of your menu that your customers can take with them to make placing carryout or delivery orders easier.

- Eliminate bottlenecks in the production process caused by delays at strategic locations. When things aren't flowing smoothly, figure out why. Be sure your equipment is adequate, well-maintained, and located in the proper place for the task.
- Recognize that the misuse of space is as damaging to your operation as the misuse of machinery and labor.
- Eliminate backtracking, the overlapping of work, and unnecessary inspection by constantly considering possibilities for new sequences and combinations of steps in food preparation.

Set up the dishwashing area so the washer can develop a production line. The person responsible for washing dishes should rinse them in a double sink, then place them into racks on a small landing area next to the sink. From the landing area, the racks full of dishes are put through the commercial dishwasher, then placed on a table for drying. The size and capacity of your dishwasher will depend on the needs of your operation.

Receiving and inventory storage spaces will take up to about 8 percent of your total space. These areas should be located so they're accessible to delivery vehicles. Use

These Mats Were Made for Standin'

An important piece of equipment in every food-service operation is matting. Rubber mats reduce employee fatigue and prevent falls from spills. Place quality mats in all areas where employees such as cooks, dishwashers, preparation staff, and bartenders will be standing for long periods. Also place mats wherever spills may occur, such as at wait stations, near storage areas, and in walk-in refrigerators and freezers. A good 3-by-5-foot anti-fatigue mat will range in price from $30 to $65.

double doors at your receiving port, and always keep a dolly or hand truck available. Locate your dry-storage area and walk-in refrigerator and freezer adjacent to the receiving area.

Since most food-service businesses require employees, you should also have a private room for them that includes a table, a few chairs, a closet or garment rack (to hang coats and street clothes after staffers have changed into their work clothes), lockers for safe storage of personal belongings and valuables, and a restroom. The staff facility should not take up more than 5 percent of your total space.

You'll also need a small area where you or your manager can perform administrative tasks, such as general paperwork, bank deposits, and counting out cash drawers. This space is essential even if you have another office at home where you do the majority of your administrative work.

Ventilation

Pollution control is tightening across the country, and new regulations are being introduced every year. This has had a significant impact on ventilation requirements for restaurants. New, more efficient systems that meet the stringent requirements have increased the cost of starting a food-service business. Expect to pay $175 to $450 per linear foot for the hood and grease filter and $20 to $50 per linear foot for the ductwork. While ventilation systems are expensive to install, they offer a tremendous opportunity for energy conservation. The more efficient systems are worth their extra cost because they result in substantially lower monthly utility expenses. Check with HVAC (heating, ventilation, and air conditioning) system manufacturers and installers to find the best options for your particular facility.

You have three basic ventilation system options. The first is reducing the quantity of exhaust air, which will decrease the exhaust fan size and ultimately lower your purchasing and operating costs. In conjunction with this option, you can also reduce the amount of makeup (fresh) air you have to introduce to compensate for the amount of exhaust air you release. This, in turn, will reduce the size of the makeup air fan you need and result in lower purchasing and operating costs. Finally, you can change the method of introducing makeup air so it doesn't have to be conditioned. This will significantly reduce the air-handling costs.

One of the best ways to achieve a reduction in exhaust air and makeup air is to install a high-velocity, low-volume system,

> ## Bright Idea
> Food doesn't have to be served on traditional plates or in an expected setting. One California barbecue chain, for example, serves a full meal family style in a wooden wagon. It's different, memorable, fun, and keeps the customers coming back.

▲

Shedding Light on the Subject

Throughout your facility, be sure you have adequate and appropriate lighting. The kitchen and work areas should be brightly lit to assure productivity, accuracy, and safety. Your dining and waiting areas and other customer spots should be lit in a way that's compatible with your theme and overall décor. Keep safety in mind at all times. A candlelit dinner is certainly romantic but not if your patrons trip and fall on their way in or out because they can't see where they're going.

which reduces the exhaust air output by 40 percent. This directly affects the makeup air quantities—since makeup and exhaust must be in balance—and results in savings in processing the makeup air. A key benefit of such a system is that it introduces raw, unconditioned air directly into the exhaust ventilator, a process that eliminates the cost of heating or cooling a portion of the makeup air.

Merchandising

How you present your food and beverages is as important to sales as how those offerings taste. You can have the most delicious sirloin steak in town, but if you don't present it to the customer properly, it won't be as enjoyable as it could be. Presenting food in an attractive manner is called "merchandising," and it's a powerful marketing tool that successful restaurateurs use to improve sales.

Merchandising is an art that requires a creative mind that can anticipate public likes and dislikes. Your concept, for instance, is a form of merchandising. So is how you present the dishes on your menu and the drinks in your bar. Arranging each of your dishes so the food looks appealing will not only please the customer who ordered the dish, but it will also attract the attention of other customers.

Many restaurants use parsley as a basic garnish, but an increasing number of establishments are turning to more creative options ranging from fresh fruits and herbs to little ornaments and even edible flowers.

Just as important as the garnish you use is selecting the right plate or glass for your food and beverages. For instance, you can serve a regular cut of prime rib on one type of plate and a deluxe cut on a different plate. This also applies to drinks: You might have one type of glass for regular beer and a better glass for premium beer and imported classics. You could, for example, serve a German beer in a stein.

Furniture and Fixtures Checklist

The furniture and fixtures you'll need depend, of course, on the specific type of food-service business you start. Your shopping list may include all or part of the following:

- ❏ Bar(s)
- ❏ Benches
- ❏ Chairs
- ❏ Hat racks/coat racks
- ❏ Highchairs/booster seats
- ❏ Host stand

- ❏ Merchandise display cases
- ❏ Planters
- ❏ Room dividers
- ❏ Stools
- ❏ Tables

Good merchandising is a great way to increase your sales. It's also a way to enhance your image and develop that all-important word-of-mouth advertising.

Pricing Menu Items

Before pricing each item on your menu, you must first account for how much it costs to purchase the ingredients. Then you should incorporate your overhead and the labor costs for preparing and serving the food into the price of each item. Finally, you can add your profit. The net profit restaurants expect on food ranges from 8 to 20 percent, depending on the item. In many cases, the menu price is about three times the food cost. However, this is just a general guideline. There will likely be situations where the market will allow you to charge more, especially if you have a high-quality, in-demand item.

Your net profit before taxes on drinks can be quite high: as much as 60 percent—or even more—of your total selling price. You should generally charge anywhere from 1,500 to 4,000 percent of your cost for drinks, depending on the particular drink and your location.

"Take a look at the balance between the commodity [food] pricing and what you spend on labor for preparation and

Bright Idea

Check the dirty dishes when they're returned to the kitchen to evaluate waste and determine whether you're serving too much. You may be able to increase profits by reducing portion sizes.

presentation," says Paul Mangiamele, president and CEO of Bennigan's. "You need a margin that's acceptable but also communicates value to your customer."

You may want to do some price testing to be sure that not only are you charging an amount that your customers are willing to pay but also one that will generate an acceptable profit for you. However, be careful: "I do not think the old adage that you keep raising prices until the customer can't bear it anymore holds true," says Mangiamele. "The greedy people in this business are usually the ones that go out of business first. There needs to be a balance between a number of issues, such as who else is in your niche, your competitors' pricing, your unique selling proposition, and the experience you are delivering. It's more than just the food aspect because you can get food anywhere. You have to deliver an experience and value as well."

Setting prices can be tedious and time-consuming, especially if you don't have a knack for juggling numbers. Make it your business to learn how to estimate labor time accurately and how to calculate your overhead properly so that when you price your menu, you can be competitive and still make the profit you require.

Menu Nutrition Labeling

Federal law requires restaurants and similar retail food establishments with 20 or more locations to post nutrition information on their menus. Many states and local governments also require food service operations to make this information available to customers. For complete details on what you need to do to be in compliance, visit the U.S. Food and Drug Administration's website at www.fda.gov.

Keep It Clean

In the food-service business, cleanliness is absolutely essential and a lot easier to achieve if you keep it in mind from the beginning. See Chapter 15 for more on restaurant sanitation issues.

Restaurant

The mainstay of the food-service industry is the general-category restaurant. The popularity of restaurants stems primarily from the fact that people have to eat. But there's more to it than that.

The rise in single-parent families, dual-income couples, and individuals working more than one job are all factors driving

▲

into restaurants customers who don't have the time or desire to cook for themselves. Of course, time issues aren't the only reason people dine out. Restaurant customers also benefit from the relatively low inflation of menu prices; competition in the industry in recent years has kept menu prices at fairly reasonable levels.

Restaurants are also great places to entertain or conduct business. Going to a restaurant with friends or associates takes the pressure off people who want to concentrate on interacting rather than on preparing a meal. Many restaurants offer private rooms, large tables, and banquet facilities for these customers.

The Three Food Groups

Restaurants are classified into three primary categories: quick-service, midscale, and upscale. Quick-service restaurants are also known as fast-food restaurants. These establishments offer limited menus of items that are prepared quickly and sold for a relatively low price. In addition to very casual dining areas, they typically offer drive-thru windows and takeout service.

When people think of fast-food restaurants, they often envision hamburgers and French fries, but establishments in this category may also serve chicken, hot dogs, sandwiches, pizza, seafood, and ethnic foods.

Midscale restaurants, as the name implies, occupy the middle ground between quick-service and upscale restaurants. They offer full meals but charge prices that customers perceive as providing good value. Midscale restaurants offer a range of limited- and full-service options. In a full-service restaurant, patrons place and receive their orders at their tables; in a limited-service operation, patrons order their food at a counter and then receive their meals at their tables. Many limited-service restaurants offer salad bars and buffets.

Midscale restaurants embrace a variety of concepts, including steakhouses, casual dining, family dining, and ethnic restaurants, such as Italian, Mexican, Asian, and Mediterranean. Even in full-service midscale operations, the ambience tends to be casual.

Upscale restaurants offer full table service and don't necessarily promote their meals as offering great value. Instead, they focus on the quality of their cuisine and the ambience of their facilities. Fine-dining establishments are at the highest end of the upscale restaurant category and charge the highest prices.

Beware!

Consider your options carefully before deciding to open a themed restaurant. Some theme operations—especially those owned by celebrities—have enjoyed popularity, but the allure of theme operations appears to be on the wane. One restaurant analyst says the problem with theme restaurants is that most people visit them once, twice, or maybe three times but don't go back. It doesn't matter how good the food is if you can't pull in repeat customers because they take a "been there, done that" attitude toward your operation.

Many restaurants cater to customers who want a certain dish but for whatever reason—perhaps a lack of culinary skill or the inability to find ingredients—are unable to prepare it for themselves. Ethnic restaurants or restaurants that serve exotic desserts often attract customers with such strong cravings.

Finally, beyond the food itself, many customers want to enjoy the atmosphere of the restaurants they visit. Ethnic restaurants and specialty-themed restaurants are examples of operations that meet this particular market need.

Before starting any type of restaurant, you must know who your customers are and where they're located. With that information, you can decide on the best site and move forward with your plans. However, restaurateurs don't always agree on the best approach to concept development and site selection.

Some restaurateurs believe you must determine your concept and market before choosing a location. For example, you may want to start an Italian restaurant, so you research the market for this type of cuisine, and then, based on what you find out, choose a general area and later a precise location for the restaurant.

Others believe that finding the location is the most important task and place secondary emphasis on concept and market. For instance, an entrepreneur may find a great building in a downtown business district, decide that it's perfect for a restaurant, and then determine the best concept for the location.

When it comes to restaurants, it doesn't really matter whether you research your market or your location first; what's critical is that you take the time to research both thoroughly.

Choosing Your Concept

Restaurant patrons want to be delighted with their dining experience, but they don't necessarily want to be surprised. If you're anticipating a family-style steakhouse (based on the name or the décor of the establishment), but you find yourself in a more formal environment with a bewildering—and pricey—gourmet menu, the surprise may keep you from enjoying the restaurant. Concepts give restaurateurs a way to let patrons know in advance what to expect and also provide some structure for their operation. In this section we'll explore some of the more popular restaurant concepts.

Seafood Restaurants

Quick-service seafood restaurants generally offer a limited range of choices, often restricted to fried seafood. Midscale and upscale seafood restaurants offer a wider selection, prepared in ways other than fried, such as baked, broiled, and grilled. Most seafood restaurants also offer a limited number of additional menu items, such as steak and chicken.

Seafood can be a risky area on which to focus, as prices are always changing, and many kinds of seafood are seasonal. Also, quality can vary tremendously. When shopping for seafood, make sure that the items are fresh and meet your standards of quality. If you're not happy with what a distributor offers, you can be sure your customers won't be, either.

The décor of a typical casual seafood restaurant consists of marine-related décor, such as fishing nets, buoys, and aquariums. Finer seafood restaurants usually have minimal marine-related furnishings. Seafood restaurants are often located on or near a waterfront, which adds to the nautical ambience.

Steakhouses

Steakhouses are part of the midscale and upscale markets. Midscale steakhouses are typically family-oriented and offer a casual environment with meals perceived as good values. In terms of décor, comfort is emphasized, and Western themes are popular.

Upscale steakhouses offer a more formal atmosphere and may serve larger cuts of meat that are of better quality than those served in midscale restaurants. Upscale establishments also charge higher prices, and their décor may be similar to that of other fine-dining establishments, offering guests more privacy and focusing more on adult patrons than families.

Although red meat is the primary focus of steakhouses, many offer additional items,

> **Bright Idea**
> Choose a site for your restaurant that's near a well-known landmark. It will be easier for customers to find you if they can use a landmark as a reference point.

such as poultry, seafood, and pasta selections. Salad bars are popular at midscale steakhouses.

Family-Style Restaurants

As the name implies, these establishments are geared toward families. Since they charge reasonable prices, they also appeal to seniors. They offer speedy service that falls somewhere between that of quick-service places and full-service restaurants. Their menus offer a variety of selections to appeal to the interests of a broad range of customers, from children to seniors. Family-style restaurant prices may be higher than those at fast-food restaurants, but these establishments provide table service to compensate.

The décor of family-style restaurants is generally comfortable, with muted tones, unremarkable artwork and plenty of booths and wide chairs. Booster seats and highchairs for children are readily available.

What's on the Menu?

Your restaurant's menu is an important sales and communication tool. It must portray your restaurant's theme clearly and consistently. It also must clearly describe the dishes you offer and their prices. Some restaurant owners also use the menu to describe the history of their operation or to provide other information that customers may find interesting. Be sure to make your menu attractive and easy to read.

If you run an upscale, fine-dining establishment, use a paper menu with a cloth binder. Many midscale and upscale restaurants use paper or laminated menus. If you plan to make changes to your menu throughout the year, a cost-effective method is to use plastic menu covers and insert paper menus that can be changed whenever necessary. The plastic menu covers are easy to clean and preserve paper menus for extended use.

Be sure to clean your menus regularly. Menus can be a haven for germs and a stained or sticky menu does not get a dining experience off to a great start. At Stefano's Trattoria, menus are cleaned twice daily (after lunch and dinner).

Casual-Dining Restaurants

These establishments appeal to a wide audience, ranging from members of Generation Y to Generation X to baby boomers with families to seniors, and they provide a variety of food items, from appetizers and salads to main dishes and desserts. Casual-dining restaurants offer comfortable atmospheres with midrange prices. Many center on a theme that's incorporated into their menus and décor.

Ethnic Restaurants

Ethnic restaurants enjoy a significant share of the U.S. restaurant market. They range from quick-service places with limited menu selections to upscale eateries with a wide variety of menu items. Their menus typically include Americanized versions of ethnic dishes, as well as more authentic food. Most ethnic restaurants also include a few American cuisine dishes.

The three most popular kinds of ethnic restaurants are Italian, Mexican, and Chinese. Other popular ethnic restaurant types include Indian, Thai, Caribbean, English, French, German, Japanese, Korean, Mediterranean, and Vietnamese. An even wider variety of ethnic restaurants can thrive in areas with a culturally diverse population, such as large metropolitan areas.

Setting Up Your Facility

The major factors to think about in terms of a restaurant's design are the size and layout of the dining room, kitchen space, storage areas, and office. Dining space will occupy most of your facility, followed by the kitchen and preparation area and then by storage. If you have an office on the premises—and you should—that will most likely take up the smallest percentage of your space.

You may want to hire a food-service consultant or designer to help plan your layout, or you can do it yourself. Remember that all the components—dining room, kitchen, menu, etc.—have to work together, which is why it's a good idea to get some assistance from an expert. In his Melting Pot franchises, Brian Neel begins with his own ideas and then works with the franchisor's in-house architect and interior designer. "Make sure you like it,

> **Tip...**
>
> **Smart Tip**
> Before hiring a consultant, determine exactly what you want help with, then get a complete proposal in writing, including the scope of the work, a timetable, and a fee schedule.

but definitely get help from a designer and a consultant," he advises. "Professional restaurant designers have a very good understanding of the flow of traffic patterns. They know how to create a mood. People dine at restaurants for three things: food, service, and atmosphere. It's very difficult for one person to be completely knowledgeable about all these categories. You ought to get as much help as you can from professionals who have been successful."

The design of your restaurant should promote an efficient operation. The kitchen should be close to the dining room so the waitstaff can serve meals while they're still hot—or cold. The office is the least important factor in the design. You can locate it in the back of the restaurant or even in the basement, along with the storage area. Consider which personnel will need access to which items, then try to locate those items as conveniently as possible to the appropriate workstations. See the "Sample Restaurant Layout" at the end of this chapter.

Customer Service Area

This area is important because it determines the first impression your restaurant will make on your guests. It must accurately convey the atmosphere of the restaurant in a way that takes advantage of the space available. Your customer service area should include a waiting area for customers, a cashier's station, public restrooms, and a bar, if you choose to have one.

The waiting area and cashier's station should be located near the entrance. The cashier's station can be designed as a small counter with a cash register, or you can use more space to display merchandise or any baked goods you might sell.

If you decide to set up a small retail center, your cashier's station will take up a little more room, and you'll have to invest in a counter with a glass casing or shelves. This is a small investment, however, when you consider the potential return on the additional sales.

You can use your cashier's station as the host or hostess station, or you can set up a separate station at the threshold between the customer service and dining areas. A host or hostess stand usually consists of a

Bright Idea

A popular and effective marketing technique used by quick-service restaurants is offering value meals. These meals typically include a main item, side dish, and beverage, all packaged at a price lower than a customer would pay to buy each item separately. For example, a hamburger restaurant may offer a value meal of a burger, fries, and soft drink. A Mexican restaurant might offer a burrito, side salad, and beverage. Like fast food in general, value meals offer convenience and savings to the customer.

▲

Getting to Know You

Use technology to get to know and remember your customers. In his Melting Pot restaurants, Brian Neel maintains a database on every customer. "When they make reservations, we ask them if they're celebrating anything, and if they are, we make a note of it," he says. "When they come in, we greet them and acknowledge whatever they're celebrating. We put a little card on the table, congratulating them again, and the server will acknowledge it as well."

In addition, Neel says, servers make notes on each guest's preferences. "If they really loved a particular wine, or a dish, or the booth where they were seated, we put it into the computer so the next time they call for a reservation, we can ask if they'd like that bottle of wine waiting for them or if they'd like us to reserve the booth they enjoyed so much."

The idea is to create a memorable dining experience that customers will want to repeat. "Not only do you have to provide great food, but you've got to provide great service and have an atmosphere that's warm and inviting," says Neel. "And then you've got to do the little extra things to make the guest remember you and remember their experience."

small wooden podium with a ledger or computer keyboard and monitor for recording the names of waiting guests.

The waiting area itself should have a few benches lining its walls. Don't skimp on these seats. They should be cushioned, unless your theme dictates otherwise, so your customers are comfortable during their wait. If the wait turns out to be long, and if your seats are hard and uncomfortable, chances are you'll lose customers and generate some bad word-of-mouth.

In some restaurants, a bar will generate a good portion of the operation's revenue. Profit margins on beverage sales are much higher than they are on food sales, so a bar will help improve your bottom line. Generally speaking, you should have one bar seat for every three dining seats. For example, if you have 150 dining seats, your bar should have about 50 seats, including bar stools and seats at tables. Allow about 2 square feet of floor space per stool. Your tables should have about 10 to 12 square feet per customer.

A bar also provides an additional waiting area for your restaurant. It's a good place for your customers to relax and enjoy themselves while their table is being prepared.

The Dining Area

This is where you'll be making the bulk of your money, so don't cut corners when designing and decorating your dining room.

Visit restaurants in your area and analyze the décor. Watch the diners. Do they react positively to the décor? Is it comfortable, or do people appear to be shifting in their seats throughout their meals? Make notes of what works well and what doesn't, and apply this to your own décor plans.

The space required per seat varies according to the type of restaurant. For a small casual-dining restaurant, you'll need to provide about 15 to 18 square feet per seat to assure comfortable seating and enough aisle space so servers have room to move between the tables.

The Production Area

Too often, the production area in a restaurant is inefficiently designed, and the result is a poorly organized kitchen and less-than-top-notch service. Your floor plan should be streamlined to provide the most efficient delivery of food to the dining area.

Keep your menu in mind as you determine each element in the production area. You'll need to include space for food preparation, cooking, dishwashing, trash disposal, receiving, inventory storage, and employee facilities, and an area for a small office where daily management duties can be performed.

The food preparation, cooking, and baking areas are where the actual production of food will take place. Allow about 12 percent of your total space for food production. You'll need room for prep and steam tables, fryers, a cooking range with griddle top, small refrigerators that you'll place under the prep and steam tables, a freezer for storing perishable goods, soft drink and milk dispensers, an ice bin, a broiler, exhaust fans for the ventilation system, and other items, depending on your particular operation.

Arrange this area so everything is only a couple of steps away from the cook. You should also design it in such a way that two or more cooks can work side by side during your busiest hours.

You'll want to devote about 4 percent of your total space to the dishwashing and trash areas. Place your dishwashing area toward the rear of the kitchen. You can usually set this up in a corner so it doesn't get in the way of the cooks and servers. Set up the dishwashing area so the washer can develop a production line.

Customer Areas

The areas that have the greatest impact on your customers are the dining area, waiting area, and restrooms. Essential items for your dining area include china or dishware, glasses, napkins (either cloth or paper), flatware, and an assortment of containers for foods not served on plates. Make sure all your tableware is compatible with your overall concept. Plan to pay about $2,000 to $4,000 for a complete set of dinnerware.

The furniture and fixtures in your dining area should match your concept and be appropriate to the market you're trying to attract. For example, a family-style restaurant needs to have comfortable tables and booths that can accommodate children's booster seats and highchairs. A fine-dining establishment should be more elegant, with tables situated to provide your patrons with privacy.

Develop a uniform atmosphere all through the public areas of your restaurant. That means the décor of your waiting area, dining room, bar, and even restrooms should match.

Equipment

Getting your restaurant properly furnished and equipped requires a substantial investment, both financially and in terms of taking the time to make the best choices. It's important not to skimp when it comes to developing a customized plan for your operation. Use the information in this section as a guide; there is also a "Restaurant Equipment and Fixtures Checklist" on page 50.

Production Equipment

Regardless of the type of restaurant you're opening, you're going to need production equipment. While specific equipment needs will vary from one restaurant to another, most establishments serving hot meals will have to equip a service and preparation kitchen.

If you're entering a facility that already has a kitchen, it may already have much of the equipment you need. You can modify what's there to meet your needs and add any other pieces.

Outfitting your preparation kitchen requires a substantial amount of equipment.

> **Bright Idea**
>
> If you have a large facility, consider wireless headsets to allow various staff members to communicate quickly and efficiently.

Stat Fact

Nearly 7 out of 10 adults (66 percent) visit a restaurant on their own or someone else's birthday, making birthdays the most popular occasion to dine out, followed by Mother's Day (38 percent) and Valentine's Day (28 percent).

Budget anywhere from $30,000 to $45,000 for your heavy-production equipment. Before you buy anything, study all the developments that have taken place in the industry and look for versatile, cost-effective equipment.

Most full-service restaurants will have a mixer, a slicer, preparation sinks, hand-washing sink(s) (check with your local health department for minimum requirements), a portion scale, a food cutter, baker's bins and tables, a meat grinder, a blender, a griddle-top range with an oven, a convection oven, a fryer, a cheese melter, a broiler, a pressureless steamer, a steam kettle, and a refrigerator and freezer in their preparation kitchens.

Figure on spending another $1,200 to $2,700 for small-production items like ladles, tongs, spoons, pans, potholders, spatulas, can openers, and other items.

The service area of the kitchen is typically where the final touches are put on the plate and where side orders like salad, soup, sandwiches, and so forth are prepared. A kitchen helper or the server will generally be responsible for food preparation in the service kitchen.

A complete service kitchen should consist of a prep and steam table, a toaster, heat lamps, a microwave oven, a utensil rack, a roll warmer, and a sandwich table. You'll also want to place your beverage center in or near your service kitchen. You'll need a coffeemaker, an ice machine, a beverage stand, a soda system, an ice cream cabinet, and a water station. You'll end up spending from about $11,000 to $20,000 to equip this area.

Dishwashing Equipment

A three-stage dishwashing machine is probably the best way to tackle your dishwashing needs. The machine will cost from $2,000 to $25,000. Installing the equipment, complete with landing area, dish table, garbage disposal, and three-compartment sink, will run you anywhere from $5,000 to $25,000.

Receiving and Storage Equipment

The largest and most costly piece of equipment in your receiving and storage area will be your walk-in refrigerator/freezer, which will cost between $3,000 and $8,000. This will be your main storage area and one of your most important pieces of equipment, because it will preserve your food and keep it fresh. Don't cut corners here.

▲

Your receiving area will also need a scale, a breakdown table, and shelving for the walk-in refrigerator/freezer. You should be able to pick up these items for $2,000 to $4,000.

Bar Equipment

Outfitting a lounge area in a restaurant can be almost as taxing as buying equipment for the restaurant. The first thing you'll need, of course, is the bar. You can buy a standard bar with a refrigerator underneath from an equipment dealer, or you can have one custom made. Either way, plan to spend about $5,000 to $9,000 for the bar.

Equipping the bar will require a cash register, a three-compartment sink with a drain board, an ice bin, an ice machine, a beverage-dispensing system, a beer-dispensing system, glasses, mixers, blenders, ice crushers, bottle openers, and miscellaneous tools. Altogether, the bar equipment will cost between $12,000 and $22,000.

One of the most important pieces of equipment for your bar is your beverage-dispensing system. You'll want one that performs a variety of functions. Two types of automatic beverage dispensers are available: one for mixes and one for liquor. A seven-valve dispensing system that can calibrate the amount of mix served will be sufficient when you start out. You can lease this piece of equipment for $150 to $350 per month, and leasing makes it easier to upgrade the equipment if demand warrants.

You can also pour liquor by hand. To help with portion control, you can attach prepour plastic spouts to each open bottle. These prevent overpouring by dispensing a measured amount of liquor into a drink. Bar equipment manufacturers usually sell these spouts for $28 and up apiece.

Tableware and Miscellaneous Supplies

Purchase your tableware, dishes, and glasses based on the seating capacity of your operation (see "How Much Do You Need?" on page 49, for quantity guidelines). In addition, you'll need salt, pepper, and sugar containers for each table, plus about a dozen sets for backup. You'll also need about a dozen sets of tongs and a dozen large pans.

You'll need paper products such as napkins, doggie bags, to-go containers with covers, place mats, towels, and tissues. Suppliers can advise you on how large an order you should place based on your seating capacity and anticipated volume.

Other important items are ashtrays (if smoking is permitted), potholders, spatulas, a wire whisk, a can opener, towel dispensers, garbage cans, a first-aid kit, a mop, a bucket, a broom, a dustpan, and bus boxes.

Uniforms

Most restaurants require their staff to wear uniforms, giving the employees and the restaurant a more professional appearance. Your cooking staff may need aprons, chef's hats, hairnets, and other items. Uniforms for serving personnel are available in a wide range of styles and colors. Choose attractive uniforms, and, if possible, pick uniforms that reflect the theme of your establishment.

Inventory

A restaurant's inventory consists of items used in the preparation of meals and other restaurant fare. This includes fresh food items such as milk, produce, and meat and preserved items such as canned vegetables and frozen sauces. Nonfood items, which also make up part of a restaurant's inventory, may include garnishes, miniature umbrellas for drinks, and disposable bibs for customers who order messy dishes like ribs or lobster. Restaurant supplies, such as napkins, paper towels, cups, plates, and flatware are considered equipment rather than inventory because they're not actually food.

Your basic stock must fulfill two functions: First, it should provide customers with a reasonable assortment of food products. Second, it should cover the normal sales demands of your business. To calculate basic stock accurately, you must review sales during a set time period, such as a full year of business. Of course, during your startup phase, you'll have no previous sales and stocking figures to guide you, so you'll project your first year's stock requirements based on your business plan.

How Much Do You Need?

Use the following chart to determine how much tableware to buy for your restaurant. Multiply the quantity needed by your restaurant's seating capacity.

- ❑ 2 spoons and knives
- ❑ 1 iced tea spoon
- ❑ 1 soup spoon
- ❑ 3 forks

- ❑ 2 cups, saucers, and plates
- ❑ 2 salad plates
- ❑ 1 12-ounce soda and iced-tea glass
- ❑ 1 ice cream/salsa dish

Restaurant Equipment and Fixtures Checklist

- ❑ Bakers' bins and tables
- ❑ Bar
- ❑ Beverage-dispensing system
- ❑ Blender
- ❑ Broiler
- ❑ Can openers
- ❑ Cash register
- ❑ Cheese melter
- ❑ Coffeemaker
- ❑ Convection oven
- ❑ Dishwasher
- ❑ Food cutter
- ❑ Freezer
- ❑ Fryer
- ❑ Garbage disposal
- ❑ Griddle-top range with oven
- ❑ Hand truck (dolly)
- ❑ Heat lamps
- ❑ Ice cream cabinet
- ❑ Ice machine
- ❑ Ladles
- ☒ Meat grinder
- ❑ Microwave oven
- ❑ Mixer

- ❑ Pans
- ❑ Portion scale
- ❑ Potholders
- ❑ Prep and steam table
- ❑ Preparation sinks
- ☒ Pressureless steamer
- ❑ Refrigerator
- ❑ Roll warmer
- ❑ Sandwich table
- ❑ Security system
- ☒ Signage
- ❑ Slicer
- ❑ Soap dispensers
- ❑ Soda system
- ❑ Spatulas
- ❑ Spoons
- ❑ Steam kettle
- ❑ Storage shelves
- ❑ Three-compartment sink
- ❑ Toaster
- ❑ Tongs
- ❑ Utensil rack
- ❑ Ventilation system

Depending on the size and type of your restaurant, during your first year, you can expect to spend anywhere from $12,000 to $85,000 on food, $3,500 to $25,000 on beverages, and $700 to $2,000 on paper products.

Staffing

There are several categories of personnel in the restaurant business: managers, cooks, servers, buspersons, dishwashers, hosts, and bartenders. Each has a specific function and contributes to the operation of the restaurant. When your restaurant is still new, you may find that some of the duties will cross over from one category to another. For example, the manager may double as the host, and servers may also bus tables. Because of this, be sure to hire people who express a willingness to be flexible in their duties.

Your payroll costs, including your own salary and that of your managers, should be about 24 to 35 percent of your total gross sales. If payroll costs are more than 35 percent of gross sales, you should look for ways to either cut those costs or increase sales.

> ### Smart Tip
> Tip...
>
> Be sure your entire wait-staff is familiar with everything on the menu. They should know how items are prepared, how they taste and if special requests can be accommodated. Spend at least 15 minutes with your entire crew every day before the restaurant opens going over the menu, the specials, and any special events that will be occurring that day.

Most restaurant employees typically work shifts from 10 A.M. to 4 P.M. or 4 P.M. to closing. One lead cook may need to arrive at your restaurant early in the morning to begin preparing soups, bread, and other items to be served that day.

Manager

The most important employee in most restaurants is the manager. He or she can help you with your duties or handle them entirely if you plan to be an absentee owner.

Your best candidate for the job will have already managed a restaurant in your area and will be familiar with local buying sources, suppliers, and methods. A manager should be able to open and close the restaurant; purchase food and beverages; open the cash register(s); track inventory; train and manage the staff; deal with suppliers, develop and implement a marketing strategy; and handle other miscellaneous duties. Beyond these responsibilities, the manager must reflect the style and character of your restaurant. Don't hire a cowboy to manage your fine-dining establishment.

A good manager should have at least three years of nonmanagement restaurant experience in addition to two years of managerial experience. It's often best to hire a manager with a background in small restaurants because this type of person will know how to run a noncorporate eatery. As a rule, restaurant chains buy in mass quantities from central suppliers, which means chain managers probably won't have the buying experience your operation requires.

You'll also want a manager who has leadership skills and the ability to supervise personnel in the kitchen, service area, hospitality entrance, bar, lounge, and restrooms, and who can also make customers feel welcome and comfortable.

Restaurant managers typically work long hours—as many as 50 to 60 hours a week—which can contribute to a high burnout rate. To combat the potential of burnout and to reduce turnover, be careful not to overwork your manager, and be sure he or she has adequate time off to relax.

To get the quality of manager you want, you'll have to pay well. Depending on your location, expect to pay a seasoned manager $35,000 to $55,000 a year, plus a percentage of sales. An entry-level manager will earn $28,000 to $32,000 but won't

How Many Servers Does It Take . . .

The number of servers you need depends on the type of service you want to offer, your table turnover rate, the size of your restaurant, and the type of technology you're using. In the past, when everything was done by hand, there were two forms of service: In the first, the server worked alone with maybe 15 seats to handle. A single server took the order, got the drinks, served the food, and wrote the check with only the help of a busboy. The other form was more elaborate, with a captain, a front and back waiter, and a busboy for each station. A team could handle 25 to 30 seats.

But technology has changed the way many restaurants approach staffing and service. Computers are streamlining the ordering and serving processes, with one server taking the order and entering it into the computer, where it's transferred to the kitchen, and then, when the food is ready, it's delivered by a runner who may have no further contact with the guests. A restaurant may have one or two runners whose sole job is to deliver food as it comes out of the kitchen.

Try to design a floor plan that will let you create flexible stations that can be adjusted based on your volume and staffing. If you're using runners to support the servers, and the server is doing everything except delivering the food and bus-ing the tables, limit each server to 25 seats, or "covers." If you're not using runners, limit the number of seats per server to no more than 15.

have the skills of a more experienced candidate. If you can't offer a high salary, work out a profit-sharing arrangement; this is an excellent way to hire good people and to motivate them to help you build a successful restaurant.

Chefs

At some restaurants, the star attraction is the chef. A chef creates his or her own culinary masterpieces for you to serve. Chefs command salaries significantly higher than cooks, averaging $1,300 to $1,800 a week, and sometimes more. You may also find chefs who are willing to work under profit-sharing plans.

Cooks

When you start out, you'll probably need three cooks—two full-time and one part-time. One of the full-time cooks should work days, and the other should work evenings. The part-time cook will help during peak hours, such as weekend rushes, and can work as a line cook, doing simple preparation, during slower periods. The full-time cooks can also take care of food preparation before the restaurant opens, during slow times and after the restaurant closes.

Hire your cooks according to the type of restaurant you want. If your goal is a four-star, fine-dining establishment, you'll want to hire a chef instead of a short-order cook. If you plan to have an exciting and extensive dessert menu, you may want to hire a pastry chef. Cooking schools can usually provide you with the best in the business, but look around and place ads in the paper before you hire. Customers will become regulars only if they know they can expect the best every time they dine at your restaurant—and to provide that, you need top-notch cooks and chefs.

Salaries for cooks vary according to their level of experience and your menu. If you have a fairly complex menu that requires a cook with a great deal of experience, you may have to pay anywhere from $575 to $650 a week. You can pay part-time cooks on an hourly basis; check around to see what the going rate in your area is. College students can make good part-time cooks.

Dishwashers

As the job title implies, dishwashers keep clean dishes available in your restaurant. You can probably get by with two part-time dishwashers, one working the lunch shift and the second covering the dinner shift. If you're open for breakfast, you can go with either one full-time and one part-time person or three part-time dishwashers. Expect to pay minimum wage to minimum wage plus $1.50 an hour.

Serving Staff

Finding the right serving staff is just as important as finding the right manager. The servers are the people with whom your customers will have the most interaction, so they must make a favorable impression to keep customers coming back. Servers must be able to work well under pressure, meeting the demands of customers at several tables while maintaining a positive and pleasant demeanor.

In general, there are only two times of day for waitstaff: very slow and very busy. Schedule your employees accordingly. The lunch rush, for example, usually starts around 11:30 A.M. and continues until 1:30 or 2 P.M. Restaurants are often slow again until the dinner crowd begins arriving around 5:30 to 6 P.M. Volume will typically begin to slow at about 8 P.M. This is why some restaurants are only open for peak lunch and dinner times. During slow periods, your waitstaff can take care of other duties, such as refilling condiment containers.

Because servers in most types of establishments earn a good portion of their income from tips, they're usually paid the minimum wage for tipped employees (which is lower than the standard minimum wage) or slightly above. It's also customary for the waitstaff to share their tips with the buspersons who clean the tables at their stations. In fact, some restaurants require their servers to pay the buspersons assigned to their sections 10 percent of their tips.

When your restaurant is new, you may want to hire only experienced servers so you don't have to provide extensive training. But as you become established, you should develop a training program to help your employees understand your philosophy and the image you want to project.

As part of your serving staff, you may want to hire runners who are responsible only for delivering food from the kitchen, freeing up the servers to focus on the customers.

Hosting Staff

Depending on the size and style of your restaurant, you may need someone to seat guests, take reservations, and act as cashier. You may want to hire someone part time to cover the busy periods and have the waitstaff or manager handle these duties during slower times. Hire people-oriented, organized individuals for host positions; after all, they will determine the first impression your customers form of your service staff. Students often make great hosts. Pay for this position typically ranges from minimum wage to minimum wage plus $1.50 an hour.

Buspersons

Buspersons are responsible for setting up and clearing tables and filling water glasses after customers are seated. Your buspersons should be assigned to stations, just like your waitstaff; in fact, buspersons and servers should work together as a team. Buspersons should be trained to pay attention to their stations, refilling water glasses as necessary, making sure condiment containers are clean and full when the table is turned, and generally supporting the server.

Typically, buspersons will be part-timers who work during peak periods. Servers can handle busing tables during slow times. Consider hiring high school and college students as buspersons. These positions usually earn minimum wage plus a portion of the tips received by the servers they assist.

Bartenders

If you have a small bar in your restaurant and it's only open at night, one bartender will probably be sufficient. Of course, if you expect to earn a good portion of your business from the bar, you'll need two bartenders—one full- and one part-time person to assist during peak periods. If your bar attracts customers during both the lunch and dinner periods, you'll need two or three bartenders, or you might try a combination of a full-time bartender or bar manager, plus two or three part-time helpers.

The bartender begins his or her day by prepping the bar, which includes preparing the condiments and mixers for the entire day as well as ordering supplies. The bartender also needs to check the liquor requisition sheet and the liquor inventory and restock the bar. If you use a computerized beverage-dispensing and inventory management system, the bartender will check the meters and hook up the necessary bottles.

The night bartender will close the bar. Last call for drinks should occur 30 minutes before the legally required closing time. The closing process usually includes packaging the garnishes and placing them in the refrigerator, wiping down the bar area and stools, and restocking the bar.

It's important to look for a bartender who knows how to pour regular well drinks as well as special requests. Experienced bartenders can make small talk and relate to people individually while juggling several drink orders in their heads. They also know when to stop pouring drinks for intoxicated customers and call a taxi or other transportation to take such customers home. Bartenders are usually paid an hourly wage—often $7 to $11 an hour—plus tips.

Finding, recruiting, screening, and hiring employees is discussed in more detail in Chapter 14.

Sample Restaurant Layout

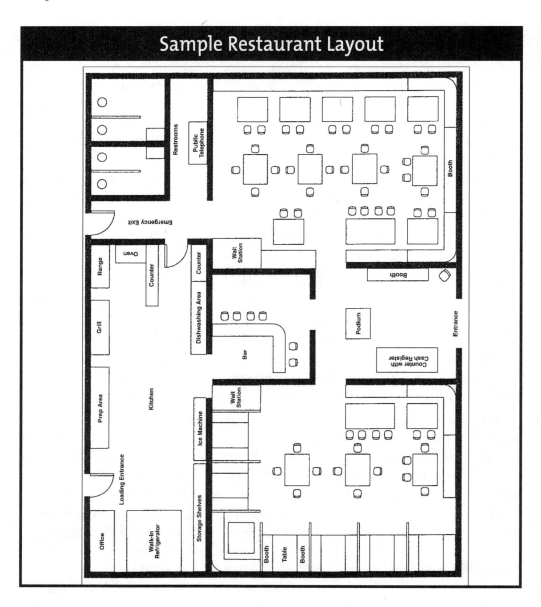

6

Pizzeria

The first pizza restaurants appeared in the United States during the 1930s. In the decades that followed, pizza went from novelty to fad to habit. Originally an Italian dish, pizza is now one of the most popular American fast foods. It's enjoyed as lunch, dinner, and even as a snack by consumers of all age groups and socioeconomic backgrounds. People flock to try new varieties, such as Chicago or Sicilian style, stuffed crusts, double crusts, and creative topping combinations. But as popular as pizza is, the competition is intense—and a successful pizzeria is much more than a great pie.

You have two primary choices when starting a pizzeria. One is a to-go restaurant in a modest facility with a specialized menu highlighted by pizza and beer, limited seating, and a self-service atmosphere. The other is a full-service pizza restaurant with a menu that features not only a variety of pizzas and beer and wine but also Italian entrées like spaghetti, ravioli, and lasagna; side dishes, such as salads (or even a salad bar), and a few desserts.

Within these generalities, specialization is the key to success for any pizzeria. A to-go pizzeria will specialize in pizza and beverages, perhaps with a limited selection of salads and simple sandwiches. Of course, even a full-service pizzeria will specialize in pizza, though you may offer a wider range of sandwiches, pasta dishes, garlic bread, and salads. If your goal is to open a pizzeria, don't try to grow your operation into a full-service Italian restaurant. This will detract from your image as a pizzeria and will probably reduce your profits.

An operation that usually works well by itself and can easily be multiplied into a chain is the to-go concept, with anywhere from 30 to 55 seats for a small section of sit-down customer dining but without any table service.

The Art of the Pie

Here's the key to it all: how to make the pizza. Roll out the dough about 2 inches larger than the pan. Press it into the curves of the pan, then pull some slack dough into the center to compensate for shrinkage, and trim the edges around the pan. With a ladle, spread the sauce over the entire surface to the edges. Use more cheese on the plain cheese pizzas and less on those with other toppings. Add the toppings chosen by the customer, spreading them evenly. Never overload the pie, because it will take so long to cook through to the middle that the bottom will burn.

The oven should be set at 500 to 550 degrees—hotter if you're busy and opening the oven door often. If you're using fresh dough, cook the pizza in the pan until the top is golden brown, then slide the pie off the pan to brown the bottom. Remove the pizza from the oven, slide it onto a cool pizza pan, cut and serve.

If you don't have the extra money necessary for the sit-down portion of the business when you start, you'll be able to grow into it after things are rolling. Just be sure to plan for that growth, and be sure your facility has the space to accommodate it. Many to-go pizza stores also deliver and find the revenue from this portion of their market substantial. With a little advertising and two or three licensed drivers from a local high school or college, you, too, can offer the convenience and reap the profits of home and office delivery.

The Pizza

The foundation of a pizzeria is, of course, the pizza. Many pizzerias also serve salads, sandwiches, pasta, desserts, and other Italian dishes, but the pizza is paramount. If you don't know how to make a good pizza, hire a pizza cook who does. Without a good product, you're sure to fail, regardless of what else you do. Invest in top-quality ingredients and preparation methods, and make every pizza as if you were going to eat it yourself. Do that, and your customers will keep coming back.

Should you offer thick or thin crust? It depends on your market. A thick, doughy crust tends to be popular in the Eastern United States, while in the West, the crust of choice is generally thin and crisp. However, you'd be wise to provide customers a choice and offer both types. For thinner crusts, you can use preformed shells, but make the thick ones yourself.

You might also want to offer a choice of crust flavors. For instance, you could try to sprinkle special toppings or spices—such as garlic, Parmesan cheese, or poppy seeds— on the crust before baking. The market response to these "specialty" crusts has been tremendous, and you can offer them for free or for a nominal extra charge, because they cost you practically nothing extra, yet they make your pizzas more flavorful. If you offer a variety of crusts, be sure to promote them on your menu and other marketing materials.

Stefano LaCommare, owner of Stefano's Trattoria, says the right amount of spices and seasonings are critical to good pizza dough. It's also important to adjust your dough recipe based on the season and environment. For example, when the humidity is high, you might need more yeast; or in the winter, you might use warm water but very cold water in the summer.

Beyond the basic crust is the style of pizza. Sicilian- and Chicago-style pizzas are

Stat Fact

Research by *Pizza Today* shows that 74 percent of pizzeria operators have dining rooms, 94 percent serve appetizers, 56 percent serve pasta meals and salads, 48 percent serve beer, and 38 percent serve wine.

▲

varieties with thick, chewy crusts. Chicago-style pies are baked in a deep dish, while Sicilian is baked on a flat pan. But the ingredients are essentially the same, so you can try experimenting with both traditional and other styles to see what sells best in your market. But don't get carried away with variety: You don't want to overburden your cook with too many shapes and sizes that have different cooking times, require customized pans, or need special dough-rolling procedures.

Setting Up Your Facility

A to-go pizzeria has minimal space requirements (see the "Sample Layout of a To-Go Pizzeria" on page 71). Most range in size from small takeout and home-delivery operations of only 800 square feet to larger, limited seating-capacity operations of 1,500 square feet. For a full-service pizzeria, you'll need a facility between 2,500 and 4,000 square feet (see the sample layout of a full-service pizzeria on page 72). Depending on the type of facility you want to open and your own resources, expect to spend $70,000 to $1.5 million to get your pizzeria ready for your grand opening.

There are no textbook ratios for distribution of space in a pizzeria, but a good formula is to allocate 20 percent for your customer service area (25 percent in a strictly to-go/home-delivery operation), 45 percent for the dining area, and 35 percent for your production area. Of course, if you don't provide a dining area, your production area will be adjusted upward to 80 percent.

For dine-in pizzerias, allotting 60 to 65 percent of the space for dining and customer service allows adequate room for quality food production. If you let the production area fall below 35 percent, you run the risk of limiting yourself in a way that could result in poor-quality food.

Customer Service Area

Your customer service area determines the first impression your customers will have of your pizzeria's atmosphere. Use this space to create an appropriate ambience that takes maximum advantage of the available space. The customer service area should include a waiting area for customers, a cashier's station, and public restrooms.

The exact layout will depend on whether your operation is a to-go or full-service pizzeria. With both types, the waiting area and cashier's station will be located directly at the entrance to the facility, but this is where the similarities end.

And to Top It Off

What do Americans want on their pizzas? Besides cheese, their favorite topping is pepperoni. Other popular toppings are tomatoes, onions, mushrooms, extra cheese, sausage, chicken, bacon, green peppers, and olives. Anchovies rank last on the list of favorite toppings.

In addition to traditional toppings, pizza lovers are experimenting with a variety of gourmet toppings such as a variety of cheeses, oysters, crayfish, dandelions, sprouts, eggplant, shrimp, artichoke hearts, tuna, and even potatoes and nuts. Approximately two-thirds of Americans prefer meat toppings, while the remaining one-third prefer vegetarian toppings. Women are twice as likely as men to order vegetarian toppings on their pizza.

In addition to the waiting area and cashier's station, a to-go pizzeria will have an order/pickup counter that serves both the takeout and sit-down customers. This counter will usually stretch wall-to-wall across the facility to separate the production area from the customer service and dining areas. The cashier's station should be incorporated into the order/pickup counter so customers can pay when they order.

Line the walls of the waiting area for takeout customers with bench seats. Don't skimp on quality here; provide cushioned seating so your customers are comfortable during their wait. Think about it: Even a short wait seems like a long time when someone needs to get back to the office at lunchtime or is tired, hungry, and in a hurry to get home in the evening. Hard seats or no seats in an uncomfortable waiting area can generate unfavorable word-of-mouth advertising and may send customers to your competition. You may also want to have a television for customers to watch while waiting.

In a full-service pizzeria, make the cashier's station a small counter that parallels one wall at the entrance. To conserve space, the cashier's station can double as the host stand, or you can set up a separate host stand at the threshold between the customer service area and the dining area. A small wooden lectern with a ledger-type book to record the names of waiting guests, and perhaps a storage area underneath for menus, is usually sufficient for a host stand. As in a to-go pizzeria, the waiting area should have a few bench-style seats lining its walls.

Location Is Everything

Most pizzerias are located near business sections of cities and towns. The industry leaders—Pizza Hut, Domino's, Papa John's, and Little Caesars—look for strong lunch business, as well as early-dinner, dinner, and post-dinner-crowd business. Your best location choice is one with a strong day and nighttime population, easy access for both cars and pedestrians, and a consistent traffic flow.

In the past, most pizzerias were in freestanding buildings, but that trend has shifted. Now pizzerias are springing up in all sorts of locations, including shopping centers and mall food courts. You may find it profitable to locate your business either in a mall or in a freestanding building next to a mall, which will let you share the mall's traffic. Another good location would be one that's convenient to commercial office developments. You can turn almost any space into a thriving pizzeria if you have the customer base, the knowledge, and the capital to make it happen. Just be sure your market research supports your final location decision.

Locate your beverage center behind the customer service counter toward the end. If you choose to have customers serve themselves beverages—as many fast-food and self-service restaurants are doing these days—place the dispenser near the front counter so your employees can keep an eye on it. You need to make sure it's clean and functioning properly at all times.

If you have sit-down customers, you'll need to provide public restrooms, which are usually located close to the dining area.

Dining Area

Whether your pizzeria is self-service or full-service, a sit-down dining area increases your profit potential. That's why it's imperative that you don't cut corners when designing and decorating your dining room. This is, after all, the area that has the most impact on your customers.

The space required per seat will vary depending on your type of operation. In

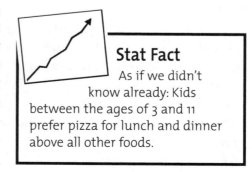

Stat Fact
As if we didn't know already: Kids between the ages of 3 and 11 prefer pizza for lunch and dinner above all other foods.

a to-go, self-service pizzeria, the amount of space per seat should range between 12 and 15 square feet. A full-service pizzeria will need between 15 and 18 square feet per seat. This ensures comfortable seating and enough aisle space so servers have room to move between tables.

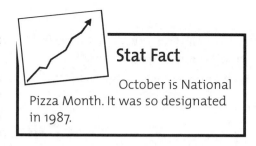

Stat Fact

October is National Pizza Month. It was so designated in 1987.

Essential service items for your dining area include dishware, glasses, flatware, and an assortment of containers to hold foods not served on plates. Salt and pepper shakers and napkin holders for each table are optional. If you decide to present them on request, be sure you have enough for at least half the tables at any given time. If your menu includes bread with most meals, you'll need as many bread baskets as you have tables.

Keep your overall concept in mind when choosing your dinnerware. Many to-go pizzerias place paper plates and plastic forks, spoons, and knives on a self-service table and serve the beverages in mugs. A full-service pizzeria can't get away with this cost-cutting approach. For a full-service pizzeria, plan to spend about $2,500 to $4,000 for a complete set of dinnerware.

Production Area

You need enough room in the food preparation area to accommodate prep tables, pizza oven(s), a range, microwave oven(s), a small refrigerator with a freezer, an exhaust fan for the ventilation system, utensils and smallware, and other food production equipment. To-go pizzerias might require less food prep space than full-service operations, depending on menu offerings and specific equipment needs. In any case, arrange this area so everything is positioned within a few steps of the cook. It should also be designed so that two or more cooks can work side by side during rush periods.

Stat Fact

The pizza industry generates $36 to $38 billion in annual sales. There are between 65,000 and 75,000 pizza restaurants and approximately 10,000 Italian restaurants in the United States. More than 3 billion pizzas are sold in the United States each year, and another 2 billion are sold around the world.

Dishwashing and trash areas should be located toward the rear of your operation, near the receiving port. Allow about 4 percent of your total space for these areas. Dishwashing equipment can usually be situated in a corner so it doesn't get in the way of food-service personnel. A to-go pizzeria may not need a commercial dishwasher, but you'll need a three-compartment sink and adjacent counter space and racks for washing cooking utensils and the small amount of tableware you use.

▲

Your production area will also need receiving and inventory storage facilities, an employee room, and a small office or administrative area (see Chapters 4 and 5 for more on setting up your facility).

Equipment

Aside from building preparation, equipment will be one of your biggest startup expenses. New equipment to run your pizzeria will cost anywhere from $60,000 to $125,000, depending on the type of operation you choose. The good news is that you don't have to buy everything new. This section will explain the process of deciding what you need, how and where to find it, and how to acquire it for as little as possible. The "Pizzeria Equipment and Fixtures Checklist" on page 65 will help you focus on what you need.

Equipment selection for a pizzeria is a complex process and will require some time and research beyond the scope of this guide. For example, some ovens can perform a multitude of cooking procedures, from baking pizza and cooking meats to reheating entrées and melting cheese on appetizers. Ice machines, on the other hand, have only one use: They make ice. Some equipment is basic to every food-service operation; other items are unique to pizzerias. The prerequisite to purchasing equipment is knowing exactly what you need to prepare the foods on your menu. It will also help you to know how other pizzerias are equipped, so visit other establishments, observe as much as you can, and ask as many questions as possible. Talk to people who own and work in pizzerias, as well as equipment sales representatives.

You may want to spend some time talking with a restaurant consultant before making your final purchase decisions. Don't rush into choosing your furniture, fixtures, and equipment—especially if you're not sure exactly what you want or require or how it will all blend together.

Food Production Equipment

While the equipment needs of a to-go pizzeria and a full-service facility will vary,

> **Tip...**
>
> **Smart Tip**
> Budget between $30,000 and $45,000 for the heavy production equipment in your pizza kitchen. Before you buy, study all the new developments in the industry, as new technologies and methods are being developed constantly and you need to know what's out there so you can make the best choice for your operation. Read trade magazines and industry newspapers to keep up on the latest equipment advances and design innovations.

Pizzeria Equipment and Fixtures Checklist

- ❑ 45-gallon bakers' bins on wheels (2)
- ❑ Beer/wine serving equipment
- ❑ Breakdown table
- ❑ Cash register
- ❑ Coffeemaker
- ❑ Company vehicle
- ❑ Dinnerware
- ❑ Dishwasher
- ❑ Dolly/hand truck
- ❑ Dough mixer/blender
- ❑ Dough roller
- ❑ Dry-storage shelving
- ❑ Fixtures (booths/tables)
- ❑ Gas hot plate/range
- ❑ Grinder
- ❑ Hand slicer/electric slicer
- ❑ Hotboxes
- ❑ Ice machine
- ❑ Microwave oven
- ❑ Office equipment
- ❑ Office furniture
- ❑ Pasta machine
- ❑ Pizza oven(s)
- ❑ Portion scale
- ❑ Prep table
- ❑ Production area refrigeration units
- ❑ Scale for receiving area
- ❑ Security system
- ❑ Service counter
- ❑ Signage
- ❑ Softdrink system
- ❑ Three-compartment sink

one piece of equipment essential to both is a pizza oven. Your oven should be able to heat to 650 degrees and have a minimum deck space of 32 inches deep and 42 inches wide, with a 7-inch mouth. A new single-deck oven can be purchased for $2,500 to $7,500. If you anticipate a sales volume of $1,500 or more per week, buy a double unit for $4,500 to $14,000. Because gas ovens heat more intensely than electric ovens, most pizza chefs prefer them.

In addition to the oven, you'll need a range or hot plate for cooking sauces and pastas. You can buy a used household range for about $125 or a used commercial gas hot plate for about $100. If you opt to buy new, you'll pay $400 to $2,800. Whichever you choose, set it up next to the pizza oven for the cook's convenience. Other necessary items include a toaster oven for preparing garlic bread and a microwave oven for reheating pasta.

The service area of the kitchen is typically where the pizza will be made and side orders (such as salads and bread sticks) prepared. The cook should be in charge of preparing the pizza, and a kitchen helper or the servers (if you have them) can handle side orders.

A complete service area for a pizza kitchen usually contains a prep table, a slicer or grinder, a portion scale, a dough mixer/blender, a dough roller, production hardware, and a utensil rack.

Your health department may require a stainless-steel top on the prep table. If so, a 6-foot table will cost about $125 used and $300 to $1,000 new. Otherwise, you can buy a Formica top or work counter for about $50 used. It's a good idea to have an inexpensive second table to use for cutting and boxing orders.

Some pizzerias grind their toppings, others slice them. It doesn't seem to make a lot of difference to customers, so the choice is yours. A slicer is a must, however, if your menu will include Italian sandwiches. A new electric slicer will cost $300 to $3,000 and should last for several years. You may consider a hand slicer with various attachments for smaller jobs. You can expect to pay $100 to $400 for that.

You'll need a small grinder or cheese grater to grate the cheese for your pizzas. You should invest in a good professional grinder, which will range in price from $1,000 to

---

Get Real

Pizzeria operators are responding to consumer demand for natural ingredients by changing their recipes and promoting the new ingredients in their marketing. While it might make one wonder exactly what was used before, consumers appear to be responding positively to the switch.

Pizza Hut began its migration to real ingredients in 2008. The company's research indicated that 73 percent of those tested agreed that foods that are natural have flavor the way it was meant to be. Pizza Hut says the ingredients are all-natural with no artificial preservatives, no nitrites or nitrates added, no artificial colors or flavors, and real beef with no fillers. Pizza Hut also offers a multigrain crust, responding to consumer demands for more whole grains in their diets.

$4,000. Don't try to "make do" by grating cheese by hand; you'll wear yourself out and probably won't be able to keep up with the demand.

Assuming you're going to make your own pizza dough but don't want the upper-body workout mixing dough by hand provides, you'll need a dough mixer/blender. This isn't a necessity when starting, but it will probably become crucial as your business grows. A new heavy-duty dough mixer/blender will cost from $600 to $5,000 or more, used ones can be found for as low as $400.

When rolling out your pizza shells, you can either do it by hand or purchase a mechanical roller. The speed and efficiency of a mechanical roller lets you prepare shells as you need them. If you're going to do it by hand, however, you can roll the shells in advance and refrigerate them until you're ready to use them. Don't roll more than you can use in two or three hours, though, as shells get tough and gummy if left sitting around too long.

Smart Tip

To maintain consistent quality and give your inventory control procedures a fighting chance, you'll need a portion scale. It's not enough to buy the scale—make sure your employees use it. This will help you estimate the amount of each ingredient required to prepare each dish efficiently and with accuracy. If your chefs are "guesstimating" on portions, they'll probably use too much inventory, and you'll be serving your profits rather than taking them to the bank. Dollar for dollar, the $30 to $150 you'll spend on a portion scale may well be the wisest investment you make in your pizzeria.

If you're planning on a full-service restaurant and your menu will include a variety of pasta dishes in addition to pizzas, consider investing in a pasta machine. This purely optional investment lets you make your own noodles from scratch rather than buying premade pasta from grocery wholesalers. Because your main menu focus is pizza, a home-kitchen-style pasta machine should be sufficient. You can expect to pay about $300 for a high-quality machine.

Bakers' bins are especially useful in a full-service operation. These will make preparing your pizza crusts, pasta, and other products much easier. Your prep table should have enough space underneath for these large containers. Also, the bins should be on rollers so they can be moved around easily. You'll spend $200 to $400 on bakers' bins.

Utensils and Miscellaneous Equipment

The cost of the small stuff can add up, so pay close attention to what you really need in this area. In a typical pizzeria, you'll need 12 plastic or stainless-steel bins

Where the Ovens Are

You have three choices when it comes to pizza ovens: electric, gas, and wood fired. Electric is the least desirable because it doesn't generate enough heat to cook the pizza crust properly. Gas generates a good hot, dry heat, which can produce a consistently good product, but many pizzeria operators say wood fire beats gas and electric hands down because you can get the temperature almost twice as hot as you can with a gas oven. Even the nonconnoisseurs who routinely order pizza from takeout chains can tell the difference between a conventionally cooked pizza and a wood-fired pizza.

Though wood-fired ovens may be best, they're not cheap. You can easily spend $12,000 or more for wood-fired ovens.

(about $3 each) for pizza ingredients; four 12-inch, four 15-inch, and four 18-inch pizza pans (about $5 each, used) for baking pizzas and sorting dough; and one peel ($10 used to $40 new), which is the large, long-handled wooden spatula that is used to lift the pizzas from the oven. You'll also require a large pot (20- to 40-gallon variety) for cooking sauce, two four-quart pots (for weighing dough ingredients, etc.), one rolling pin, one can opener, one pizza cutter, one large ladle (for spooning sauce), and knives. Plan to spend $1,000 to $1,400 on these items.

You may or may not want to insist on uniforms for your cooking staff, but your employees will at least need aprons, chef's hats, and hairnets. Uniforms for servers are available in a variety of styles, colors, and price ranges.

Stat Fact

Collectively, Americans eat approximately 100 acres of pizza each day, or 350 slices per second. People across America eat an average of 46 slices (23 pounds) of pizza a year, and 93 percent of Americans eat at least one single-serving pizza per month.

Beverage Center

Your beverage center can be located completely in the service kitchen or split between the service kitchen and the customer service area if you offer self-service drink machines. The typical beverage center will include a coffee machine, an ice machine, a water station, and a soft drink-dispensing system. If you sell beer, the tap should be behind the counter under your employees' control. Bottled beer and wine should also be stored in coolers out of the reach of customers. Expect to spend $7,000 to $12,000 on beverage equipment.

Inventory

Your menu will determine your inventory, but there are some specialty items you must purchase for your pizzeria. Here are some of the more typical inventory categories you'll be dealing with:

- *Meats*. You'll need sliced and processed meats as part of your pizza toppings selection. Some of the more common meats are pepperoni, sausage, and Canadian bacon. You may also need ground beef if you'll be offering dishes with meatballs or pasta shells filled with meat (such as ravioli).

- *Dairy products*. Pizzerias use great quantities of cheese as a primary pizza topping. If you're going to make your own pizza crust, garlic bread, or pasta, you may also be using milk and eggs in large quantities.

- *Sauces*. You'll need a variety of sauces, both for pizzas and for other Italian dishes. Sauces can be purchased by the can in bulk quantities or made from scratch. Most restaurateurs buy canned sauces and add various herbs to spice them to taste and give them a unique flavor.

- *Fresh produce*. You'll use fresh vegetables as pizza toppings, in salads, and as side dishes.

- *Pastas and breads*. If you make your own pizza dough, pastas, and breads, you'll use a great deal of flour. Some of these products are available either premade or partially prepared, which can speed up your production process.

- *Condiments and dressings*. You will need salt, pepper, cooking oil, garlic, oregano, red pepper flakes, Parmesan cheese, and many other items that help finish off your dishes. If you offer salads, you'll want to stock canned and packaged items like olives, pickles, kidney beans, and garbanzo beans. Unless you're serving only antipasto salads, you'll need a selection of dressings, such as Italian (of course), blue cheese, French, Thousand Island, and perhaps an herb or honey-mustard flavor. At least one dressing should be low fat.

- *Beverages*. Soft drinks are considered necessary beverages for a pizzeria. You'll also need to serve coffee, tea, and milk. Beer and wine are very profitable, but state and local licenses may be expensive and aren't always easy to obtain.

- *Paper and plastic products*. You'll need a variety of paper and plastic products for your takeout and delivery orders, as well as for your dining room service. The list includes straws, napkins, paper cups, bags, plastic tableware, pizza boxes, spaghetti/pasta cartons, and salad containers. Most of these items are available from paper products distributors. Check your local online or paper Yellow Pages or do an internet search for distributors in your area.

- *Hot-food bags.* If you offer delivery, you'll need insulated food bags to keep the pizza and other food warm during transit. Hot-food bags run $15 to $55 each, and you'll need three or four for each driver.

Staffing

How you staff your pizzeria will depend, of course, on the size and scope of your operation. You'll definitely need a cook to make the pizzas and other menu items, and a cashier. If you offer sit-down dining, you'll need a host or hostess and waitstaff. If you offer delivery, you'll need drivers. You may also need buspersons and other cleaning staff.

Keep security in mind when planning your staffing. Even a small to-go operation should have at least two people on duty at all times.

Pay scales will vary depending on region and whether the position is likely to earn tips. A glance through the help-wanted section of your local newspaper or online job postings will give you a fairly accurate idea of what you can expect to pay. You can also check sites such as www.salary.com.

Bright Idea

Consider using manufactured pizza shells. While pizza connoisseurs say premade crusts don't have the taste of those made with fresh dough, manufactured shells simplify a pizza operation. Try some and see for yourself. There might be a manufacturer in your area that uses a formula that surpasses the run-of-the-mill recipes. You can expect to pay 35 cents to $1 wholesale for a 12-inch (small) pizza shell and more for larger sizes. To find a supplier, look under "Food Products" and "Restaurant Supplies" in the Yellow Pages online.

Sample Layout of a To-Go Pizzeria

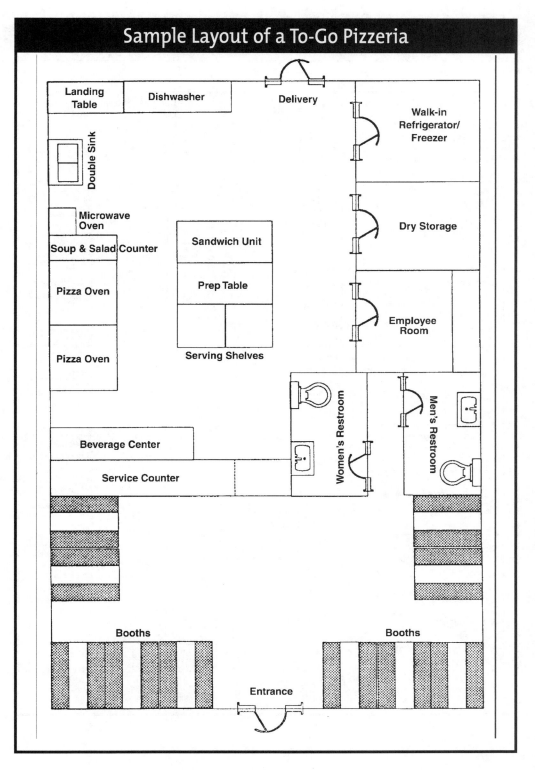

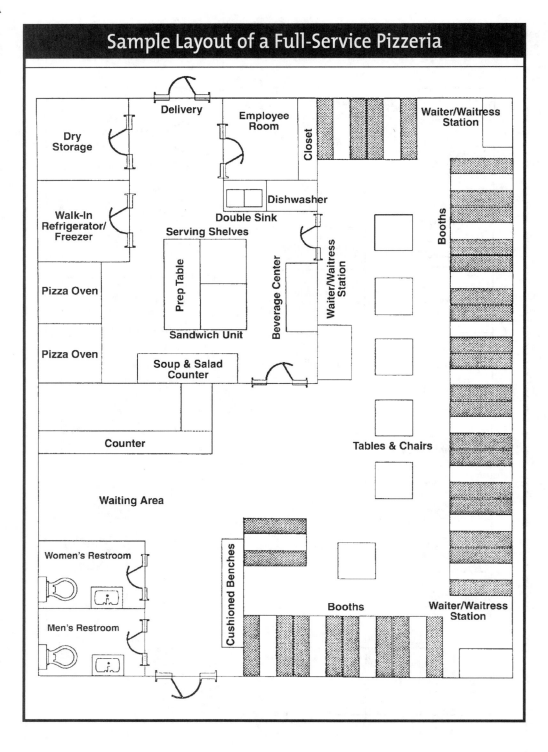

Sample Layout of a Full-Service Pizzeria

Delivery

Dry Storage

Employee Room

Closet

Waiter/Waitress Station

Walk-In Refrigerator/ Freezer

Dishwasher

Double Sink

Serving Shelves

Prep Table

Booths

Pizza Oven

Beverage Center

Waiter/Waitress Station

Sandwich Unit

Pizza Oven

Soup & Salad Counter

Tables & Chairs

Counter

Waiting Area

Women's Restroom

Cushioned Benches

Booths

Waiter/Waitress Station

Men's Restroom

Sandwich Shop/ Delicatessen

The wide appeal of sandwiches, both nationally and internationally, ensures the stability of sandwich shops and delicatessens. Sandwiches, after all, have been around for a long time. In fact, the sandwich is named for the fourth Earl of Sandwich, John Montagu. This English nobleman of the 1700s is said to have eaten sandwiches while at the gaming table so he didn't have to take time out for a formal meal.

For centuries, sandwich shops have lined the streets of Europe. You can't walk down a street in Paris, for instance, without passing a sandwich shop or a bakery that sells *baguettes* (French long bread) and sandwiches. The *croque monsieur* (melted ham and cheese on bread) is a popular sandwich in France. Italians, on the other hand, often make their sandwiches with *focaccia* (a spiced bread), vegetables, salami, and mozzarella cheese. Sandwiches are no less popular in the United States. Philadelphia, for example, is well-known for its "Philly cheesesteak" sandwiches.

One reason sandwich shops are so successful is that they enjoy high profit margins. Sandwich shops and delicatessens can also change their menus quickly and easily to adapt to the current tastes. For example, with the growing interest in health and nutrition in the United States, sandwich shops and delicatessens have started to offer more low-fat, healthy ingredients in their sandwiches, salads, and other menu items. They've also added a range of low-carb items. In addition, many sandwich shops and delis have been able to keep up with American workers who eat at their workplaces by adding delivery and catering to their sit-down and takeout operations.

Catering to Their Every Whim

Offering delivery services and small-scale catering can generate additional revenue for your sandwich shop or deli. You can provide delivery of standard menu items to a specified geographic area around your shop for no charge or a small charge, depending on the market demand.

A catering operation could consist of sandwich and party platters or more elaborate menus. Include both of these options in your market research to determine demand. You'll also need to consider whether your startup budget allows for the equipment you'll need to provide these additional services. You may want to start out with a small shop and expand your service offerings later. However, knowing your eventual goals will help you make better choices on your initial equipment purchases. Maxine Turner, owner of Cuisine Unlimited in Salt Lake City, started with a catering operation and added three delicatessens. Today, each deli has a catering menu prominently displayed. See Chapter 10 for more information on starting a catering service.

Sandwich shops and delicatessens can be differentiated by the foods they serve. Most sandwich shops serve only sandwiches, possibly with some side dishes or desserts. A delicatessen, meanwhile, usually serves a more extensive menu, including sandwiches, prepared meats, smoked fish, cheeses, salads, relishes, and hot entrées. The word "delicatessen" comes from the French *délicatesse*, meaning "delicacy."

A full-scale delicatessen will usually have a dining area and offer sit-down service as well as takeout, while a sandwich shop may only offer takeout. This chapter will discuss both types of businesses, and you'll need to decide whether you want to open a sandwich shop, a deli, or a combination of the two.

Factors that contribute to the fast growth of sandwich shops and delis are their startup and operating costs, which tend to be lower than those of other fast-food enterprises. Many sandwich shop franchises promise startup packages for as low as $150,000, and some are only $40,000. Low-end independent establishments have started their businesses for as little as $36,500. The average startup cost for a sandwich shop is approximately $100,000.

Competition

Your competition in most locations will consist of other quick-service outlets (such as fast-food, specialty and ethnic restaurants, and other sandwich shops and delis), grocery store deli departments, national sandwich shop chains, and some sit-down restaurants.

- *Quick-service/fast-food restaurants*. One major advantage a sandwich shop or deli has over many fast-food restaurants is the ability to provide both quick service and healthier food choices. You can promote this as a strong selling point.

  You should also be able to compete easily against fast-food restaurant prices. You may not be able to match an 89-cent burger, but you should be able to come close to matching prices for chicken or steak sandwiches, which usually sell for $2.50 or more. If you offer a pickle or coleslaw with your sandwiches, you can sell a more satisfying meal to your customers than some of the fast-food chains, which usually sell only the sandwich.

> **Bright Idea**
>
> If your sandwich shop/ or deli will offer party platters or catering as a service, be sure to ask if prospective customers ever buy party platters or use caterers when you conduct your initial market research.

- *Grocery store deli departments.* Because they buy in volume and appear to have a captive audience, an in-store deli may seem like strong competition, but don't let it scare you. Many people just don't think of going to the grocery store for lunch, and they will find your easy-in, easy-out shop preferable to going into a supermarket.

- *National sandwich shop chains.* National chains may have huge advertising budgets, but you have a number of competitive advantages. For one thing, you can offer an innovative menu that's customized to local preferences, and you can provide high-quality food. Personalized service is another plus for an independent operator, and it pays to get to know your customers by name and greet them when they come through the door. Eye contact, good service, and a smile go a long way toward building customer loyalty, whether you're competing against a national chain or another independent business.

Setting Up Your Facility

Whether you plan to open a takeout sandwich shop with a limited menu or a full-scale sit-down deli, you will need enough space for a production area (a kitchen or sandwich preparation area), a customer service area, a receiving and storage area, and at least one employee restroom. You'll also need some kind of office, though some sandwich shop and deli owners use a homebased office to keep commercial space requirements to a minimum. A dining area and public restrooms may also be included in your facility. You'll probably need a space with somewhere between 500 and 3,000 square feet.

Converting an existing food-service operation (such as a bakery, deli, or small restaurant) can lower your initial investment. In any case, if you'll specialize in serving customers on the go, you can probably get by with 500 to 750 square feet, including kitchen space (see the "Sample Layout of a 700-Square-Foot Sandwich Shop" on page 88 and the "Sample Layout of a 1,200-Square-Foot Sandwich Shop" on page 89). If you want to offer a more extensive menu and allow space for customer seating, you'll want a facility as large as 3,000 square feet.

In a strictly takeout operation, allow 75 percent of your space for your production area, 15 percent for customer service, and 10

Smart Tip Tip...

Be sure to keep the front of your display cases clean and clear. As customers make their selections, they're likely to touch the cases and will naturally leave fingerprints behind. After every meal period, wipe off the sides and tops of your counters and cases.

percent for storage, restrooms, and a lounge. If you plan to have a combination takeout/ sit-down operation, allow about 35 percent of your space for the production area, 5 percent for customer service, 50 percent for the dining area, and 10 percent for storage, restrooms, and the lounge.

Customer Service Area

A principal requirement for the customer service area is that it be large enough to accommodate customers, display case(s) or service counter(s), and at least one cashier station. In a strictly takeout operation, you may want to devote as much as 15 percent of your space to this area to accommodate several waiting customers during busy periods. If you plan to offer sit-down service, the customer service area should only occupy about 5 percent of your space, which is just enough for takeout customers to place orders and for sit-down customers to wait to be seated (if need be).

In a deli, your refrigerated display cases will be important marketing tools, as they'll be displaying and thus advertising much of your menu. The salads and ingredients should be attractively displayed, and the case should be well-lit. The glass should be spotless, and the chrome should be shiny and clean.

Likewise, the counter area in a sandwich shop should always be clean. Since the customer service area will be the first thing patrons see when entering your shop, cleanliness will make a good first impression.

As for the cashier's station, all you need is enough space for the cash register at the end of the counter nearest the entrance.

Dining Area

Dining areas in delis and sandwich shops range from small self-service sections set aside almost as a courtesy to customers (with perhaps three to five tables, each with two to four chairs) to full-scale dining rooms with booths lining the walls, tables, and chairs in the center of the area, and a waitstaff to serve patrons. The latter borders on being a full-service restaurant; if that's your goal, use the information in Chapter 5 to guide you in setting up and managing your operation.

For a typical sandwich shop or deli in a small facility of 500 square feet, consider having 6 to 8 small tables with a total of 12 to 18 chairs. For a larger facility of, say, 1,200 square feet, consider having 10 to 12 tables with 20 to 36 chairs. You don't want the chairs to be overly comfortable; look for chairs that discourage lingering.

Turnover is key in this business, which must capitalize on a few peak periods—or even one period, namely lunch—per day.

Production Area

The production area will include space for sandwich and salad preparation. Depending on your menu, it may require space for preparing hot items, as well. If you decide to offer sit-down service and a full menu, you'll probably want to set up both a service kitchen and a preparation kitchen. (A service kitchen is simpler than a preparation kitchen; it's used to prepare sandwiches and basic items such as soups. A preparation kitchen is more elaborate, allowing you to prepare a wide variety of hot items.) Many sandwich shops and delis can get by with a relatively simple setup.

For example, in a sandwich shop, the customer service and production areas are usually separated by a simple service counter. A deli should have a three-tiered, refrigerated, glass-fronted case (instead of a counter) to display the wider variety of cheeses, salads, and various types of fish.

Against the wall behind either the service counter or display case could be your sandwich preparation area. This section can contain bread boards on which sandwiches will be made, a meat slicer, and shelving for frequently used ingredients. Toward the rear of the production area, on the same side of the wall, you could have a sandwich warmer, a double sink unit, and a refrigerator. On the other side of the sandwich preparation area, nearest the entrance, you could place your softdrink dispensing system and coffeemaker.

Whether you use this layout or a more traditional layout with both service and preparation kitchens, your primary concern is to make sure the production area is as streamlined as possible to ensure the efficient delivery of food to waiting customers. A poorly designed area reduces the effectiveness of both equipment and personnel.

Receiving and Storage, Office, and Restrooms

About 5 to 10 percent of your total space will be used for receiving and storing food. Your receiving area should be accessible to delivery vans. It should also have double doors and a dolly for the easy transport of goods. Your dry-storage area should be located next to your receiving area. This section might include a second freezer and an employee restroom. Contact your county or state health department for area regulations that govern how many employee restrooms are required.

For a sit-down shop, you'll probably want to provide at least one, if not two, public restrooms, each fully equipped for access to people with disabilities. Contact your city or county building department for the building and plumbing codes that apply.

Your restrooms don't need to be fancy or elegant, but patrons will expect them to be attractive and clean.

A large storage room can double as your back office. You'll need enough space for a desk, a phone, a small filing cabinet, and shelves. If you have the room, you may also want to provide some lockers in the storage area for your employees to use.

Image

The image of any food-service operation is important to attracting and keeping customers. Always balance professionalism and cleanliness with a comfortable atmosphere.

Research shows that you have less than 10 seconds to attract the attention of a passerby, so your signs and the exterior of your facility must have high impact. There's a variety of decorating ideas and thematic treatments you can use to set your operation apart from the sterile look of fast-food restaurants.

In shopping center takeout operations, proprietors often use eye-catching displays with large, high-quality product photos and unique logos. Be sure to replace photos regularly; a tattered or limp picture of a faded sandwich is unappetizing.

A clever, attention-getting device used by many sandwich shops is having the production process clearly visible to passersby. Displaying the ingredients and showing the sandwiches being made has proved to be an effective technique for drawing customers.

Inside, create a warm, inviting setting with inexpensive hanging plants (live, not artificial), posters, photographs, and so on. Paintings, murals, wall plaques, and pictures can effectively establish a theme, but you don't need to spend too much money on decorations. Creativity and cleanliness are more important than spending thousands of dollars on themed decorations.

Because spotlessness is essential, choose surfaces that are durable and easy to clean, such as washable wall coverings, tile floors, and walls covered in enamel-based paints.

Equipment

A key advantage of starting a simple sandwich shop is that your equipment needs will be minimal compared with those of a full-scale restaurant. Many sandwich shops serve only cold sandwiches and don't do on-site cooking, so their equipment costs are comparatively low. A deli or sandwich shop serving hot entrées requires a larger investment.

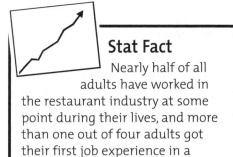

There's some equipment that all restaurants need, such as preparation tables, slicers, cutlery, pots and pans, ovens, refrigerators, and freezers. Whether you decide to bake your own bread, offer an extensive menu, or provide sit-down service will determine what further investment you'll need to make in equipment and fixtures. Most likely, it will be somewhat lower than for the typical dine-in restaurant, which will require additional equipment listed in the "Sit-Down Dining Tableware Checklist" below.

Production Equipment

A service kitchen, which you'll use for simple tasks such as preparing sandwiches, requires a preparation and steam table, a toaster, heat lamps, a microwave oven, a utensil rack, a roll warmer, and a sandwich table. You'll also need to install your beverage center near your service kitchen, where you should have a coffeemaker, an ice machine, a beverage stand, a soda system, an ice cream cabinet, and a water station. In all, you'll end up spending from $12,000 to $20,000 to equip the service kitchen.

Sit- Down Dining Tableware Checklist

If you're going to offer sit-down dining, use the following guide to determine the amount of tableware you'll need. Simply multiply the quantity listed below by your facility's seating capacity.

- ❑ 2.5 spoons and knives
- ❑ 1.5 iced tea spoons
- ❑ 1 soup spoon
- ❑ 3 forks
- ❑ 2.5 cups, saucers, and plates

- ❑ 2 salad plates
- ❑ 1.5 12-ounce soda and iced-tea glasses
- ❑ 1 ice cream or salsa dish

In addition, you'll need salt, pepper, and sugar containers for each table, plus a dozen sets as a backup.

Setting up your preparation kitchen will require a lot more equipment and a lot more capital, so you should budget anywhere from $30,000 to $45,000 for your heavy production equipment. Most sandwich shops and delis have some or all of the following: a slicer, preparation sinks, a portion scale, a food cutter, bakers' bins and tables, a meat grinder, a blender, a griddle-top range with oven, a convection oven, a fryer, a cheese melter, a broiler, a pressureless steamer, a kettle, and a refrigerator with a freezer. Your cooking staff may need aprons, chef's hats, hairnets, and other items, and if you have serving personnel, you'll want to provide them with uniforms.

> **Smart Tip** — Tip...
>
> If you use live plants as part of your décor, be sure they're healthy and well-maintained. Droopy or brown leaves or plants infested with insects won't contribute to a positive dining experience.

You'll also need a variety of kitchen cookware, such as measuring cups and spoons, ladles of various sizes, spatulas, wire whisks, a can opener, tongs, and large kitchen spoons. Other miscellaneous items you'll need include potholders, towel dispensers, garbage cans, first-aid kits, a mop and bucket, a broom and dustpan, and dish containers for busing tables. Plan to spend from $1,200 to $2,500 for cookware and miscellaneous items (see the "Sandwich Shop/Deli Equipment Checklist" on page 82 to help you plan what you need to purchase).

Retail/Service Area Equipment

The specific equipment you'll need for this area depends on the type of shop you plan to open. For many sandwich shops, a 6- to 10-foot service counter or display case can also serve as the customer service area. Customers order their sandwiches and pay for them at one end of the counter. Your staff makes the sandwiches and calls customers' numbers when they're ready, and the customers pick up their order at the other end of the counter.

As mentioned earlier, a deli will probably display cheeses, salads, meats, and fish in three-tiered, refrigerated, glass-fronted cases, which can range in cost from about $1,600 (for used equipment) to $9,000 or more (for new equipment). At Cuisine Unlimited in Salt Lake City, caterer/deli owner Maxine Turner uses two refrigerated delicatessen cases: one for salads—including green salads, fruit salads, specialty pastas, and natural grains—and one for what she calls "savory" items, such as chicken tortes, quiches, stuffed manicotti, and lasagna rolls.

Whether you place it on your service counter or have a separate stand for it, you'll also need a cash register in this area.

Sandwich Shop/Deli Equipment Checklist

- ❏ Bakers' bins and tables
- ❏ Beverage center
- ❏ Blender
- ❏ Breakdown table
- ❏ Broiler
- ❏ Cappuccino maker
- ❏ Cheese melter
- ❏ Coffeemaker
- ❏ Convection oven
- ❏ Dinnerware
- ❏ Dishwashing machine
- ❏ Display case(s)
- ❏ Equipment for dishwashing
- ❏ Fax machine
- ❏ Food cutter
- ❏ Freezer
- ❏ Fryer
- ❏ Griddle-top range with oven
- ❏ Heat lamps
- ❏ Hot-water machine
- ❏ Ice cream cabinet
- ❏ Ice machine

- ❏ Kettle
- ❏ Lighting
- ❏ Meat grinder
- ❏ Microwave oven
- ❏ Panini grill
- ❏ Portion scale (for food)
- ❏ Preparation and steam table
- ❏ Preparation sinks
- ❏ Pressureless steamer
- ❏ Refrigerator
- ❏ Roll warmer
- ❏ Sandwich table
- ❏ Scale (for receiving area)
- ❏ Service counter
- ❏ Shelving
- ❏ Slicer
- ❏ Tables and chairs
- ❏ Toaster
- ❏ Utensil racks
- ❏ Ventilation system
- ❏ Water station

Dining Area Equipment

Preparing your dining area (if you have one) will be another expense. You can expect to spend as little as $300 for tables and chairs for a small sandwich shop and up to $6,000 for tables, chairs, and booths for a larger establishment.

Other necessary items for the dining area include dishware, glasses, flatware, and an assortment of containers to hold foods not served on plates. These items should match your overall theme or image. A very casual sandwich shop or deli may use paper or plastic plates and cups. For a more formal establishment, you will need flatware and dishware. Figure on your dinnerware costing up to $3,000.

Dishwashing Equipment

If you're going to use disposable tableware, flatware, and cups, you'll only need to wash pots, pans, and preparation utensils. A dishwashing machine would be easiest, but you can make do with a three-compartment sink and do the washing by hand. You'll spend $600 to $2,000 for a sink.

If you're going to be using regular dishes, flatware, and glasses, you'll need a small, three-stage dishwashing machine. Your dishwashing area, complete with landing area,

Know the Locals

Some owners buy for their restaurants the same way their customers buy for themselves—on impulse. This isn't necessarily a bad practice, as long as your tastes coincide with a sound knowledge of your patrons' preferences and your estimates closely resemble your actual inventory requirements. Even so, it's better to shop with a plan. In general, a wide array of foods will attract a diversified clientele. With practice and diligent market research, you can identify your strongest menu items and order inventory accordingly.

drying table, garbage disposal, three-compartment sink, and small machine will run you anywhere from $6,500 to $20,000.

Receiving and Storage Area Equipment

If your volume warrants, you may want to purchase a walk-in refrigerator and freezer for your storage area. This will cost between $7,000 and $10,000, but it's not necessary for most smaller shops. Most sandwich shops and delis can get by with just a scale, a breakdown table, and shelving in the receiving and storage area. If your operation is on the small side, you can probably equip this area for less than $1,500.

Inventory

Your specific inventory will, of course, depend on your menu. Caterer/deli owner Maxine Turner says one of the challenges she faces is offering enough variety to keep nearby businesspeople returning for lunch on a daily basis while maintaining an efficient inventory system. When you're starting out, keep your inventory low until you can work out a suitable ordering pattern. You'll probably open with about $9,000 to $12,000 in inventory, and your full food and beverage inventory should turn over about once every two weeks.

Let's take a look at the basic food categories you'll probably be dealing with:

- *Bread.* The basic ingredient of every sandwich, bread can make or break your sandwich shop/deli. You may be tempted to buy packaged breads and rolls from distributors, but the most successful sandwich shops and delis purchase freshly baked bread daily from a local baker or bake their own breads on-site. While "home baking" your breads can be an excellent marketing tool, you may not have the budget to invest in the necessary equipment and labor. The equipment alone will cost between $20,000 and $150,000, depending on the quantities of bread you plan to bake each day. If you can't afford to make the investment, don't worry. Virtually all cities and towns have bakeries known for their delicious products. Make arrangements with them to buy the bread and rolls you need at wholesale prices. You'll also want to have wraps as an alternative to bread. Plain tortillas work well, or you can offer flavored wraps such as spinach or tomato basil.

- *Meats.* Your meats must be of the highest quality—and fresh—so plan to reorder at least every other day. High-volume shop owners use 150 to 300 pounds of roast beef, ham, and salami each week as well as about 75 to 100 pounds of pastrami, turkey, and other meats. Shop carefully to find the best quality at the best prices.

- *Additional deli items.* Delis usually offer a complete selection of salads (such as potato, three-bean, coleslaw, cucumber, pasta, and green), various types of fish (including cod, salmon, herring, sturgeon), and an extensive selection of cheeses. Sandwich shops may have a more limited menu.

  Both sandwich shops and delis may serve hot entrées, such as soup, chili, stew, quiche, barbecued ribs and chicken, and so on. Dessert items may also be included to round out a sandwich shop or deli menu. Purchase these extras in limited quantities at first, until you can determine demand.

- *Beverages.* Some delis and sandwich shops offer canned soda, pints of milk, and glasses of iced tea, lemonade, or carbonated drinks. Virtually all serve coffee, and some serve hot chocolate during the winter. You might also want to invest in an espresso or cappuccino machine and provide a variety of hot teas. Some beverage suppliers provide the beverage-dispensing systems for free or at a reduced cost to high-volume operations, provided you buy their beverages. Check with a variety of beverage suppliers, and negotiate for the best deal possible.

  If you decide to include shakes, malts, frozen yogurt, floats, and ice cream sodas (or soft-serve ice cream), all the ingredients you'll need should be available from the same distributor that supplies your milk. These ice cream items can dramatically increase your dollar-per-customer sales figures.

  Many sandwich shops and delis serve beer by the bottle and wine by the glass or bottle. Most don't serve hard liquor; a limited beer-and-wine license meets their needs and is easier to obtain than a full liquor license.

- *Fresh produce.* It's easiest to order your fruits and vegetables through a fresh-produce supplier, although some shop owners like to visit a farmers' market themselves. Although vegetables are available year-round, they're seasonal and subject to climatic conditions. Be flexible in your buying, and look for items in plentiful supply. Take advantage of price swings by modifying the makeup of your salads or sandwiches according to the season and produce availability. But regardless of the season, you'll use several cases of lettuce and tomatoes and several pounds of cheese each week.

- *Canned, frozen, and packaged foods.* If you offer soups and salads, you'll need canned and packaged items like soups, olives, pickles, kidney beans, garbanzo beans, and some canned condiments. Purchase these items from a processed-foods distributor, and start with their minimum order, which is usually a case of each.

The Paper Chase

In addition to your food and beverage supplies, you'll need a wide array of paper and plastic products, as well as miscellaneous items unique to your type of restaurant.

Paper goods will be a significant monthly expense. Disposable plastic or paper plates, napkins, and cups range from 8 to 16 cents per setting, depending on your business volume. Negotiate with several paper products distributors (they're listed in the Yellow Pages or you can find them online) to get the best prices.

It's not necessary to order paper products with your shop name and logo printed on them. This adds considerably to the cost of these products and doesn't do very much to advertise your business or boost your bottom line. It may work for large chains that order in huge quantities, but it doesn't make sense for the owner of a single shop just starting out.

You'll also need several dressings for salads, such as blue cheese, French, Thousand Island, Italian, and honey mustard. Make sure you provide low-fat options. You'll probably want to buy them commercially since homemade dressings generally require too much time and labor. Offer a variety of salad toppings, including olives, chopped vegetables, nuts, bacon bits, grated cheese, soybeans, raisins, and sunflower seeds.

Condiments for sandwiches and other menu items (mustard, ketchup, salt, pepper, cooking oil, relish, etc.) can be purchased through a processed-foods distributor.

If you include French fries on your menu, you can either buy potatoes from a fresh-produce supplier and cut them yourself (which may be too time-consuming) or buy precut, precooked frozen French fries by the pound. You might also want to offer onion rings, which can be purchased precooked and frozen.

Staffing

Your staffing needs will vary depending on the size of your operation. If you're planning to work full time in your sandwich shop or deli, you could probably open with just one full-time employee: an experienced sandwich maker. As your business grows, you'll probably want to cover busy periods with part-time workers. For security reasons, try to have at least two employees in the shop at all times. Of course, if you're planning a full-service deli with a dining area, you'll need to staff more along the lines of a typical restaurant.

Look for employees who are pleasant, people-oriented, and well-groomed. Food prepared by sloppy employees won't be appealing to your customers.

Most sandwich shop and deli positions don't earn significant tips, although some shops have a tip jar by the cash register. Wage scales vary by region, but you can expect to pay 50 cents to $2.00 above minimum wage. A glance through your local newspaper's help-wanted section or online job sites will give you an idea of the going rates in your area.

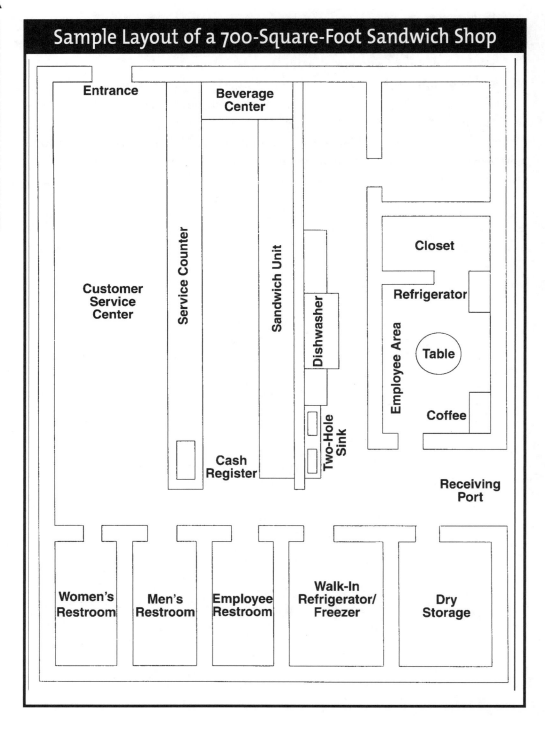

Sample Layout of a 700-Square-Foot Sandwich Shop

Entrance

Beverage Center

Customer Service Center

Service Counter

Sandwich Unit

Dishwasher

Closet

Refrigerator

Employee Area

Table

Coffee

Cash Register

Two-Hole Sink

Receiving Port

Women's Restroom

Men's Restroom

Employee Restroom

Walk-In Refrigerator/ Freezer

Dry Storage

Sample Layout of a 1,200-Square-Foot Sandwich Shop

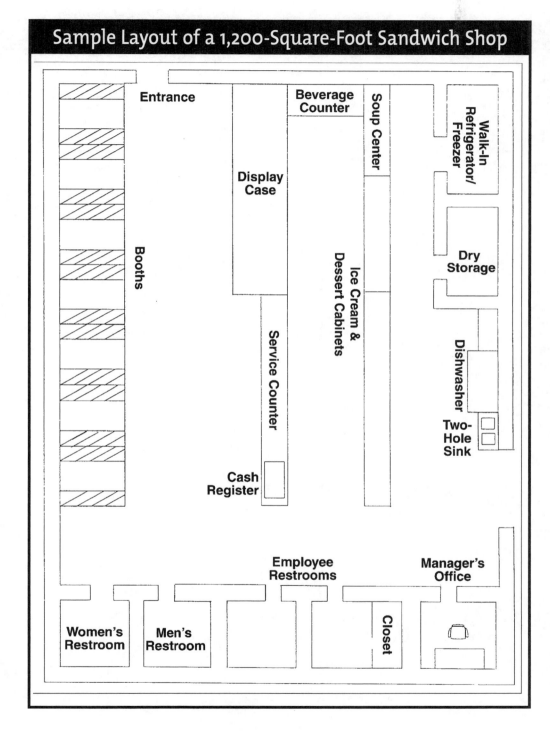

Entrance

Beverage Counter

Soup Center

Walk-In Refrigerator/Freezer

Display Case

Booths

Ice Cream & Dessert Cabinets

Dry Storage

Service Counter

Dishwasher

Two-Hole Sink

Cash Register

Employee Restrooms

Manager's Office

Women's Restroom

Men's Restroom

Closet

Coffeehouse

Coffee connoisseur or neophyte, aficionado or abstainer, you've probably noticed the tremendous growth in the specialty coffee industry. New incarnations of this previously background beverage have taken center stage in restaurants and shops around the world. Coffee has become a culture—complete with its own language and accessories—that offers a wide-open retail opportunity.

Coffee is a global industry that employs more than 20 million people worldwide and ranks second only to petroleum in terms of dollars traded. With more than 400 billion cups of coffee consumed every year, it is the world's most popular beverage.

The first coffeehouses opened in Constantinople nearly 450 years ago and did so well that by the 1630s, European coffeehouses had become the center of cultural and social activities. Coffeehouses also enjoyed some popularity in colonial New England, but Americans didn't accept the coffeehouse as a place for social or cultural gatherings until well into the second half of the 20th century. Before the 1970s, Americans either drank their coffee at home or in a restaurant and settled for the canned variety that was brewed in a percolator.

In the 1960s, coffeehouses and folk musicians appeared on the scene. Although the coffeehouses seemed to focus on the counterculture, they managed to create a demand for fresh coffee beans that people could grind and thus brew their own coffee at home. However, starting in the late 1960s, the number of people who consumed coffee declined sharply. "In 1962, 75 percent of the population drank coffee on a typical day," says Robert F. Nelson, president of the National Coffee Association (NCA). "In 1997, it was 49 percent." He blames that decline on dwindling social support for coffee, negative publicity about the effects of coffee and caffeine on health, and competition from other beverages, such as soft drinks. In the late '90s, that trend started to reverse. Today, more than half the U.S. adult population drinks coffee every day, representing more than 150 million daily drinkers. About two-thirds of Americans drink coffee with breakfast; 30 percent drink it between meals; and 5 percent drink it with meals other than breakfast. An estimated 17 percent of the U.S. adult population consumes gourmet coffee beverages, such as specialty coffee, mocha, latte, cappuccino, espresso-based beverages, and frozen and iced coffee beverages.

While most of the statistics on coffee consumption focus on adults, teenagers represent a growing market for coffee. Many don't care for the taste of coffee, but enjoy frothy, sweet, milkshake-like frozen coffee drinks. "In the past, coffee was a commodity, and there was very little innovation [in the industry]," Nelson says. "It was seen as an old-fashioned beverage for older folks. In the '90s, the social supports [re-emerged] for coffee. [Now] it's seen as a relevant, contemporary beverage." About coffee's impact on health, he observes that "today,

> ### Smart Tip
> Although just about every business guru advises choosing a business where the owner can combine profitability with passion, the requirement to love the product is especially true in the coffee industry. Learn everything you can about the culture of coffee and how to identify and produce quality beverages.

the consumer takes a much more pragmatic approach to healthy eating and living." It's possible and common for a healthy lifestyle to include coffee.

In many situations, coffee is replacing alcohol as the social beverage of choice, with people meeting for coffee instead of cocktails. It's acceptable for people to meet for coffee at any time of day, rather than just "cocktail hour."

Beyond the beverage itself, people frequent coffeehouses and espresso bars for a variety of reasons. Some go to meet with friends, socialize, and perhaps enjoy some live music or conversation; some are looking for a quick lunch and a drink that will help them weather the afternoon doldrums; others simply want a great cup of coffee to start each morning. Coffeehouse patrons tend to be sophisticated, and they often want unusual, exotic coffees that are expertly prepared.

These days, coffeehouses are meeting a strong social need. They give people a place where they feel like they belong, where they see the same faces regularly. It's often called the "third-place phenomenon": People have home and work, and they need a third place to go to. That place needs to be somewhere they can go regularly so they can form relationships with other people—in this case, with other customers and staff. While most people don't go to their favorite restaurant every day, they will go to a coffeehouse every day. Today's coffeehouses cater to a marketplace as varied as the coffee flavors themselves. Some target the breakfast and lunch-on-the-go market; others operate as evening destinations, with food items and perhaps entertainment and a wide range of styles in between. Many—especially those with free wireless internet access—have also become regular meeting places for homebased workers who want to get out of their houses to meet with clients, as well as workplaces for students and telecommuters.

"There continues to be innovation, and there continues to be expansion in the whole gourmet and specialty shop area. That will continue to have a positive impact on the consumption of coffee," the NCA's Nelson says.

Another plus for the industry is the growing sophistication of the American coffee drinker. "As more and more [types of] coffee are introduced to consumers and more and more coffee beverages are available, the consumer is developing a more educated palate and becoming more educated about the beverage itself," says Nelson. He points out that coffee drinkers consume different types of coffee beverages at different times of the day. "You may have one type of coffee at home for breakfast, a different type at lunch, and maybe an espresso after dinner. What the industry has tried to do is respond to consumers by providing them with different varieties so people can choose what they like."

Most successful coffeehouses have heavy foot traffic and high-volume sales. The majority will serve up to 500 customers per day and manage up to five customer turnovers during the lunch hour, despite having limited floor space and modest seating capacity. Profit margins for coffee and espresso drinks are extremely high—after all, you're dealing with a product that is more than 95 percent water. At the same time, customers' average purchase amount is $3 to $5, so you need volume to reach and maintain profitability.

Though most restaurants try to have either very fast turnover and low prices with basic food or slower turnover and higher prices with fancy food, coffeehouses break those rules. People will hang around a coffeehouse for an hour or more, sipping a $2 cup of coffee, but because of the huge profit margins coffee drinks can bring, even relatively low-volume operations can turn a profit if the business is run correctly.

Besides specialty roasted coffee by the cup, most coffeehouses also have espresso-based drinks (such as cappuccinos and lattes), assorted teas, bottled water, and fruit juices, along with an inviting assortment of baked goods such as biscotti (Italian dipping cookies), bagels, croissants, muffins, and a selection of desserts. Many also sell beans by the pound so customers can enjoy their favorite brews at home. Adding flavors to coffee drinks continues to be popular. Customers are ordering varieties ranging from simple chocolate and vanilla to raspberry, fudge ripple, and even more exotic tastes. Flavorings can be roasted into the beans or added in the form of syrups at the time the coffee is served. Flavoring syrups are available in regular and sugar-free versions.

Competition

You may find the competition from large chains such as Starbucks intimidating, but industry experts insist there's a place for everyone in the business. In fact, the independent retailer probably has the potential to be most profitable because it can ride on the marketing coattails of giants like Starbucks, yet its size provides a level of flexibility that larger organizations simply don't have.

Many smaller operators don't see the giant chains as a threat but rather as a marketing engine that can help educate the public about specialty coffee. Each individual shop then competes on its own—and you need to know what the other shops are doing. Small operations may not be able to compete in terms of marketing dollars spent, but they can compete with top-quality products, people, and presentation. You can get coffee anywhere you go—restaurants,

Smart Tip

Tip...

High-volume coffee sales help offset the high cost of food preparation. That means at least 30 percent of your total sales should be in coffee.

Grab 'Em by the Nose

Since location, high-volume foot traffic, and repeat business are the real keys to success, don't spend more than 5 percent of your advertising budget on conventional advertising. Instead, you can do several inexpensive promotions to help get the traffic started and keep it coming.

When you walk into a coffeehouse, you're immediately struck by the distinctive aroma of fresh-roasted coffee beans. This is what entices many people to go inside and linger over a hot cup of coffee, a delicious cappuccino, or a shot of espresso. People passing by can't resist slowing down a bit to see what's brewing inside.

Take a tip from cookie shops and bakeries: Grab customers by the nose. Savvy owners help nature along by having an open setup that will push aromas out the door with the help of strategically placed fans and vents. A fan mounted in a door transom is one of your best bets.

The smell of coffee will permeate the store even if you lock the beans in air-tight bins. It's crucial that you make sure the smell—and the beans themselves—always stays fresh, which is why it's so important to use the correct display and storage equipment.

---

bars, nightclubs, department stores, boutiques, gift shops, hair salons, automotive repair shops, even hardware stores. It's a universal drink that appeals to the majority of the population, and it's inexpensive to prepare. But not all these locations should be considered competitors.

Your four primary competitor groups are other coffeehouses, bakeries and doughnut shops, retail coffee and tea stores, and mobile coffee/espresso carts. Study what they're doing, and then put together a product, service, and ambience package that your target market will prefer.

Industry Trends

If you're going to operate a coffeehouse, you'll be interested in the following trends and predictions.

- *Product categories are solidifying their niches.* According to industry experts, straight (unblended) coffees will continue to move toward "estate marks," in which the specific geographic location—not simply the country—of the coffee's origin will play a key role in product marketing. Dark-roast coffees will remain popular for espresso-based beverages, and product quality will improve as the

> ### Bright Idea
> Set aside some room for coffee tasting. This can consist of a simple setup of thermoses of the coffees you sell at the end of the counter. Provide small tasting cups, stirrers, cream, and sugar. Encourage customers to sample coffee before they place their orders.

  roasting community achieves greater sophistication. Though blends don't demonstrate the same strength as other categories, local roasters will blend coffees that sell well in their marketing area because of regional taste preferences or local water conditions that may affect taste. In the future, we can expect to see a broader range of decaffeinated coffees, and flavored coffees will continue to be popular. We'll also see a significant increase in the market for organically grown coffees.

- *Coffee cafes will set the pace for new outlet creation.* The fastest-growing distribution channel will be coffee cafes, including espresso bars and espresso carts. This rapid growth will be fueled by three factors: the high gross-profit margin of selling coffee by the cup, the fact that espresso-based beverages are difficult for consumers to prepare correctly at home, and the fact that existing food-service outlets will be slow to upgrade their product quality to the level of specialty coffee operations.

- *Retail roasters are a driving force in product lines and marketing.* "Microroasteries" remain popular. (Micro-roasting is when coffee beans are roasted in small batches so that the roasting can be fine-tuned for the specific bean, from batch to batch.)

- *Consumers will continue their two-tier system of shopping.* Consumers patronize both establishments that sell bulk items, typically at a discount, and specialty stores. The specialty coffee product category is expanding rapidly.

- *Consumption of iced and frozen coffee is on the increase.* Iced coffee is cooled coffee served over ice; frozen coffee is served as either a blended or granita (a granular dessert ice with a sugar-syrup base) ice drink. Frozen coffees can be made in machines designed for that purpose or in basic blenders, which makes them easy to add to a menu. When you use blenders, you can make these drinks to order. Some consumers are looking for "lite" versions of various frozen coffees, so you may want to consider adding some low-fat frozen coffee options.

Setting Up Your Facility

Just as coffeehouses aren't restricted to serving a particular market group, neither are they limited to occupying a certain kind of facility to be profitable. Given the markets you're going to target, your hours of operation, the volume of coffee you expect to sell, and the geographical locations under consideration, you can choose from freestanding buildings, downtown or center-of-town storefronts, and mall spaces. A typical coffeehouse is 800 to 3,000 square feet. If coffee- and espresso-on-the-go will be your specialty, you won't need as large a facility as someone who intends to run a coffeehouse and bookstore. Likewise, starting in a large facility of 2,500 square feet or more is ideal for an entrepreneur who wants neighborhood regulars to be able to lounge around drinking coffee for hours and not feel rushed or crowded (see the two sample coffeehouse layouts on pages 111 and 112).

> ### Smart Tip
> Coffee experts advocate storing beans so they'll be protected from light and air. To let your clients know your beans are properly stored and therefore are of high quality, display only beans that aren't going to be sold in transparent containers.

When allocating space, a good formula to follow is to allow 55 percent of your space for the seating area, 25 percent for your production area, and 20 percent for your customer service area, including the bar. If you let the production area fall below 25 percent, you run the risk of having problems with service.

Depending on the amount of cash you have to invest, you can spend $20,000 to $200,000—or more—on your facility. This depends on whether you're starting from scratch or converting an existing food-service business and what you plan for a theme and décor.

Customer Service and Seating Area

This area must convey the atmosphere you've chosen in a manner that takes advantage of the available space. Large coffeehouses use a waiting area and cashier's station located at or near the entrance to avoid causing traffic jams at the service counter. The cashier's station is usually parallel to a wall. You can design it as just a small counter with a cash register or use the space to display specialty items such as coffee grinders and mugs, bags of coffee beans, and perhaps some of the baked goods you offer. As an alternative, you can set up your cashier's station at the threshold between the counter and the seating area.

Stat Fact

Coffee drinkers consume an average of 3.1 cups of coffee per day, and the average coffee cup size is 9 ounces.

If you're tight on space, you can skip the display areas. Any accessories you sell can go on shelves within customers' reach. More expensive items, such as espresso and cappuccino makers, can go behind and above service counters.

When considering the layout of your service area, keep this in mind: While long lines out the door generally convey the fact that quality goods are inside, they can also deter busy shoppers or commuters who want to pop in and out. Try to leave space to allow for a two- or three-line service approach, with enough room for those who have ordered to stand off to the side if necessary. Also, be sure your coffee production equipment is placed near the service counter, not away from it, so that efficiency in serving beverages is maximized.

Assuming you want to have a coffee bar, you'll generally want to have one bar seat for every three table seats. A coffeehouse with 75 table seats, for example, should have about 25 seats at the bar. For bar stools, allow about 2 square feet per stool, while tables should have about 10 to 12 square feet per seated customer.

A bar is a good idea because it also serves as an additional waiting area for people looking to grab a table when one opens up. You'll also need to provide public restrooms, which should be located close to the dining area.

Coffee on Ice

One way to add some variety to your menu is to serve iced coffee drinks. Making delicious iced coffee takes a special knack. It's not enough to just brew coffee and chill it. One coffeehouse owner we spoke with uses a "cold drip" method. She combines the ground coffee with cold water for an extended period of time, and the process extracts the flavor and aromatics but not the acidity from the coffee. It then forms a concentrate, which can be diluted to make iced coffee drinks.

Because the resulting beverage has no acidity, it's creamy and works better as a cold beverage. However, keep in mind that acidity is an important part of the coffee profile. If you were drinking a cup of hot coffee with no acidity, you would find it bland or flat. But using a cold drip process and no acidity for iced coffees makes for a better cold drink.

Production Area

Your coffee and food production area should promote the efficient delivery of food and coffee to the customer area. Your menu should be your prime consideration when you design your production area. By taking what you serve into consideration, you'll be able to cut down on the amount of space and equipment needed to run an efficient operation. Generally, you'll need to allow approximately 25 to 35 percent of your total space for your production area. This includes room for receiving, storage, food and drink preparation, cooking, baking, trash, dishwashing, an employee-only area, and a small office. Receiving and food storage will take up about 8 percent of your total space. These areas should be strategically located as close to the front or rear door as possible. Your dry storage area should be adjacent to the receiving area.

If you've decided to serve food as well as coffee, you'll need about 12 percent of your total space for food preparation, cooking, and baking (depending on what you plan to serve). Your equipment might include prep tables, fryers, a cooking range with a griddle top, a refrigerator with a freezer, soft drink and milk dispensers, an ice bin, a broiler, and exhaust fans for the ventilation system. Arrange this area so everything is positioned within reach and two or more people can comfortably work side by side

You've Got to Know Beans About Beans

When it comes to storing and displaying your beans, you may be tempted to go with something attractive, such as natural wood cases, barrels, and bins, instead of something practical, such as nonporous wood or plastic. Wood is the worst type of material for coffee bean storage, because it can promote staleness and bad taste. It's notorious for absorbing coffee oils, which penetrate the wood grain and then go rancid. When you add fresh coffee beans, they absorb the rancid oils and are ruined.

If you go with a wood décor, get a guarantee from the manufacturer that the wood is nonporous, or line the bins with heavy-duty nonporous plastic. Replace the plastic routinely to ensure freshness. Remember, coffee is best stored away from light and air.

For displaying limited quantities of beans, your best option is to use nonporous display bins made of acrylic, glass, or plastic. Be sure to wash them on a regular basis.

when you're at maximum production. You can center the prep area in the middle of the kitchen or, for smaller cafes and bars, below or behind the counter. For more on setting up prep or full-service kitchens, study the chapters on restaurants, sandwich shops/delicatessens, and bakeries, and adapt that information to the size and scope of your menu.

Most coffeehouses use interesting-looking and sometimes ornate espresso machines, so they locate their beverage centers directly behind the counter in full view of the customers. Customers want to be able to smell the aromas, watch you prepare drinks, and make sure they're getting exactly what they want. This also allows employees to get the order to the customer quickly.

Arrange your dishwashing area toward the rear of the kitchen, perhaps in a corner so it doesn't interrupt the flow of employees in the prep area. Your dishwashing equipment needs will depend on whether you use traditional tableware or disposable products.

Your facility must make it as easy as possible for you and your employees to serve a large number of customers quickly. By allowing customers to seat themselves and approach the counter when they want to order, you can eliminate most of the problems traditional restaurants and other labor-intensive food-service operations face.

Equipment

For an average-size coffeehouse, equipment costs range from $12,000 to $70,000 or more, depending on the number of coffee and espresso machines purchased and the extent of food-service operations (see the "Coffeehouse Equipment and Fixture Checklist" on page 103 for a comprehensive list).

Coffee and Espresso Machines

Coffee and espresso machines are the heart of a coffeehouse. You can operate profitably without a convection oven or a walk-in refrigerator, but good coffeemakers and espresso machines are absolutely mandatory.

Coffeemakers are used for brewing straight coffee, and espresso machines are used for brewing espresso and for making espresso-based drinks that require steamed or frothed milk. Although they're notoriously expensive and temperamental, industrial espresso machines have come down in price over the years, and their reliability has improved. Still, the most frequent and costly problems coffeehouse and espresso bar owners face are usually with their espresso machines. Sales either stop when the machines go down, or owners have to do what they can with a backup system, which annoys customers who expect prompt service. Daily cleaning and regular maintenance of these machines is a must. Many parts of the machine can be quickly rinsed with hot water and/or wiped down after each drink. You may want to have your machines serviced completely on a monthly or semimonthly basis.

There are four key features to look for in an espresso machine:

> **Smart Tip** ◯ Tip...
>
> Read every book and trade magazine you can find on the subject of coffee and coffeehouses. Become as familiar as you can with the business, the industry, and your target markets. Make reading industry magazines and newsletters an important part of your day so you can keep up with the changing commodities market and how it will affect the price of coffee. Most metropolitan newspapers track commodities in their business sections.

1. *Volume*. How much espresso can the machine make each day? Here's how to tell: Espresso machines differ chiefly in the number of "groups" they have. The group is the part of the machine that acts as a stationary lock to fix the removable handle or "head" to the machine. The finely ground coffee is placed in a perforated metal cup known as a portafilter. The filter is placed into the head, and the head locks into the espresso machine at the group. Most of today's machines are single-group or two-group, with one group and one corresponding head that locks into place or two groups and two corresponding heads, respectively. Heated water comes out of the espresso machine's tank at the group and is forced, at 10 atmospheres (a unit of pressure equal to air pressure at sea level) of pressure, through the coffee grounds.

   Most coffeehouses and espresso bars that do any volume of business have two-group machines, which range in price from $3,000 to $9,000. You'll probably never need anything larger. Using a single-group machine with a twin head (having two spouts at the bottom of the head instead of one, which doubles your capacity), you can make 100 to 200 espresso-based drinks a day. However, keep in mind that a busy coffeehouse can sell upward of 300 espresso drinks a day.

   In the beginning, to save on your initial cash outlay, a single-group machine may provide sufficient capacity. After you're established and your business begins to grow, you may find that you need to buy a second single-group machine.

2. *Warranty*. Any machine you buy should come with some kind of warranty—at least 90 days and preferably a year. Warranties vary tremendously among espresso machine manufacturers. If you buy a foreign machine, there's no guarantee that

you'll be able to find someone who can fix it unless you buy it through an American distributor.

3. *In-line filters.* If you use an outside water source to provide water for your espresso machine, you won't know much about the water's chemical composition. If the water in your area is high in minerals and other compounds, those substances will begin to collect in your water line much like they do in your reservoir. Espresso machines that come with simple in-line filters will slow the rate at which deposits begin to collect in the machine, allowing it to run better and require less maintenance.

4. *Reservoir or tank.* Look for machines with reservoirs made of stainless steel rather than copper. Stainless steel is better at retarding the buildup of calcium and other mineral deposits along the tank walls.

Coffeemakers are far more readily available than espresso machines, and they're relatively easy to operate. With a few exceptions, they all work the same way: Heated

---

Bright Idea

Team up with other food-service businesses to create your menu. Find a bakery that can provide your morning pastries, croissants, sweet breads, bagels, and muffins as well as your midday sweet snacks, such as cookies, brownies, and even dessert items. Look for a deli or a caterer that will sell you premade sandwiches that you can sell from a refrigerated case.

Grinding It Up

A key piece of equipment will be your coffee grinder. Grinding coffee to the right consistency has a lot to do with the quality of the finished product. Electric mills have dials indicating the kind of coffee grind that's right for various coffeemakers.

You can buy a new coffee grinder with several grind selections for $700 to $1,300, or you can lease one for $20 to $35 per month. Your coffee supplier will either have them on hand or know where you can get one.

Most coffee mills are 24 to 36 inches high. Place the mill on your rear display counter, and position it so your clerks can use it easily. When customer traffic increases, add a second grinder. As with your espresso machine, cleaning and maintenance of your grinder is crucial.

Coffeehouse Equipment and Fixture Checklist

- ❑ Bakers' bins and tables
- ❑ Beverage center
- ❑ Blender
- ❑ Breakdown table
- ❑ Broiler
- ❑ Cappuccino maker
- ❑ Cheese melter
- ❑ Coffee grinder(s)
- ❑ Coffee machines
- ❑ Convection oven
- ❑ Dishwashing machine
- ❑ Display cases
- ❑ Equipment for dishwashing
- ❑ Espresso machine(s)
- ❑ Food cutter
- ❑ Freezer
- ❑ Fryer
- ❑ Griddle-top range with oven
- ❑ Heat lamps
- ❑ Hot-water machine

- ❑ Ice cream cabinet
- ❑ Ice machine
- ❑ Kettle
- ❑ Lighting
- ❑ Preparation and steam table
- ❑ Preparation sinks
- ❑ Pressureless steamer
- ❑ Refrigerator
- ❑ Roll warmer
- ❑ Sandwich table
- ❑ Scale (for receiving area)
- ❑ Service counter
- ❑ Shelving
- ❑ Tables and chairs
- ❑ Tableware
- ❑ Toaster
- ❑ Utensil racks
- ❑ Ventilation system
- ❑ Water station

Note: This checklist is appropriate for a coffeehouse with a fairly elaborate menu. A coffeehouse with a limited menu would only need a portion of this equipment.

▲

Add It Up

When it comes to extenders and additives, such as chicory and other spices, the best route is to sell them selectively. Many flavors such as cinnamon, orange, chocolate, and anise go well with coffee, but if you routinely order coffee spiced with these, you'll probably run into a serious inventory problem. The same holds true for chicory, which isn't roasted with coffee but is added afterward.

Offer spices and coffee extenders (available through coffee suppliers) for consumers to add to their own beverages or that they can purchase to take home. Spiced teas are another matter, since many teas are at their best and are most popular with certain spices. Let a good tea supplier put you on the right track on that front.

water is forced at 10 atmospheres of pressure through finely ground coffee beans to infuse them. Regular coffee has about 7 percent soluble solids, while espresso contains roughly 25 percent.

Your expected business volume will determine the number and kind of coffeemakers you should purchase. Coffee machines are fairly standard. Most use paper filters (some use metal) to hold the coffee grounds as the water filters through, and each pot holds 50 to 70 ounces of coffee. Prices for commercial coffeemakers range from $300 to $1,200. You may want equipment that looks good sitting behind the counter, but reliability and quality

Bright Idea

An essential element of success in the coffee business is to remember that the anchor is coffee, but it pays to explore options that will enhance the primary product, such as pastries and other baked goods, additional beverages, gift baskets, and so on.

output should be the two factors that influence your purchasing decision the most.

Inventory

Your initial inventory will depend largely on how much startup capital you have available. For a 600- to 1,000-square-foot coffeehouse or espresso bar, plan to spend

$4,000 to $9,000 on coffee and $1,700 to $5,500 on accessories (if you sell them) to get started.

Your inventory costs will probably fluctuate during the year. If you serve food, you'll likely buy more produce during the summer when you're serving lunches with fresh vegetables. In the winter, coffee sales will soar because of the cold weather and gift-giving holidays.

Order coffee beans once or twice a week from local suppliers to ensure freshness. Most roasters do their best to accommodate clients and deliver in whatever quantities are needed. Remember that coffee beans begin to go stale the moment they're roasted and will keep for only one to three weeks if stored properly.

Your inventory should include coffees from several countries. To start, offer at least five decaffeinated coffees, plus at least a dozen regular coffees (your wholesaler can give you suggestions about the best selling types). For the sake of variety, don't focus strictly on blended coffees or devote your entire inventory budget to select estate-grown beans. Create as much diversity as you can with the amount of startup capital you have. You should begin with a coffee inventory of 400 to 700 pounds.

Here's a list of the different kinds of coffee, decaffeinated coffee, tea, and accessory items that can be used to stock your coffeehouse:

- *Coffee.* House blend (your choice), espresso roast, French roast, Italian roast, Vienna roast, Colombian supremo, Colombian popayan, Brazilian santos, mocha java, Mexican, Guatemalan high-grown, Java estate, Costa Rican terrazu, royal Hawaiian kona, El Salvadorian, Kenya Nairobi AA, Antiguan, Arabian mocha (Yemen), yirgacheffe, Ethiopian sidamo, Bolivian, Honduran, Nicaraguan, Panamanian, Paraguayan, Venezuelan, Tobago, Celabese, Ecuadorian, Peruvian, Haitian, Madagascar (Malagasy), Indonesian, Jamaican blue mountain, Tanzanian, Ugandan, Ivory Coast, Rwanda/Burundi, Sierra Leone, Zaire, Singaporian, Philippino, Liberian, Sumatra mandehling, Sumatra linton, and Zimbabwe code 53.

- *Decaffeinated coffee.* Espresso, Colombian, Costa Rican, El Salvadorian, Brazilian santos, Sumatran, mocha java, Vienna roast, and French roast.

- *Tea.* Earl Grey, chamomile, English breakfast, oolong (Taiwanese jasmine), black jasmine (from mainland China), Lapsang, Pingsun, Congou, Keemun, Darjeeling, Assam, Ceylon, rose hips, Russian,

Smart Tip

Keep a reasonable supply of tea and hot chocolate on hand at all times so people who don't drink coffee can still enjoy your coffeehouse.

spearmint, peppermint, lemon mist, lemon lime, orange pekoe, golden-tipped pekoe, lemon, apple cinnamon, cherry, orange nutmeg, and cinnamon.

- *Miscellaneous.* Sugar, artificial sweetener, cream, nondairy creamer, ground cinnamon, vanilla and chocolate powder, flavored syrups, and lemon slices.

- *Accessories.* Consumer coffee mills (electric), filter coffeemakers (various sizes and styles), tea eggs and filters, various coffee filters, insulated carafes, tea kettles (including copper), nonelectric espresso makers, mugs, cups, creamers, sugar bowls, and tea services.

- *Retail and other supplies.* Sealable bags (for selling coffee beans by the pound), labels (for coffee bags), plastic or metal scoops, paper cups and lids, stirrers, and napkins.

Staffing

It's not enough to have the right equipment and properly roasted coffee. You also need people who understand coffee and know how to make the beverages with skill.

A key member of a coffeehouse staff is the barista, the person who prepares espresso. Baristas are extremely well-versed in the language of coffee, and espresso-based drinks are their specialty.

If you expect to stay open more than 12 hours a day, you'll need two baristas, one working full time and one part time. The part-time person can help tend the counter during peak hours or work the early-morning or late-evening shifts. Baristas are usually paid an hourly wage and keep whatever tips they generate, which can be substantial if they make exceptionally good espresso. As with a good bartender, you can hire a qualified barista at a reasonable $7.50 to $10.50 per hour, depending on your location. The best place to find talent is at your competitors—espresso bars, restaurants, and other establishments that sell espresso drinks.

Look for someone who knows how to make all the standard espresso drinks as well as concoct their own creations and fill customers' exotic drink requests. Your espresso expert should be quick pouring, consistent, and especially personable—more so than any other server in the house. Just like good bartenders, experienced baristas possess the ability to make small talk with people while juggling several drink orders in their heads.

> **Bright Idea**
> If your coffeehouse is extremely successful and you want to increase your evening and late-night business, consider adding alcoholic beverages to your menu. You can increase sales significantly by selling coffee drinks, desserts, and brandy.

The remainder of your staff will depend on the size and style of your establishment and the range of your menu. The chapters on restaurants and sandwich shops/delis can help you determine how many people to hire based on the kind of establishment you want to open.

The Coffeehouse Market

Even chain coffeehouses vary in style, design, and menu offerings, depending on the particular market they serve. For an independent operator, it's critical that you understand your target market and tailor your operation to meet its needs.

Just about everyone over the age of 15 is a potential coffee/espresso bar patron. But such a vague market description won't help you build a successful coffeehouse. Consider targeting one or more of the following customer groups:

- *Local consumers*. Area residents are clearly a prime market for most coffeehouses. Those who live in the neighborhood are in proximity for all or part of the day and therefore constitute a substantial group of potential customers. If you plan to set up shop in a rural area, a suburban neighborhood area, or an urban area with a large residential population nearby, this is the first market to target.

- *Commuters*. A coffeehouse offers precisely what most morning commuters are looking for: a good cup of coffee and a bite to eat. Coffee is the universal breakfast drink, and a muffin, croissant, or pastry is the perfect accompaniment. While competition for the breakfast market among doughnut shops, fast-food chains, and traditional coffee shops is fierce, a business that specializes in coffee has a competitive advantage over the more generic breakfast places that serve low-grade coffee. The only substitute for good coffee, as far as coffee drinkers are concerned, is better coffee. Coffeehouses can offer quick breakfast foods, and often serve the best coffee in town.

  At the end of the day, coffeehouses in urban areas can target customers who work in the area but live elsewhere and don't have time to go home before meeting up with people for dinner or evening entertainment. Given the

> **Bright Idea**
> During peak periods, consider adding an express line to accommodate customers who just want a basic hot or iced coffee and a simple pastry or snack so they can get in and out quickly. The customer who wants the cappuccino, the latte, the double iced mocha, or other type of labor-intensive beverage can go through the regular line and get full service.

choice between battling other drivers on the highway or spending a relaxing hour in a cafe until traffic dies down, many commuters will choose your cafe. The evening is ideal for promoting "happy hour" coffee specials.

- *Campus folk.* Some of the most profitable coffeehouses in the country are located near schools and universities. High school and college students, as well as faculty members, are a strong market. Despite apparently limited spending power, students have embraced coffeehouses and are putting in long hours drinking coffee, studying, and talking within their walls. Coffeehouses near

> ### Beware!
> Coffee roasting is a complicated process, and it shouldn't be undertaken lightly or without a great deal of study. Roasting is truly an art—it's what transforms the beans into a flavorful brew. Though there are numerous advantages to roasting your own beans (lower cost and quality control, for example), don't move into this area until you have sufficient industry experience and capital to support the required investment.

campuses are typically open well into the night. In addition, the coffee and foods they serve are inexpensive, and unlike bars, both the atmosphere and the menu are conducive to industrious behavior. Because coffeehouses don't serve alcohol, they don't enforce age limits, and that means students under 21 who can't go to bars have a place to gather.

- *Entertainment crowd.* Those who travel to shopping districts and commercial centers seeking entertainment are also usually in search of some food or refreshment. A coffeehouse located near an entertainment venue is a convenient place for a snack, a quick meal, or just a cup of coffee before or after the main event.

- *At-home gourmets.* Many people who call themselves gourmets enjoy experimenting with new coffee flavors and espresso drinks at home. You can encourage these individuals to try different varieties and expand their awareness of unblended or "straight" coffees and espressos. One of the big appeals of a specialty coffee operation is that customers can pick and choose their own coffee beans to take home or to the office.

About Beans

Many coffeehouse patrons are well-versed in the language of coffee, which means they understand the difference between arabica and robusta beans, and they know how an espresso, cappuccino, or latte is supposed to taste. Coffeehouse patrons are usually acutely aware of the consumer choices they make, buying food products for prestige, nutritional value, and distinct taste. For instance, they're most likely to buy estate coffee, which is labeled with the name of the estate on which it is grown and carries the same status and appeal of fine wines. Having become accustomed to the taste of high-quality coffee, coffee connoisseurs don't consume the low-grade, mass-produced coffee brands sold in supermarkets.

As a coffeehouse owner, you must at least match, if not surpass, the coffee knowledge of your patrons. While this book will provide you with information on the mechanics of starting and running a successful coffeehouse, you should dedicate yourself to in-depth research on your product before you invest your time, energy, and financial resources in opening a shop of your own. Despite its apparent abundance, only a small amount of the total coffee harvested each year is true gourmet coffee, made with premium arabica beans instead of low-grade robusta beans.

You'll need to decide what types of beans you'll offer and use in your beverages. Some people love dark-roasted coffee; others believe it kills the natural taste of the drink. Will you offer one or the other, or will you offer the full spectrum? How many types of whole beans will you make available?

Starting Each Day

At the beginning of the day, you should inspect your facility to be sure everything is as you or your manager left it the night before. The next step is to make a working plan of the day's events.

By the time your doors open in the morning, all your preparation work should be done. The better your setup routine, the easier it will be for you and your staff to focus on serving customers and the less you'll have to worry about whether you're going to run out of inventory and supplies in the middle of a rush. For heavy coffee and espresso production, you need to be prepared. If you're going to have a slightly different menu each day, which is a good idea, as customers will appreciate the change, all the ingredients that go into the day's menu items—certain coffee beans, milk, sugar, cream, flavorings, toppings, ice, condiments, etc.—must be ready. Give yourself enough time to make sure you have everything you need.

Most coffeehouses have about five varieties of coffee brewed and ready at the bar. It's important to keep the coffee fresh and warm. Some shops use the warmers that come with coffee machines or hot pads to help maintain heat, while others prefer to take the coffee immediately from the machine and pour it into insulated dispensers or carafes. Warming plates, because of their high temperatures, tend to keep coffee so hot that it loses freshness and develops a burned flavor after 30 minutes or so. That means you don't want to serve coffee that's been kept on a burner for more than a half hour.

You'll need to grind beans every morning and at intervals throughout the day. To ensure the freshest coffee, you should grind beans for each pot of coffee you make. For espresso, the rules are a little different. Because it's made by the cup, you're better off grinding perhaps half a pound or a pound at a time to accelerate the process. Your customer traffic and your menu will determine what you need to grind and how many pots should be ready for customers.

An over-the-counter coffee bar that seats 35 people may need to keep five varieties of coffee (four regular roasts and one decaf) brewing in five pots at any given time, while operating a single-capacity espresso machine. A popular 100-seat coffeehouse

A Matter of Taste

The language of coffee is complex, and you'll need to do some in-depth studying to be able to communicate comfortably with true coffee aficionados. Professional coffee-bean tasters use a process called cupping to determine the quality, acidity, and aroma of beans for selection in their blends. Here are some basic tasting terms you'll need to be familiar with:

❍ *Acidity.* This is the sensation of dryness that the coffee produces under the edges of your tongue and on the back of your palate. Without sufficient acidity, coffee tends to taste flat, so acidity is a desirable characteristic. Don't confuse acidity with being sour, which is a negative flavor characteristic.

❍ *Aroma.* Smell is a very powerful sense, and fragrances contribute to the flavors we discern on our palates. The aroma of brewed coffee has a wide range of nuances.

❍ *Body.* The feeling, or the texture, of the coffee in your mouth is its body. An example of body is the difference between the way whole milk and water feel in your mouth. Coffee body is related to the oils and solids extracted during brewing.

❍ *Flavor.* Acidity, aroma, and body combine to create the overall perception of the coffee in your mouth, and that is its flavor. General flavor characteristics are richness, which refers to body and fullness; complexity, which is the perception of multiple flavors; and balance, which is the satisfying presence of all the basic taste characteristics.

may have 15 different coffees ready to drink throughout the day (perhaps 11 regular and 4 decaf) and have a barista working a double-capacity espresso machine constantly.

Sample Layout of a Coffeehouse with Seating at Nine Tables and a Side Area for Coffee Accessories, Restrooms, and Storage

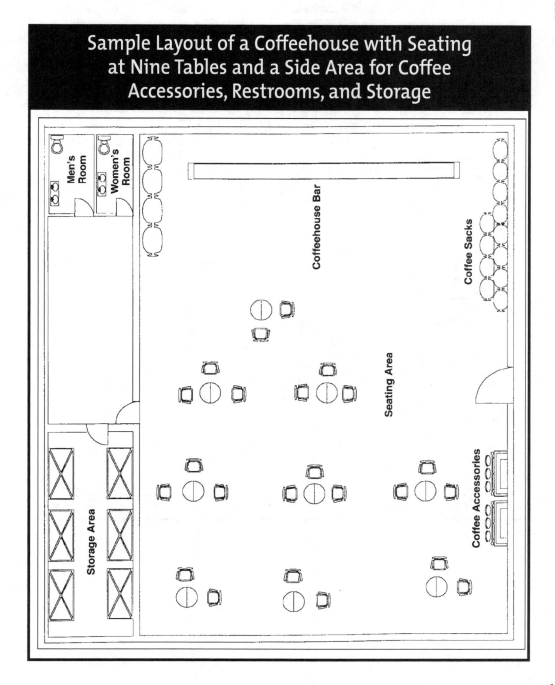

Sample Layout of a Coffeehouse with a Kitchen, Storage Area, Restrooms, Waiting Area, Cashier Station, and Seating Area with 14 Tables

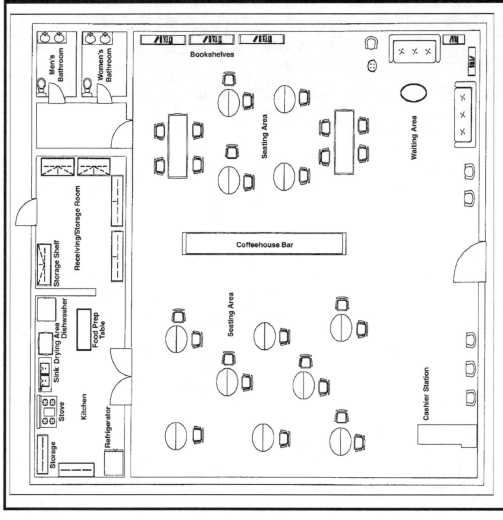

Bakery

Bread: Its role in our lives is larger than simple nourishment. Bread has always been a fundamental part of our world. Thousands of years ago, people learned to soak wheat kernels, beat them to a pulp, shape them into cakes, and cook them over a fire. Crushed cereal grains—a precursor to flour—have been found in the 8,000-year-old remains of Swiss lake dwellers. By 1680 B.C., the

Egyptians had invented leavened bread as well as the bakery. They established a hierarchy of breads: wheat for the rich, barley for the middle class, and sorghum for the poor. Centuries later, the English Parliament enacted a series of laws that limited the profits bakers could make from bread and required that every baker put his mark on his loaves. And that was the beginning of the trademark.

As colonists settled in the New World, their wheat crops flourished and so did bread innovation. The first successful threshing machine was invented, and milling processes were refined, creating better-quality flour. By 1850 there were more than 2,000 commercial bakeries in the United States.

> **Bright Idea**
>
> You can sell more bread and increase profits by selling hot, buttered rolls or bread by the slice. This is an attractive concept to customers, especially if you're located in a shopping area and also offer a selection of beverages. The taste of a fresh slice of warm, buttered cinnamon bread will keep shoppers coming back. Most bakers charge at least 50 cents per slice.

With the emergence of strip malls and competition from supermarkets that have in-store bakeries, "bread only" retail bakeries have almost disappeared from the United States. In addition to selling bread, bakeries today offer cakes, scones, bagels, and coffee drinks, and sometimes even offer full menus, including sandwiches, hot entrées, beer, and wine. Consumers love fresh bakery goods, but the market is extremely competitive. As you develop your particular bakery concept, keep in mind that you'll need something to differentiate yourself from other bakeries in town.

Before you start, survey the market. People strongly prefer some breads over others. Age, income level, and ethnic background of your market are important considerations when deciding what breads and other items to offer. Begin by checking area supermarket shelves to see which breads are fast movers and which end up on the day-old rack. Don't be afraid to ask grocery-chain buyers what the best sellers are.

In the Western United States, exotic breads remain popular. In the South, soft white bread is the best seller, and cakes also make up a significant portion of bakery sales. People in the Midwest seem to favor white bread as well, and sales of cakes, muffins, and cookies are also strong in this area. The preferred bread in the Northeast is the traditional Italian loaf; cakes, doughnuts, and bagels are also popular.

You'll need to decide whether you're going to bake hearth or pan breads or both. Hearth breads are made directly on a shelf or oven bottom, while pan breads are made in loaf pans. French, rye, and Italian varieties are leaders of the "hearth" breads. Your product mix will depend in part on how much of a purist you want to be and how much your customers like natural foods.

Easy Bake

Staggering baking schedules throughout the day guarantees fresh product for the customer. To set up your daily baking schedule efficiently, start by baking breads with high yeast levels or shorter proofing times. Get these first batches in the oven so they can bake while you're mixing breads with longer proofing times. You'll be ready to take a batch out of the oven at the same time another batch finishes the final proofing stage.

The average batch of bread takes about 1 hour and 45 minutes to bake. However, you can bake 15 to 20 varieties a day by baking all the wholewheat breads together, for example.

The best location for a bakery is a middle- to upper-middle income area with a population of at least 100,000. In less affluent neighborhoods, buyers might not want to pay the extra money for a loaf of specialty raisin bread when they can get plain white bread for substantially less at the supermarket.

Keep in mind that breads are low-margin items. It's possible but not likely that you would be able to make a living on high-volume bread sales alone. It's better to offer a wide variety of products.

Once you get your systems in place, producing at high volume shouldn't be a problem. After about four months in business, you should easily be able to produce 35,000 loaves of bread a month. That said, baking thousands of loaves a day is one thing, but selling them is another. Set realistic production and sales goals based on customer flow and projected growth. Also, become familiar with your customers' buying patterns. Demand for certain products will be different on different days of the week.

Smart Tip

Tip...

If you're going to sell wholesale, don't try to serve the commercial supermarkets. Most buy in huge volume, drive hard pricing bargains, and can change suppliers with no notice. Find wholesale customers who appreciate the quality you provide. Jim Amaral, owner of Borealis Breads in Portland, Maine, for example, sells to independent groceries, sandwich shops and delis, health-food stores, schools, corporate cafeterias, and restaurants. "We stay away from big stores because they treat the product like a commodity," he says. "We've had them come to us, and we've turned them down."

You can get formula recipes from suppliers, some flour mills, and, of course, from cookbooks. Many people who start bakeries are already avid bakers and spend a lot of time baking at home. Even many large multimillion-dollar wholesale bakeries began with a person who baked as a hobby. Tried-and-true home recipes can be adapted for large-scale baking.

Competition

The key to combating your competitors is knowing their business as well as you know your own. Here are some of the places where you can expect competition:

- *Supermarket bakeries.* In-store bakeries at supermarkets offer shoppers the convenience of one-stop shopping. What these bakeries usually lack, however, are high-quality baked goods and personal service. Many supermarkets use mixes or even buy ready-to-sell baked products rather than baking them from scratch. The items they do bake fresh are usually made early in the morning, so the store doesn't have that bakery-fresh aroma throughout the day.

  Supermarket bakers may not market their services as aggressively as independent bakeries might. While supermarkets may mention these departments in their weekly ads and announce in-store bakery specials over the intercom, they generally don't focus strongly on this segment of their business. With aggressive promotion, you should be able to compete successfully with such bakeries.

- *Chain bakeries.* Chain bakeries have the advantage of strong advertising campaigns to promote the chain name so it's recognizable. By purchasing a franchise, the franchisee automatically gets the benefit of the franchisor's marketing skills and ad budget. Chain bakeries also usually sell high-quality food at competitive prices. They should provide good service, but depending on how busy they are, they might not always do so. They don't always get to know their customers as independent bakeries do. This is where you have an advantage.

Not by Bread Alone

Bread may be the staff of life, but it is certainly far from the only item produced by bakeries. For example, a baker may also bake pies, cakes, cheesecakes, cookies, doughnuts, rolls, pretzels, croissants, bagels, muffins—the list goes on. You may want to offer a range of items, as does Jim Amaral, owner of Borealis Breads in Portland, Maine, or you may want to specialize in a very narrow product line, which is how

Kenny Burts built Kenny's Great Pies in Smyrna, Georgia. Burts started his company making key lime pies exclusively, but after 10 years in business, the company began expanding to other flavors.

If you choose to focus on a narrow product line, it needs to be outstanding. "We had people tell us early on, you can't survive on this one product," Burts recalls. "But I knew it was so special and so good that we could. Where we were able to excel was that we have something very unique and something nobody else was doing."

Your product line will be guided by a variety of factors. Amaral, for example, loves sourdough bread, and that's what he started his bakery with. Burts loves key lime pie and was making it as a hobby when friends urged him to go into business.

In addition to your own personal preferences, consider the demands of your market. Who will your customers be and what type of baked goods do they buy? This information should have been revealed by your initial market research.

Consider your available space and equipment. Be sure they are adequate for the product line you choose. Can your equipment do double or even triple duty? Will you have to spend a lot of time cleaning equipment and work areas to switch from making one product to another? And how will that affect your productivity and profitability?

Credit Where Credit Is Due

Most of your retail sales will be paid in cash, check, or credit card. You'll want to get a deposit or full payment in advance for special orders. But if you're selling wholesale, your customers will likely expect you to extend credit. Accurate record keeping is critical to maintaining your profitability.

Create a permanent record of credit sales and maintain it separately from your sales slips and invoices. This record should show the date, the invoice number, the amount of any new charges, a running balance of the total amount owed, the date and amount of each payment received, and a record of any invoices, collection letters, and collection phone calls made to this customer.

Make sure your invoices are clear, accurate, and timely. Send them to the right address and correct person. The prices on invoices should agree with the quotes on purchase orders or contracts, and disputes should be handled promptly. Your invoice and contracts should also clearly state the terms of sale, such as "net 30 days".

▲

Think about how your products work together and about the collective image they project. For example, if you bake a variety of breads and have only one dessert or sweet item, that product doesn't really fit in with your primary image. Or, if you're promoting your business as a whole grain or natural foods bakery, you don't want to have items that include highly processed or artificial ingredients.

Setting up Your Facility

You have several options when selecting your facility. If you'll specialize in serving customers on the go, you probably won't need a very large facility: 1,000 to 1,500 square feet, including kitchen space, should suffice. On the other hand, if you choose to offer a full menu and allow space for customer seating, you may want a space as large as 3,000 square feet. Keep in mind that having more square footage doesn't necessarily mean higher sales, so you may want to start small and expand or move if business warrants.

Plan to spend anywhere from $20,000 to $200,000 or more on the facility, depending on whether you're converting an existing facility or building from the ground up. There's no one-size-fits-all bakery layout, which is why we haven't provided a sample layout in this chapter. If you'll be starting a retail bakery, your front setup will be similar to the layout of the sandwich shop/deli (see Chapter 7 for information on setting up this type of facility). The back will depend on what you're baking. It's best to check out similar operations for guidance. This advice also applies to setting up a wholesale bakery.

> **⚠ Beware!**
> Just knowing the mechanics of bread making is not enough. You and your staff should be able to distinguish a good loaf of bread from a bad one, or even an average one. French bread should have a crisp, golden crust. Italian breads should have a denser consistency and a less-crisp crust. A good sourdough has a tough, chewy crust, slightly grayish-white crumbs, and a strong, distinctive flavor.

Kitchen/Production Area

The kitchen is usually located in the back of the store and includes all your bread-baking equipment, such as a mixer, divider, roller, proof box (a device that maintains the right temperature and humidity for dough to rise), oven, and walk-in refrigerator or cooler. You'll need counter space for baking and decorating activities and enough space for your employees to move around comfortably. Arrange production equipment according to the sequence of operations so you eliminate backtracking, reduce materials handling, and streamline the flow of work. Most bakeries allot at least 40 percent of their space to the kitchen.

Front Retail/Display Area

In the front of your operation, you'll have a retail area that includes such things as pastry display cases, a checkout counter, at least one cash register, and maybe a few pieces of equipment behind the counter, such as a cappuccino machine, coffee machine, soft drink dispensers, or other refreshment machines. The presentation of your storefront should be appealing to draw in customers.

You may also want to provide tables and chairs for customers, either inside or on a patio, so they can eat on the premises. Devote about 35 to 40 percent of your space to this area.

Restrooms

You'll need at least one restroom that's accessible to employees and possibly to customers. You may want to have two—one for men and one for women—especially if you offer a sit-down eating area. Your local health department can advise you on the legal requirements that apply to restrooms.

Office/Shipping/Receiving Area

See the guidelines in the chapters on opening a pizzeria (Chapter 6) and a sandwich shop/delicatessen (Chapter 7) for details on setting up this area.

Other Areas

Your bakery may feature a hot case in the sandwich area for prepared hot foods such as lasagna; a dimmed area with spotlights at each decorator station; and some successful supermarket-style presentations, such as self-service racks for bread and rolls and half-sized or quarter-sized cakes.

Equipment

The only way you'll meet high-volume production goals is with ultramodern automated equipment, such as Jet Air ovens, which move air for faster baking; rotating rack ovens; a drum grater/shredder that allows for continuous loading; high-speed bun lines and molders (for pan breads, baguettes, rolls, soft pretzels, and other items); conveyor belts designed for high-volume operations; and belt washers that reduce downtime. To reach this level of automation, figure on a minimum of $50,000 in total equipment costs. Of course, this equipment can be financed or leased with minimal down payments.

If you're starting on a small budget, you can buy used equipment packages that start at under $25,000. Look for ads in newspapers, trade publications, or online for bakeries for sale. Also keep an eye out for bankruptcy sales and special equipment auctions as these are opportunities for substantial savings on good used equipment. However, while this equipment can get you started, you should plan to add the up-to-date items later (see the "Bakery Equipment and Fixtures Checklist" provided on page 121).

Your main fixtures and equipment will be a refrigerator, sinks, display cases, a mixer, a dough divider, a molder (rounder), a proofer, a slicer, and a double-rack rotary or revolving oven.

Going to Sell in a Bread Basket

Your bakery can sell its wares either wholesale or retail, or both. Jim Amaral, owner of Borealis Breads in Portland, Maine, says it's easier for a wholesale baker to transition to the retail side than the other way around. Wholesale bakeries are generally larger and organized differently than retail operations. Wholesalers need to line up their commercial accounts, develop a sales strategy, and be able to service those accounts with fresh, delicious products delivered on a timely basis. Retailers need to be more concerned about generating foot traffic and attracting walk-in customers.

Retailers who try to expand into the wholesale market often find their retail facilities are inadequate in terms of space, capacity, and logistics. Amaral believes a retailer who understands this issue and is willing to open a separate wholesale location has a better chance of success.

Wholesalers who decide to expand into retail need to take the time to understand merchandising and displays and create an attractive environment for retail shoppers.

Bakery Equipment and Fixtures Checklist

❑ Bench scrapers

❑ Cash register

❑ Counters/display cases

❑ Dishwashing machine

❑ Dough divider

❑ Dough thermometers

❑ Lighting

❑ Mixer

❑ Molder (rounder)

❑ Oven

❑ Pans

❑ Proofer

❑ Racks

❑ Refrigerator

❑ Scales

❑ Showcases

❑ Sinks

❑ Slicer

❑ Tables and chairs

❑ Utensils

❑ Ventilation

A rounder is a device that smoothes the dough into the correct shape for baking. Look for a system with adjustable smoothing tracks for more accurate results. New rounders range in price from $4,000 to $9,000.

Stat Fact

The commercial bread slicer was perfected in 1928 by Otto Rohwedder, but it wasn't popular with consumers. Sliced bread grew stale faster than a whole loaf. It took packaging and improved storage techniques for sliced bread to become a truly great thing.

Dividers cut a large mass of dough, dividing it into individual pieces. Models vary in the pieces-of-dough per-hour they can process. Make certain the divider you purchase is capable of operating at the volume you anticipate for your bakery. Dough dividers can cost as little as $2,600 or as much as $10,000.

Dough is damaged somewhat by the dividing and rounding process, and the proofer gives the dough time to "relax" before the final baking stages. Inside the proofer are pockets where the dough rests. These pockets, which are typically mesh, are about the size of half a watermelon. Ranging in price from $3,000 to $60,000, proofers are available in many models.

Mixers usually come in various sizes and range in capacity from 40 quarts to about 160 quarts. For high-volume bread baking, use a spiral mixer, which holds from 100 to 200 pounds of flour. A spiral dough mixer is best.

The oven will be one of your most expensive items, at $15,000 to $26,000 or more, depending on its capacity and whether you choose a revolving oven or a pricier rack oven. In a revolving oven, the bread trays go in a revolving container, and the tray rotates, exposing the bread to all parts of the oven for even baking. Rack ovens work in a similar fashion, except vertically. You'll probably be baking many types of breads, cakes, and pastries, so buy an oven with a combustion system that easily converts from direct to indirect heat. This provides flexible control of bottom and top heat, allowing you to use different baking methods for different products. For superior-quality hearth breads, the oven should have a steam distribution system. Steam keeps breads like pumpernickel, French, and Italian from drying out and ensures a crisp crust on the outside.

Besides the major pieces of baking equipment, you'll need a wide assortment of small kitchenware items like pans, racks, scales, and utensils. Depending on the volume and type of goods you make, you may need as many as 200 pans. A hundred of these will be bread or sandwich pans of different sizes. The remainder may be used for rolls, pastries, and other items baked on a regular basis. One set of five pans can cost $60 or more. Expect to pay from $2,500 to more than $5,000 for pans, depending on whether you buy them used or new.

Inventory

When you're getting started, it's best to order your inventory conservatively until you know what will sell best. Your basic larder will include sugar, yeast, salt, dried fruits, shortening, nuts, cheese, and garlic powder. The premixed flours represent the largest single category of ingredient you'll need. At least in the beginning, you'll rely on premixes and won't need many additional ingredients.

You should budget 35 percent of your weekly gross income for inventory, and more than half this outlay will go toward

Bright Idea

Use day-old bread creatively by dicing or grinding it into croutons, stuffing mix, and bread crumbs. You could also set up a thrift counter and sell day-old bread for one-third or half off the price of fresh bread. This will allow you to at least recover the cost of the raw materials on the products you aren't able to sell fresh.

You Don't Have to Bake It All

Even though you operate a bakery, not every product you sell has to be baked on the premises. You have a range of options when it comes to buying baked goods from wholesale bakers.

You can buy other bakers' goods for your bakery but not advertise their name. Some companies sell fully baked products, which can be put right on the shelf, as well as frozen, fully baked products and frozen dough that has to be scooped, shaped, proofed, baked, cooled, packaged, and sold. The last choice lets you advertise your products as being "fresh baked."

Another option is to use the wholesaler's products and advertise the name of the supplier. This may require a licensing agreement so the supplier knows you're presenting its products in a good light. Some suppliers will also require a licensing fee. Alternatively, you could become a franchisee, operating your business according to an agreement with a franchise operation.

flour. Your monthly outlay will increase if you use a lot of special flours, like rice flour, which costs considerably more than white flour.

It's best to order flour every week or two from a nearby mill or supplier. This way, you can ensure quality control and freshness. These suppliers can also provide the paper goods you need. Polyurethane wrappings and bags represent about 3 percent of gross revenue, a surprising chunk of your business.

Staffing

If you're going to be a hands-on owner, you need to be prepared to work long hours and be comfortable working on a set schedule. "There's a lot of routine to running most bakeries," says Amaral. "You make onion bread every Tuesday, you make baguettes every day of the week." At the same time, he says, "You need some artistic sense about the food you're creating, where it's coming from, and how you're going about making it."

Unless you have baking experience, you'll need to hire a baker. The most efficient approach is to hire a baker/manager, and an assistant baker. Although the equipment does most of the work, machinery isn't entirely reliable. Many things can go wrong that only

▲

Mixing It Up

Ingredient suppliers or flour companies will provide you with bread bases, blended mixes, and plenty of advice. A premix includes ingredients like flour, shortening, milk, and salt. You only have to add water and yeast. This cuts the number of scalings (ingredient weighings) from seven or eight to three (mix, yeast, water), making it easier to produce a finished loaf quickly.

Bases require flour, yeast, and water. To make bread dough, you add three parts flour to one part base. Once you gain experience, you'll be able to cut back on some expensive mixes and experiment with your own specialties. With mixes for only three types of bread (white, wheat, and rye), you can create an enormous variety of breads by adding ingredients according to quantity recipes (known as formulas) or to your own taste. The difference between your bread and the ordinary loaf will be in these added ingredients.

The type and amount of ingredients you order will depend on the products you offer. You'll need molasses to bake a lot of sweet breads. For "healthy" breads, you'll use products such as wheat flour, honey, and organically grown fruits.

a baker would know how to correct. Dough can be overmixed, undermixed, overproofed, and so on. It takes a lot of experience and practice to develop baker's intuition.

In addition, bakers know the inventory requirements, and they're usually well-acquainted with suppliers and manufacturers. Your baker/manager can buy the inventory, deal with suppliers, and supervise production. The assistant baker will work the night or early-morning shift, depending on shop hours and volume requirements.

Experienced bakers are paid $900 to $1,300 or more per week, depending on their background and your local market conditions. Bakers' assistants will sometimes work as apprentices and can be paid less. Depending on your shop hours and volume, it's usually a good idea to have an assistant manager, too.

You'll also need salespeople to work the counter, ring up customer sales, take orders for cakes, and other specialty items, and keep the front area clean and orderly. Whether you'll need cooks and servers depends, of course, on the scope of your menu. If you sell wholesale, you'll need delivery people.

How much you'll pay in wages will depend on where you're located and the specific skill and experience level of the workers.

Food and Party Catering

Does working hard in the kitchen while everyone else is eating, drinking, and socializing in the living room sound like your idea of a good time? If your goal is to be in the catering business, the answer should be an emphatic yes.

Americans' love of dining and entertaining has created a tremendous market for off-premises caterers across the country. A wide range of social and business events are providing an opportunity for caterers to cook up tasty dishes and delicious profits. In fact, social catering has seen some of the strongest growth in the overall food-service industry in recent years, and that trend is expected to continue.

Successful caterers are organized, consistent, and creative. They enjoy working in an environment that changes every day. "Most restaurateurs hate catering for the exact reason that I love it: It's different every day," says Ann Crane, owner of Meyerhof's & Cuisine M, a catering service in Irvine, California. "A restaurateur is happy in a completely confined space where they're in control and they don't have to worry about anything leaving the building. With catering, you can get your inside operations down to the wire, but then you have to put it all in a truck and take it someplace to set it up, and you could lose control." Another appeal of catering, she says, is the strong relationship that tends to develop with clients. "This is something that's really personal. Food is a personal reflection of the host, whether it's in a corporate environment or someone's home."

> ### Bright Idea
> Catering is a great way to expand an existing food-service operation without investing a significant amount of capital. If you have a restaurant, deli, sandwich shop, pizzeria, or bakery, you can easily add a catering division. Start simply with drop-off catering, which is when the food is prepared and arranged on attractive platters and trays that are all disposable. Everything is dropped off ready to be set up on a buffet, and the containers can be thrown away after the event.

From a cost-of-entry perspective, catering is probably the most flexible of all the food-service businesses. While you need a commercial location, you can start small and build your equipment inventory as you need to. You may even find an existing commercial kitchen that you can rent, as Maxine Turner did when she started Cuisine Unlimited, her Salt Lake City catering operation. She operated in a school cafeteria for 10 years before moving into her own commercial facility.

In the beginning, if you need something unusual, such as a champagne fountain for a wedding reception, you can usually rent it rather than buy it. And your food inventory is easy to control, because in most cases you know well in advance exactly how many people you're cooking for.

Off-premises caterers—caterers who take the food to the customers rather than a catering department that operates on-site in a hotel or convention center—may offer everything from a gourmet breakfast in bed for two to elegant dinners for 20 to charity galas for more than 1,000. Some caterers specialize in one kind of food— cakes and breads, for example—while others offer a wide range of services, including floral arrangements, specialized props and costumes for theme parties, and wedding coordination.

The three major markets for off-premises caterers are:

1. *Corporate clients.* The primary need of this market is food for breakfast and lunch meetings, although there will be some demand for cocktail parties and dinners. Service can range from simply preparing a platter of food that's picked up by the client to cooking an elaborate meal and arranging it at the meeting site.

2. *Social events.* Millions of dollars are spent each year on wedding receptions—most of them on food. Other special events that are commonly catered include bar and bat mitzvahs, anniversary dinners, birthday parties, and graduations.

3. *Cultural organizations.* Opera houses, museums, symphonies, and other cultural and community organizations frequently have catered events ranging from light hors d'oeuvres to formal dinners, sometimes for as many as several thousand people.

You'll see a tremendous amount of crossover between these market groups. Turner started out with a primarily corporate clientele, serving continental breakfasts and boxed lunches. As her business grew, the corporate customers began hiring her to handle their personal social events, such as weddings and parties. And while she still does simple breakfasts and lunches, she's also catered such events as the celebration for the 100th episode of the hit TV series *Touched by an Angel,* which was filmed in Salt Lake City.

Site Seeking

Unlike a retail food-service operation, the location of your catering business isn't critical from a sales perspective. You'll be going to your clients' homes or offices to discuss the event and inspect their facilities; they'll have little or no need to visit your kitchen. Even so, be sure your operation doesn't violate any zoning ordinances or rental agreements or pose any threat to the community welfare.

Your location should be reasonably accessible by main thoroughfares, both for your employees to get to work and for you to get to various event sites. Be sure the parking lot is adequate and well-lit, as your employees may frequently be returning to their cars late at night.

Your facility needs to be able to accommodate the regular food deliveries a successful caterer will get. Having standard loading docks makes this significantly easier.

Of course, there's a wide range of additional markets and specialties. You might cook for people with specific dietary restrictions, such as kosher, macrobiotic, or other special food preparation requirements. You might focus on afternoon teas, celebration breakfasts, or even picnic baskets. Another popular niche market is cooking health-conscious meals for dual-career couples who don't have time to cook for themselves. You can either go to their homes and prepare the meals there or cook at your own facility and deliver the food ready to be served. Another option is to offer several days' or a week's worth of meals prepared in advance that your customers can simply heat and serve. Let your imagination run wild with possible market ideas, then do some basic market research to see what's likely to work.

First-rate caterers can demand and get top dollar for their services—but you and your food must be top rate. You should also keep in mind some general market trends. For the most part, extravagant meals and rich foods are a thing of the past. These days, people are eating less beef and more poultry and fish, and they're drinking less hard liquor and more wine. They're also more concerned about the bottom line than they once were. Many caterers say these trends have forced them to be more creative chefs, working with spices and ethnic dishes rather than with rich sauces.

Niche Hunt

Before you start your catering business, advises Salt Lake City caterer Maxine Turner, know your market from both the competition and customer perspectives, and find a niche no other caterer is serving. "Know every catering company and what they do," Turner says. "Find something someone else isn't providing, and focus your attention there in the beginning. Start out small. The diversity will happen as your company grows."

She advises targeting areas near office parks, because if you do a good job for a company's breakfasts, lunches, and business parties, the employees may also hire you to handle their personal social events. Ask businesspeople you know what they look for in a caterer and what they would like to have that they can't find.

You need to know what the other caterers in town are doing. Call them up and ask for their menus. Find out what services they offer, who works for them, and who their clients are. Use that information to develop your own service package and marketing strategy. "It's much easier to get started," Turner says, "when you're providing a service people want but that no one else is offering."

Setting Up Your Facility

The foundation of your catering business is your commercial kitchen. Reserve at least 75 percent of the area for food production, 15 percent for receiving and storage, and the remaining 10 percent for the office, where administrative activities take place. If you provide a lot of props and accessories for events, you may need additional storage.

The main thing to keep in mind when laying out your facility is to set up an efficient food preparation area. Organize your appliances, work surfaces, and equipment systematically so you're not trotting 10 feet to the sink to wash a handful of vegetables or carrying hot pots across the room to drain pasta.

Organize your kitchen around the major appliances and work areas for easy accessibility. For example, everything you need for cooking should be close to the stove, and all necessary peeling and cutting tools should be stored near the vegetable prep counter.

Give yourself plenty of clear workspace. Ideally, your counters should be stainless steel for both maintenance and sanitary reasons. Wooden counters are illegal in many areas because they increase the risk of food contamination. "We have a lot of linear table space," says Ann Crane. "A lot of our business will be 500 box lunches or 20,000 pieces of hors d'oeuvres for a party, and we'll need a lot of flat counter space, rolling racks and movable pieces to put them together."

Locate your dishwasher next to the sink so you can prerinse dishes and utensils. If you plan to hand-wash your dishes, a triple-sink arrangement (one sink for soaking, one for washing, and one for rinsing) is best. Keep racks on the counter next to the rinsing sink for drying the dishes, and store clean dish towels near the sink. A garbage disposal is a must for disposing of food scraps. Some municipalities require a separate sink for hand washing, so check your local health codes to be sure you set up right the first time.

The receiving area should be separate from the food preparation area and needs to be accessible to delivery vans. Ideally, it should have double doors and a hand truck for the easy transport of goods. You should also have a weighing scale set up to ensure that your deliveries are correct.

Your office area doesn't need to be elaborate. A simple desk, chair, phone, and computer should be sufficient.

If you have room, set up a small area where employees can hang their street clothes and store their personal belongings. You'll also want to put your restrooms in this space. A table and chairs for employees to use while on their breaks is a nice touch.

There's no one-size-fits-all layout for a catering operation, but check out the "Sample Layout of a 1,200-Square-Foot Commercial Kitchen" on page 151 to start

▲

Don't Try This at Home

Although some successful caterers start their businesses from home, most industry experts caution that the potential risks involved outweigh the economic advantages. Operating without health and fire department approval immediately opens you up to liability risks. Most insurance companies won't insure your business without compliance with state regulations and licensing requirements. In addition, you won't get wholesale price breaks from reputable food distributors who refuse to sell to operators without a resale license. Without adequate insurance, licensing, and payment of workers' compensation, some operators have lost their homes in lawsuits filed either by clients or injured workers. Bite the bullet, and do it right from the start.

Of course, even when they're properly licensed and located, legitimate caterers often face stiff competition from cooks operating illegally from their homes in violation of health codes. It's difficult for a caterer working out of a commercial kitchen to price competitively against such adversaries, who don't have the same overhead expenses. Even so, don't let these illegal operators drive your prices down to an unprofitable level. Focus on professional service and quality food, and you'll be around long after the homebased cooks have given up.

visualizing your setup. The best research you can do is to check out other operations and adapt their designs to your needs.

Kitchen Equipment

As you look at all the possibilities for equipping your commercial kitchen, you may find yourself overwhelmed by the quantity and potential cost of what you need. Just keep in mind that you don't need everything listed in this chapter to get started—and you may never need some of the items. It all depends on your volume and the type of food you're interested in preparing. Also, the price estimates listed here are for new equipment. Smart shopping for used items can save you a bundle.

Your major equipment purchases are likely to include:

- *Two commercial ovens.* One should be a hot top (an oven with a solid metal top that heats evenly) and the other should be a range top (an oven with the ringed metal burners you see in consumer kitchens). Expect to pay anywhere from $2,000 to $5,000 per oven, depending on size and number of burners.

- *Two convection ovens.* These ovens cook by circulating heated air and allow for efficient cooking that uses all available oven space. A double convection unit, with two ovens stacked on top of each other, will run $5,500 to $7,500.
- *Refrigerator.* A three-door commercial refrigerator will cost $3,000 to $4,000.
- *Freezer.* A two-door commercial freezer will cost $3,000 to $3,800.
- *Dishwasher.* A commercial dishwasher will be about $2,500 to $7,000.
- *Commercial-grade mixer.* This item can range from $450 to $2,200, depending on capacity.
- *Scale.* A 300-pound scale will ensure that items you purchase by weight are delivered in the correct amount. The price of $500 to $2,500 you'll pay for a good scale is well worth the investment in inventory control.
- *Ice machine.* Ice storage capacity should range from 45 to 400 pounds, depending on your needs. Prices increase with capacity, but you can expect to pay $1,500 to $4,000.
- *Food processor.* This item will cost $400 to $1,500.
- *Slicer.* This product is needed for meats and cheeses for sandwiches and deli trays. Cost is $300 to $3,000.
- *Sink.* You'll need either two or three compartments. A sink will cost between $600 and $2,000.
- *Stainless-steel worktables.* You'll pay between $300 and $1,000 each.
- *Baking equipment.* You'll need a proofing box (about $5,000, but could range from $3,000 to $60,000) and a baker's rack (between $100 and $350) if you plan to do your own baking.
- *Pizza oven.* If you plan to make pizzas, expect to pay $2,500 to $7,500 for a good pizza oven.
- *Two heat lamps.* You need these for keeping hot hors d'oeuvres warm at buffets. You'll pay $100 to $250 each.
- *Two hotboxes.* Hotboxes are necessary for transporting hot food. Expect to pay $700 to $3,000 each.
- *Carrying units.* Four to six fiberglass carrying units are needed for transporting both hot and cold food. These run $100 to $500 each.
- *Two to four coffeemakers.* Commercial coffeemakers run $300 to $1,200 each.
- *Six stainless-steel chafing dishes.* These cost $60 to $200 each.
- *Miscellaneous serving items.* You'll need assorted trays, sauce bowls, vegetable platters, meat platters, salad bowls, and punch bowls.

Cooking and Serving Equipment

In addition to major appliances and event accessories, you'll need an assortment of utensils for preparing and serving a variety of hors d'oeuvres and full meals. If you're an experienced cook, chances are you already own most of the cooking equipment you need. "The first mixing bowls I had were from my own kitchen," Turner says. "My first trays were wedding gifts I hadn't used in 10 years. My first inventory was my own personal things." Later, she began a wish list of items her chefs said they wanted or needed. When a particular item was repeatedly requested, she would budget for the purchase.

The point is that it's not necessary to go out and buy everything at once. Get the most frequently used items, of course, but give yourself some time to see what you really need before you buy an assortment of special equipment. You could easily spend $800 to $3,000 or more on miscellaneous cooking utensils, such as flatware, spatulas, garlic presses, cutting boards, and so on—but you don't have to. Don't buy needlessly. And remember: If your rate of use doesn't justify the cost of purchasing, you can always rent.

As you go along, you'll also learn to use whatever the client has for decoration, preparation, and serving. You can combine your items with theirs, particularly if you're catering an event in someone's home.

Use the following equipment list as a guide, and accept or discard the suggestions as you deem appropriate for your operation.

- *Utensils.* You'll need small and large ladles, tongs, kitchen spoons, measuring spoons (metal and plastic), measuring cups (metal and plastic), carving boards,

Miss Manners

An extremely valuable piece of "equipment" for caterers is a good book of etiquette. Amy Vanderbilt, Charlotte Ford, and others have written informative etiquette guides. You can check out these books from your local library, then purchase the one that best suits your needs. It will help clear up any questions you might have about table display, serving protocol, proper attire, and other issues that you may encounter from time to time. Your clients will expect you to know the answers to questions they may have about throwing their party in the most appropriate way, so brush up on your etiquette knowledge.

cutting boards, spatulas, wire whisks, pastry brushes, a potato peeler, a flour sifter, a can opener, a knife sharpener, an aluminum colander, funnels, a cheese grater, a radish rose, a melon ball maker, a garlic press, a pastry bag with assorted tips, a portion scale, meat and candy thermometers, an egg slicer, heavy-duty plastic food warmers, a citrus knife, chafing dish setup(s), wicker bread baskets, wicker cracker baskets, and three-prong plug adapters.

- *Knives.* A quality set of kitchen knives (with three brads holding the blade to the handle) can be bought for $250 to $350. The types of knives you need are carving, cheese, bread, paring, boning, and chef's cleaver.

- *Pots and pans.* You need frying pans; pots in ½-, 1-, 2-, 3-, 4-, 5-, 6-, and 10-quart capacities; a double boiler; a spaghetti pot; a fondue pot with warmer; omelet pans; and roasting pans.

- *Mixing bowls.* You'll need ceramic, stainless steel, and glass bowls in varying sizes.

- *Baking dishes.* Depending, of course, on whether you'll be doing your own baking or buying breads and pastries from a bakery, you'll need 9-inch pie pans, 9-inch cake pans, rectangular cake pans, cookie sheets, muffin pans, angel-food cake pans, bundt cake pans, springform pans, loaf pans, tart tins, and quiche dishes.

- *Hors d'oeuvres trays.* You should have small and large pizza pans, silver serving trays (round, square, and oblong), a coffee urn, and a candle warmer.

- *Chinaware.* Cups and saucers, soup bowls, salad bowls, salad plates, bread plates, dinner plates, base plates, and dessert plates are a necessity. White porcelain is a good choice, since it's durable, dishwasher safe, and goes well with a variety of foods and decorating themes.

- *Glassware.* You'll need water goblets, red-wine glasses (10-ounce), white-wine glasses (6-ounce), champagne flutes, martini glasses, highball glasses, old-fashioned glasses, cordial glasses, and brandy snifters.

- *Flatware.* Dinner knives, butter knives, dinner forks, fish forks, salad forks, soup spoons, iced-tea spoons, and teaspoons are essential. High-quality stainless-steel flatware will wear better than silverware and will require much less maintenance (in terms of polishing).

- *Linens.* You'll probably need napkins, round tablecloths, and rectangular tablecloths.

- *Cocktail accessories.* Pitchers, serving cart(s), strainers, shakers, stirrers, toothpicks, cocktail napkins, corkscrew(s), and ice bucket(s) are a requirement.

- *Miscellaneous.* You might also need cream and sugar sets, ashtrays, salt and pepper mills, a wheeled serving cart, scissors, candles, ribbons, matches, masking tape, paper napkins, transparent tape, garbage bags, garbage cans, paper doilies, mops, buckets, brooms, dustpans, and a first-aid kit.

Company Vehicle

For most catered events, you'll be transporting food and equipment. You can either use your personal vehicle if the amount of required supplies is small enough, or you'll have to lease or purchase a vehicle to meet your needs.

It's possible to spend $30,000 or more outfitting a new van with all the inventory and equipment a caterer might need. Some caterers have elaborate vans equipped with virtually everything but running water. Some caterers outfit their vehicles with propane tanks to cook on-site for outdoor events where electricity is unavailable and mobile warmers and refrigerators for locations where the facility is limited. But these are expensive extras that aren't necessary for someone just starting out. Your best bet is a no-frills approach: Invest in a good late-model used van. You should be able to find one for $10,000 to $20,000 if you shop carefully.

Inventory

The advantage of catering over other food-service businesses is that you always know how many people you'll have to feed. There's no guesswork, no waste, and no inventory needed in the traditional sense—at least in the beginning.

Certainly staples such as flour, sugar, grains, spices, canned goods, and frozen foods can be purchased in bulk and stocked on a long-term basis. But you won't be stocking food inventory the same way a restaurant does. Typically, you won't purchase foods until you have agreed on an exact menu with a client and determined the number of guests. Of course, as your business grows, you'll be able to stock more inventory and take advantage of the savings of volume purchasing.

The key to good shopping is organization. Sit down with your menu and make a list of everything you'll need to produce the party. If the preparation is going to require equipment you don't yet own, be sure to include that on your shopping list.

Once you've determined everything you'll need, organize your list by store and department. Then figure out the most efficient order in which to visit each store. A single shopping excursion may take you to a farmers' market, a wholesale outlet, a general grocery store, a delicatessen, a bakery, and a gourmet shop. Most of your shopping should be done the day before the party, although some fresh items (such as lettuce and bread) should be purchased the day of the event.

Wholesale or Retail?

Depending on the size of your jobs, it may or may not be worth it to buy wholesale goods. There are dealers in every major city who can supply you with fresh produce, meat, and other items in large quantities at low prices. This can mean significant savings when you're buying for large jobs or for several events at a time. Also, a big advantage of wholesalers is that most of them will deliver orders to your kitchen. But if you just need eight chicken breasts for a small dinner party, most wholesale dealers probably wouldn't be interested in making the sale. It would probably be easier to visit your nearby supermarket.

Staffing

Most catering operations have a core permanent staff supplemented by part-timers on a per-project basis. To provide quality service you'll need to understand the basic structure and division of labor at a catered affair.

The three basic kinds of catered social affairs are the formal, sit-down dinner; the informal buffet dinner; and the cocktail party. Naturally, as individual events develop personalities of their own, these three definitions often vary or converge.

The majority of business affairs will require little or no service and will mainly involve preparing platters of food for business luncheons that are either picked up from your facility or delivered to your clients. However, some business events—such as office holiday parties or formal dinners for major clients—will be run the same way as social affairs.

Typically, it takes two days to prepare food for any party. If all your ingredients are fresh and prepared from scratch at the last possible minute, those days will be full. An average party serving 50 to 125 people

Smart Tip

Tip...

Your employees should always be neat and presentable. After all, they're representing your company. They should dress unobtrusively, usually in dark pants or skirts with plain white shirts or blouses. You can add a discreet signature pin or apron to give personnel a distinctive look, but don't go overboard: You're there to serve, not to promote your company. If tuxedos are necessary for a formal affair, waiters are usually expected to provide their own garments.

135

requires one chef plus one or two kitchen helpers, depending on the complexity of the setup.

Managers and Other Employees

The key employee at any catered affair (and this is going to be you in the beginning) is the project manager. This person

organizes the food preparation and serving, hires the temporary help, and oversees the entire affair. The project manager must also be able to pitch in and prepare food in an emergency if the chef or one of the kitchen assistants fails to show up.

If you supply bartenders for an event, a good ratio is one bartender for every 50 people. You'll either employ these specialists yourself or subcontract their services, depending on your volume.

Waitstaff, buspersons, drivers, and warehouse personnel may be hired on either a temporary or permanent basis. Temporary means on a per-project basis; permanent means an employee who is paid regularly on a full- or part-time schedule. If you have 10 servers you can call to work as needed, they're typically paid as temporary workers.

Serving and food preparation personnel should be considered separate categories. A server might double as a driver and even as a busperson, but cooking and serving are

Now Presenting . . .

In addition to preparing delicious food, you must be concerned with how your meals look. Your clients hire you to create a special experience for them, to use your professional expertise and abilities to design a meal they couldn't produce themselves.

This doesn't mean simply plopping a sprig of parsley or a tomato rosette on each plate before it goes out the kitchen door. It does mean planning your garnishes and arranging your plates so that your food looks as good as it tastes. You have only two rules when it comes to garnishing: Everything should be edible, and the garnish should taste good with the food. Beyond these rules, the only limit is your imagination.

different areas of labor. Even with that in mind, you should look for employees who are flexible and who won't mind pitching in as needed in an emergency.

Clients who are trying to save money will frequently try to cut down on the number of service personnel for an event. Be firm and clear as you explain why this isn't a good idea. Guests who can't get their dirty plates taken away, get another hors d'oeuvre, or get a fresh drink are unhappy guests. Nothing will ruin a party quicker than insufficient serving personnel.

Event Staffing Guidelines

There's no better teacher than experience when it comes to knowing how to staff events. To help you get started, let's look at what experienced caterers would do when catering a party for about 100 people.

For a formal sit-down dinner with many courses, there will be eight or 10 people per table and 10 to 12 tables. You'll need two cooks or one cook, plus one or two assistants. For most parties, one server per table will be sufficient, but this can also vary. Some caterers will have one server for every 15 people; others will put two at each table to keep everything running smoothly. Another option would be to have one server for each table, plus an extra server for every two tables to remove dirty dishes and glasses. The project manager will oversee the service to all tables.

An informal buffet dinner will require three or four serving people and one cook, plus the manager. All people on the job should be versatile enough to double on tasks after the job is completed—for example, clearing tables, storing food, and loading equipment. For both formal and informal dinners, if there's cocktail service, two bartenders will be required.

For a cocktail party for 100 people, have at least one bartender on hand, plus two service personnel. If both hot and cold hors d'oeuvres will be offered, upgrade to three or four servers. If a lot of blended drinks will be served, your best bet is to have two bartenders. For a party of this size, some caterers routinely have two bartenders, two servers, and a busperson, regardless of the types of drinks being served. Still other operations have servers double as buspersons. Staffing requirements vary greatly depending on the type of cocktail party desired.

Some caterers don't provide the bartender or liquor for a cocktail party but will refer the client to reputable sources for this. Some provide ice, glasses, and bar setups, while others don't. Some provide beer and wine but no hard liquor or mixers.

Bright Idea

If you have steady clients who hire you for several events each year, change your catering menus monthly to offer variety and a new look.

These guidelines will help you plan your staffing until you are comfortable estimating your labor needs. No matter what kind of event you cater, having enough help on hand is crucial. Service can make or break a catered affair—and lack of it will surely kill your business.

Developing Menus and Setting Prices

Even though your clients will tell you what they want you to serve, you still need menus. Of course, none of those menus should be carved in stone; they must be flexible enough to accommodate your clients' preferences.

Providing sample menus will give you a solid base for meeting with clients, and they may give your clients some ideas about food combinations they wouldn't have otherwise had. Also, you can cost out your sample menus beforehand, which will make figuring prices easier. This will also allow you to give your clients a more accurate estimate. Nutritionally, you should strive to produce balanced meals with a good blend of the basic food groups. Each meal should contain about 1,000 calories.

You should also balance ingredients, textures, and tastes. If you serve leek and garlic soup as the opener, for example, you should not serve garlic chicken as the main course. Similarly, if the main course is chicken mousse, chocolate mousse would be out of place as a dessert.

When creating sample menus, include a variety of dishes and price ranges. If you specialize in Southern cooking or spectacular desserts, organize your menus to make these elements the focal point of your meals.

If you're planning to focus on the wedding market, you'll need a wide range of menus for hot and cold buffets, sit-down dinners, and other arrangements. A buffet table with a combination of hot and cold hors d'oeuvres, sliced meats and bread, fruit, and cheese and crackers is a popular choice. If you go this route, you should put together a list of hors d'oeuvres that your clients can choose from. You'll also need a wide range of wedding cakes (you can contract out to a local baker if cake decorating is not one of your talents). A photo album showing pictures of the kinds of cakes you can offer will help your clients select the cake they want. Punches, both with champagne and nonalcoholic, are also a staple at weddings.

The corporate market leans more toward platters of food that are suitable for business

> **Smart Tip** *Tip...*
>
> Coordinate menus with the season. Serve lighter foods in the summer (such as lobster and rice, Cobb salad) and heavier in the winter (such as beef Wellington and cassoulet).

breakfasts and lunches. Middle management and below will tend to want deli plates with sandwiches, cookies, vegetables and dips, fresh fruit, and similar items. If you're working with the upper echelons, you may be called on to produce something more elaborate, perhaps even cooking part of the meal at their office and supplying a server. Develop several menus based on these levels of formality.

Bright Idea

To check out the competition when you're doing your initial market research, give a few catered parties of your own. Hire the caterers you expect to be your strongest competitors so you can see exactly how they operate and what level of service they provide. It's a worthwhile investment in the future of your company.

Figuring out how much to charge is probably the most difficult thing you'll need to learn. When you're new, you may not have a solid feel for how much you can charge in your marketplace, how much ingredients for a particular dish will cost, or how much labor it will take to prepare a meal. You'll get better at this over time, but when you're starting out, it's important to cost out your menus carefully so you can make a respectable profit.

To cost out a menu, first sit down with the full menu. For each dish, break out the costs of the food by ingredients. Some dishes will be easier to price than others. For example, if a recipe calls for a boneless breast of chicken, a quick trip to the store can tell you exactly how much this item will cost. It's much harder to figure out the cost of a teaspoon of salt or other seasonings. Estimate the cost of smaller quantities and staples (such as flour, sugar, salt) as best you can.

Once you've determined the prices of all your ingredients, add them up. This is the total cost of the food you'll need to prepare the full menu. Multiply this figure by three to get the price you will charge the client. Dividing this figure by the number of guests will give you the price per head for the meal.

This is the most basic method of figuring prices, and most of the time it should cover your food costs, labor, and overhead and still leave you a net profit margin of between 10 and 20 percent.

Check your prices to make sure they're acceptable in your market by calling other caterers to find out what they charge for a comparable menu. If your prices seem to be in line with your competition, you're probably figuring correctly.

There are, of course, instances where this method won't work entirely. For example, if you're preparing a menu that's very labor-intensive, even if the ingredients aren't particularly expensive, you won't be able to pull a profit simply by multiplying your food costs because your time and employees' wages won't be adequately covered. In these cases, you should increase your prices so you and your employees are earning a decent hourly wage, based on the number of hours it's going to take to prepare the meal.

Smart Tip

Tip...

Look through cookbooks and gourmet magazines for ideas on presenting and garnishing your dishes.

Conversely, if you're making something like filet mignon, for which the main ingredient is expensive but easy to prepare, you'll have difficulty justifying high prices. In this case, you might consider multiplying the cost of the steak by two and the other ingredients by three to arrive at a fair price.

The cost per person, arrived at by multiplying the cost of the food price by three and dividing by the number of guests, is the cost for the food, labor, and overhead only. It doesn't include the cost of liquor, rental equipment, serving staff, or anything else. Be sure the final price you quote takes these expenses into consideration. Use the "Catering Price Quote Worksheet" on page 150 to figure out your price quote.

When the Customer Calls

When a client calls, you must be prepared to answer all his or her questions, make suggestions, and generally handle yourself in a pleasant and professional manner. The first phone call will rarely result in a sale for a number of reasons. First, the customer may be shopping several caterers. Second, you probably won't decide during that conversation exactly what's going to be served, so you won't be able to give a specific quote. Third, you'll want to inspect the site of the event before putting together your final proposal.

Many clients will pressure you for an exact price quote during the first phone call. Resist the temptation to do this. Even if the client knows exactly what he or she wants served, you won't know how much the cost of food and labor is going to be until you've had a chance to do your own calculations. If you make up a quote on the spot, it may either be too high, in which case you'll lose the job, or too low, in which case you'll lose money—or you'll have to raise your quote later, which isn't good for customer relations. Instead, try to satisfy the client with a general price range and promise a full written proposal later.

Use the "Initial Client Contact Form" on page 144 as a guide for taking notes during your first conversation. Many clients will be

Bright Idea

Offer to provide gifts for event attendees. You can help your clients choose a memento to be placed at each setting—perhaps something imprinted with a corporate logo—or help them choose special gifts for the guest of honor or committee members. You can purchase and wrap the gifts to provide a special service for your clients and increase your own revenue.

reluctant to tell you their budget for an event, but try to get a fairly good idea of how much money they have to spend. You should be able to adjust your menus to suit their budget, but you'll have to know what that budget is first. There are many cost-cutting methods you can use if the client seems uncomfortable with your more expensive-sounding suggestions. For example, you can substitute lower-cost ingredients with a similar flavor or use dishes that are easy to prepare rather than more labor-intensive ones.

After the first telephone conversation, your next meeting will likely be in person, preferably at the site where the event will be held. Bring your menus so the customer can review them and determine exactly what to serve. Get a firm number of guests and put it in writing; let the customer know that you will be planning your quote based on that number and that any changes will affect the final price. Determine the style of the event (sit-down, buffet, cocktail), and any particular equipment or service needs the client will have.

Take a tour of the site to see what equipment is available for your use and what you'll need to bring. Decide where the buffet will be, if there is one, and where the bar setup will go. Discuss staffing needs and be specific about who will provide what to prevent misunderstandings later. This information should also be included in your price proposal.

Take a day or two to calculate the final price, and be sure it includes everything, then call the customer with your quote. If it's acceptable, send out a detailed contract that itemizes the prices, outlines mutual responsibilities, and requires a deposit (typically 25 to 50 percent of the total amount) on signing.

Once you've received the signed contract and deposit, you're ready to start arranging for staff and purchasing food. A few days before the event, call the customer to confirm the number of guests and other details. If the customer wants to make changes to the contract, be as accommodating as possible, but don't let it cause you to lose money.

Timing Is Everything

You should have at least a week's notice for a catered event. A month's notice is common and not too much for an established caterer to ask. In fact, some catered affairs are booked as many as 10 months in advance. Of course, if a client is in a bind—for example, a business needs a deli-style luncheon for six people at the last minute—and you can handle the work, you'll build customer loyalty by doing so.

Make a Packing List

Once the food for an event is prepared and ready to go, you'll need to pack it along with the serving dishes, utensils, linens, and other necessary equipment. To be sure you don't forget or lose anything, prepare a packing list (see the "Sample Packing List" checklist beginning on page 145).

A day or so before the event, sit down with your menu. List the equipment you'll need to finish preparing each dish on-site and serve it. When you're finished, double-check your figures, taking care to properly count multiple units of items, such as when different dishes require the same serving equipment. Don't forget miscellaneous supplies, such as cocktail napkins, toothpicks, salt and pepper shakers, and so on. If you're taking care of rental furniture or flowers, make sure these are either going to be delivered to the event site or to your kitchen or will be available for you to pick up. With your completed packing list, you can start assembling the food and supplies. Pack the items you'll need first on top so you don't have to dig through several boxes to find them. Place items close together so nothing has room to shift and break. Use common sense: Don't put sacks of crushed ice on top of the bread. Make sure all containers of food are covered tightly so they won't spill if you have to turn or stop your vehicle suddenly.

The packing list will also serve as a checklist to help you collect all your items when the party is over. Leaving items behind can quickly eat up your profits. Caterer Turner puts waterproof labels on trays and other items that identify each piece of equipment for inventory-control purposes. "If something is missing, we go back through the inventory sheets to see what party it was used on last and contact the person who ordered the catering," she says. "It's amazing what we have found. One lady had coffeepots, trays, and serving pieces from a year before. It was a drop off, and we forgot to go back and pick it up. She put it in a cupboard and forgot about it."

At the Party

Once you've arrived at the event site, unpack everything and organize your service area. You'll want to arrive an average of 60 to 90 minutes in advance to make sure the food will be ready and available at precisely the right time.

If you're taking care of rental furniture, flowers, or the bar setup, make sure everything is in place and arranged attractively. Start reheating or cooking anything that needs to be served hot. Make sure every tray that leaves the kitchen has been attractively garnished and arranged. Some caterers work with tweezers in the kitchen to arrange garnishes so that all platters look like pictures. It's an extra touch that will enhance your reputation.

As the party gets under way, keep an eye on what food is being consumed, and have more trays ready to go out as the empty ones are returned. If you're serving from a buffet table, continually replenish the trays so they don't look picked over. Throughout the event, your serving staff should be collecting dirty dishes, emptying used ashtrays, returning empty glasses to the bar, and taking care of other things so the party site doesn't look cluttered and untidy.

As your servers return the dirty dishes to you, rinse and pack them for later washing. After the event is over, clean any of the client's dishes or utensils that have been used. Get out your packing list to make sure you retrieve all your own glassware, tableware, cookware, and other equipment. Also, take care that you don't accidentally take any of the client's property. Check off each item on your packing list as you load it into your vehicle.

Leftover food should be wrapped and left with the client. Floors and counters should be clean, but you shouldn't be expected to function as a maid service. Just leave the facility as you found it. You're only responsible for your own messes.

Some caterers demand payment of the balance due immediately after the event; others will send the client a bill the day after the party. Whichever you choose, be sure the client knows in advance what to expect, and make it clear that the bill doesn't include gratuities for the serving staff. If the client decides to tip, the money should be divided among the staff after the party.

While you should always be on the alert for ways to promote your business, you should never promote yourself at an event you're catering. "I never market myself at events," Turner agrees. "We're there as a support to whatever event we're doing, and that's not the proper time for us to advertise." Her company name is on the aprons the staff wears but not on anything else. And while she'll provide a business card if asked, she doesn't put her cards on display. A truly professional caterer, she believes, is virtually invisible at the event, where the focus should be on the occasion itself. "We don't intrude. We're not guests; we're there to provide a service. I tell this to

---

Smart Tip

Tip...

After you've billed each event, evaluate how things went. Collect all your receipts and figure out your total expenses. Were the costs close to the assumptions you made when you priced the event? If not, you may need to revise your menu prices or your method of estimating costs for a bid.

How smoothly did the event itself go? Did you have adequate staffing? Were the guests satisfied? What comments did you get from the guests and your client? Make notes of things that went well, so you can be sure to repeat them, and of areas where you need improvement.

my service staff. Also, I don't allow [my staff] to talk to each other when they're in front of the client, other than to take care of business. Even if they have friends who are attending the event, I discourage them from stopping to talk. They are there for a purpose, and that purpose is to serve the client."

Initial Client Contact Form

Name _____

Address _____

_____

Business phone _____ Home phone _____

Email address _____

Date of event _____

Time of event: Beginning _____ Ending _____

Location of event _____

Type of occasion _____

Number of guests _____

General age group of guests _____

General mix of guests _____

Type of service (cocktail, buffet, sit-down) _____

Foods client would like to have _____

_____

_____

Dishes to avoid _____

_____

General budget of client _____

Special services needed _____

_____

Sample Packing List

Client _____

Date of event _____

Address _____

_____

Item	Amount Needed	In	Out
Glassware			
Wine (10 ounce)	_____	❑	❑
Wine (6 ounce)	_____	❑	❑
Champagne/martini	_____	❑	❑
Old-fashioned	_____	❑	❑
Highball	_____	❑	❑
Brandy	_____	❑	❑
Liqueur	_____	❑	❑
Water goblets	_____	❑	❑
Water pitchers	_____	❑	❑
Bar Mixes			
Whiskey sour	_____	❑	❑
Bloody Mary	_____	❑	❑
Orange juice	_____	❑	❑
Grapefruit juice	_____	❑	❑
Piña colada	_____	❑	❑
Collins	_____	❑	❑
Heavy cream	_____	❑	❑
Bitter lemon	_____	❑	❑
Tonic	_____	❑	❑
Thin tonic	_____	❑	❑
Club soda	_____	❑	❑
Perrier	_____	❑	❑
Coke	_____	❑	❑
7UP	_____	❑	❑

Sample Packing List, continued

Item	Amount Needed	In	Out
Food Mixes			
Lemon twists	_____	❑	❑
Olives	_____	❑	❑
Onions	_____	❑	❑
Pineapple wedges	_____	❑	❑
Red cherries	_____	❑	❑
Green cherries	_____	❑	❑
Celery stalks	_____	❑	❑
Accessories			
Blender	_____	❑	❑
Stirrers	_____	❑	❑
Corkscrew	_____	❑	❑
Strainers	_____	❑	❑
Toothpicks	_____	❑	❑
Paper umbrellas	_____	❑	❑
Ice tongs	_____	❑	❑
Cork coasters	_____	❑	❑
Dinnerware			
Cups	_____	❑	❑
Saucers	_____	❑	❑
Salad plates	_____	❑	❑
Dinner plates	_____	❑	❑
Base plates	_____	❑	❑
Dessert plates	_____	❑	❑
Flatware			
Teaspoons	_____	❑	❑
Salad forks	_____	❑	❑
Dinner forks	_____	❑	❑

Sample Packing List, continued

Item	Amount Needed	In	Out
Dinner knives	_____	❏	❏
Soup spoons	_____	❏	❏
Serving forks	_____	❏	❏
Serving spoons	_____	❏	❏
Butter knives	_____	❏	❏
Cheese knives	_____	❏	❏
Table Accessories			
Creamer	_____	❏	❏
Sugar bowl	_____	❏	❏
Salt shaker	_____	❏	❏
Pepper mill	_____	❏	❏
Bread baskets	_____	❏	❏
Cracker baskets	_____	❏	❏
Punch bowl set	_____	❏	❏
Candles	_____	❏	❏
Candleholders	_____	❏	❏
Ashtrays	_____	❏	❏
Toothpick holders	_____	❏	❏
Pots and Pans			
Omelet pans	_____	❏	❏
Small chafing dish	_____	❏	❏
Large chafing dish	_____	❏	❏
Rectangular chafing dish	_____	❏	❏
Trays			
Pizza pans	_____	❏	❏
Cookie sheets	_____	❏	❏
Silver trays (round)	_____	❏	❏
Silver trays (oblong)	_____	❏	❏
Silver trays (square)	_____	❏	❏

Sample Packing List, continued

Item	Amount Needed	In	Out
Utility Equipment			
Coffeemaker	_____	❏	❏
Coffee grinder	_____	❏	❏
Three-prong adapters	_____	❏	❏
Chafing dish setup	_____	❏	❏
Heat lamp	_____	❏	❏
Coffee pitcher	_____	❏	❏
Serving tables	_____	❏	❏
Ice buckets	_____	❏	❏
Bus boxes	_____	❏	❏
Salad bowls	_____	❏	❏
Coffee urn and burner	_____	❏	❏
Serving carts	_____	❏	❏
Cheese boards	_____	❏	❏
Linens and Paper			
Cocktail napkins	_____	❏	❏
Dinner napkins (paper)	_____	❏	❏
Toothpicks	_____	❏	❏
Garbage bags	_____	❏	❏
Paper doilies	_____	❏	❏
Dinner napkins (linen)	_____	❏	❏
Hand towels	_____	❏	❏
Tinfoil	_____	❏	❏
Matches	_____	❏	❏
Disinfectant	_____	❏	❏
Dishwashing detergent	_____	❏	❏
Straight pins	_____	❏	❏
Safety pins	_____	❏	❏
Masking tape	_____	❏	❏

Sample Packing List, continued

Item	Amount Needed	In	Out
Clear tape	_____	❏	❏
Stapler	_____	❏	❏
Ribbons	_____	❏	❏
Staple Food Items			
Coffee (ground)	_____	❏	❏
Coffee (beans)	_____	❏	❏
Decaffeinated coffee	_____	❏	❏
Milk	_____	❏	❏
Instant milk	_____	❏	❏
Cream	_____	❏	❏
Artificial sweetener	_____	❏	❏
Sugar	_____	❏	❏
Tea bags	_____	❏	❏
Saltines	_____	❏	❏
Sesame crackers	_____	❏	❏
Pretzels	_____	❏	❏
Breadsticks	_____	❏	❏

Beginning packer _____

Double-checked by _____

Time of delivery _____

Ending packer _____

Double-checked by _____

Notes _____

_____

▲

Catering Price Quote Worksheet

Food Costs

Item	Cost
_____	_____
_____	_____
_____	_____
_____	_____
_____	_____
_____	_____
_____	_____
_____	_____
Total food costs	_____
× 3	_____
Food price to client[1]	_____
Liquor[2]	_____
Rental equipment[3]	_____
Serving staff[4]	_____
Miscellaneous	_____
Total price quote[5]	_____

1. When quoting to the client, use a per-person figure; divide the worksheet number by the total number of guests to arrive at this figure.

2. You need a liquor license to provide alcohol; it's common for clients to purchase their own liquor and for you to provide the setups. The markup on setups can be substantial; call around to other caterers to find out what the market will bear in your area.

3. Quote your client the "retail" cost of rental equipment without a markup; the rental company should give you a discount, which you can include in your profit for the event.

4. Use a standard gratuity to cover the cost of serving staff; clients may also offer a gratuity if the service was exceptional.

5. This is the sum of the food price to client, liquor and setups, rental equipment, serving staff, and miscellaneous.

Sample Layout of a 1,200-Square-Foot Commercial Kitchen

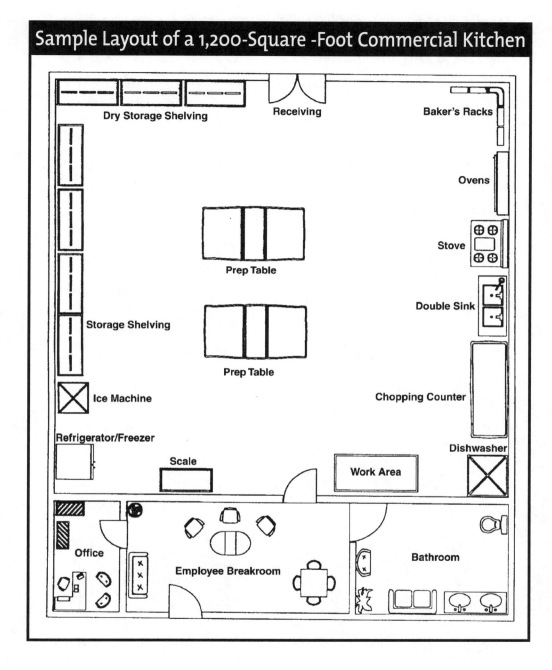

Dry Storage Shelving

Receiving

Baker's Racks

Ovens

Prep Table

Stove

Double Sink

Storage Shelving

Prep Table

Ice Machine

Chopping Counter

Refrigerator/Freezer

Dishwasher

Scale

Work Area

Office

Bathroom

Employee Breakroom

Inventory
Buying, Storing, and Tracking Supplies

Food and beverage inventory purchasing is one of the most mismanaged areas in the food-service industry, neglected by most due to lack of knowledge. Business owners who never learned to implement proper inventory purchasing and control techniques can still be successful, but they'll usually pay for this lack of knowledge with reduced profits, constant frustration, and years of repeated inventory-ordering mistakes.

There are two key components to inventory: acquisition and management. You must know how to find distributors you can count on to deliver quality products on time, you must be able to place accurate orders with them so you have enough of what you need when you need it, and you must be able to estimate how much inventory you'll consume during any given period of time—daily, weekly, monthly, or yearly.

Poor inventory management is one of the main reasons food-service businesses fail. Every shortfall or excess affects your bottom line. To succeed in this industry, you need good purchasing procedures and a system that will help you accurately control your inventory from acquisition through preparation.

"I've been at this for more than 30 years and there are a lot of new ways to do inventory," says Paul Mangiamele, president and CEO of Bennigan's. "But I've found the best way is to get out there and do a hand count. Know your product. Know your usage. You have to know your inventory very well because that's your food cost. That's a third of your business." Mangiamele recommends doing a weekly inventory of critical items and a complete inventory every month. "Use that information for cash management, profitability, and ordering. It's a big part of your business and you've got to know it backwards, forwards, and upside down."

Quality, prices, and availability often fluctuate in the seesaw food and beverage market. You need to study the market, pay attention to what's going on in the world, and track conditions so you can buy with confidence. With practice and diligent market research, you can identify your strongest menu items and order inventory accordingly.

When you calculate basic stock, you must also factor in lead time—the length of time between ordering and receiving a product. For instance, if your lead time is four weeks and a particular menu item requires 10 units a week in inventory, then you must reorder before the basic inventory level falls below 40 units. If you don't reorder until you actually need the stock, the basic inventory will be depleted, and you'll lose sales—and probably some customers, too.

One of the ways many small-business owners protect themselves from such shortfalls is by incorporating a safety margin into basic inventory figures. The right safety margin for your particular operation depends on the external factors that can contribute to delays. You must determine your safety margin based on past experience and anticipated delays.

Caterer Ann Crane says she works closely with her kitchen manager on inventory issues and discusses the challenge with other caterers. At one point, she discovered that another caterer stocked about a quarter of the amount of dry goods that she stocks. "She told me that most of her business had a week or two of lead time, so she has plenty of time to order goods. I know another caterer who does small dinners for 10 or 20 people, and she just goes to the market that morning and picks up what she needs. But a lot of my business has just 24 to 48 hours' lead time, and we can't afford the time or money to go to the store and buy all that last-minute product. For our day-to-day breakfast and lunch business, we keep an enormous amount of goods on the shelf."

Beverage Systems

Soft drinks, milk, coffee, and hot and iced tea are necessary beverages for most food-service operations. For soft drinks, you can either offer canned beverages or buy a dispensing system. Unless you expect an extremely low sales volume in this area, the dispensing system will be more profitable. You will typically pay 30 to 50 cents a can for soft drinks, which you can then sell for about $1.25 or more. While that's certainly an acceptable profit, a soft drink system will generate 10 to 15 cents more profit per drink. Syrups for colas, root beer, diet drinks, and other beverages can be obtained from your local beverage distributor.

Check with your local health department to see if you must serve milk in individual cartons or if it may be poured into glasses from a larger container. You'll make more money using the latter method.

Buy your coffee from a coffee wholesaler, which can also provide burners, coffee-brewing systems, coffee-bean grinders, and all the other equipment you need to make fresh-brewed coffee. These vendors are listed in various online and offline directories under "Coffee Break Service and Supplies." Be sure to let the company know you run a restaurant—you'll get a better price. Also, the coffee service can supply you with individual packets of sugar and artificial sweetener, nondairy creamer, stirrers, and other coffee-related items.

Avoid freeze-dried-coffee dispensers. Although they reduce waste, they'll hurt sales. They don't offer the aroma and taste of freshly brewed coffees. Also, freeze-dried-coffee systems use much hotter water, which means customers can't drink the beverage right away. Finally, these systems often produce a bitter final product because operators put too much coffee in their machines. It's worth the money to go for fresh-brewed coffee.

Bright Idea

If you have the demand, invest in an espresso and cappuccino machine. Even though these devices are fairly expensive and time-consuming to run, coffee drinks are very popular. Your coffee supplier probably has both new and used machines available.

Iced tea should be made at the start of the day and placed in its own stainless-steel dispenser (aluminum containers can alter the taste). Tea is remarkably cost-efficient. You can buy premeasured bags to make any specified amount. Just as with coffee, remember individual packets of sugar and artificial sweetener, stirrers, and lemon slices.

Where to Buy

You can purchase meats from a meat jobber who specializes in portion-controlled supplies for restaurants. A meat jobber will usually deliver five days a week so, except for weekends and holidays, you won't need to stock a large quantity on-site. Although prices from this type of specialized distributor may be slightly higher than from wholesale distributors, the quality of the meat is usually excellent, and you can benefit from their expertise.

For dairy products, try to find a wholesale distributor who can handle many of your needs and negotiate a volume discount. If you purchase a great deal of cheese, milk, and eggs—as a pizzeria would—consider a daily trip to the local farmers' market to haggle with growers face-to-face. Often this type of direct buying gives you the lowest price and the best quality available.

Canned foods can be purchased from a processed-food distributor. These vendors function as wholesale grocers that specialize in packaged products. They can be found under "Grocers—Wholesale" in your local Yellow Pages or by doing a search on the internet.

Dealing with Suppliers

Regardless of what kinds of foods you offer, developing good relations with local food distributors is essential. They'll be able to pass along vital information that will aid you in your purchasing activities. If you have a good rapport with your suppliers, they'll also work harder on your behalf to provide you with quality products at competitive prices.

This doesn't mean wining and dining your suppliers' sales reps. Having good relations simply means paying your bills on time and being upfront with your suppliers about your needs and capabilities. You'll be pleasantly surprised at what adhering to the terms of your contract will do for you, especially in an environment where so many businesses fail to live up to their part of the bargain.

Reliable suppliers are an asset to your operation. They can bail you out when your customers make difficult demands of you, but they will do so only as long as your business is profitable for them. Like you, suppliers are in business to make money. If you argue about every bill, if you ask them to shave prices on every item, if you fail to pay promptly after goods or services have been delivered, don't be surprised when they stop calling and leave you dangling.

Enough Is Enough

The ideal in inventory control is to always have enough product on hand to meet customer demand while avoiding both shortage and excess. Unavoidably, in the course of operating a business, both of these situations will occur. Rather than viewing them as mistakes, however, the smart restaurateur will use a shortage or an excess as an indicator of sales trends and alter the inventory control system accordingly.

If a shortage occurs, you can:

○ review the preparation and cooking processes to locate any problems

○ place a rush order

○ employ another supplier

○ use substitute ingredients

○ remove an item from the menu if key ingredients are difficult or exceptionally expensive to acquire

You can address overstocking by returning excess stock to suppliers or creating a promotion to stimulate demand. But don't just deal with the fallout of excess stock; analyze your ordering system to understand why the overage occurred. If you conduct purchasing and reordering correctly, you should be able to keep both excesses and shortages to a minimum.

▲

Of course, the food-service business is competitive on all levels, and you must look for the best deal you can get on a consistent basis from your suppliers. No business arrangement can continue for long unless something of value is tendered and received by everyone involved. The lesson is this: Be neither a doormat nor excessively demanding. Tell your suppliers what you need and when you need it. Have a specific understanding about costs, delivery schedules, and payment terms. Build relationships based on fairness, integrity, and trust, and both you and your suppliers will profit.

Receiving Procedures

Only you or one of your most trusted employees should receive inventory. Compare all goods received with your purchase specifications and completed price quote sheets. Weigh all products (that are sold by weight) and count all products (that are sold by count). You should also break down all the cases to check for broken or deformed containers, a full count, and spoilage. Containers of fresh produce and similar goods should be inspected thoroughly.

If you discover any shortages, spoilage, or damaged goods during the receiving process, make immediate adjustments to the invoice, which both you and the delivery person should initial. Check all mathematical calculations on the invoice, and when you're satisfied that everything is acceptable, stamp the invoice "Received."

Goods should be placed immediately into their proper storage places. If you leave products strewn all over the floor, you'll find that they'll disappear. Effective storage will help you maintain adequate stocks of goods with minimum loss and pilferage. As stock is being put into storage, check it once again against your delivery report. As with receiving, this is a task only you or a trusted employee should do.

Label all items, and place them in the appropriately marked areas for easy retrieval. Make sure your inventory is constantly rotated. Goods that come in first should be used first.

Hidden Inventory Costs

Excess inventory creates additional overhead, and that costs you money. In fact, it can cost a restaurateur anywhere from 20 to 30 percent of the original investment in inventory just to maintain it. Inventory that

Tip...

Smart Tip
Follow your receiving procedures consistently, without exception, no matter how well you get to know a vendor or delivery person or how much you trust him or her. Finding damage or a shortage after the driver has left can create an awkward situation as you try to determine who's actually at fault. Avoid potential problems by inspecting, weighing, and counting all deliveries at the time they arrive.

sits in your storeroom doesn't generate sales or profits. Rather, it generates losses in the form of:

- food spoilage from excess shelf life
- debt service on loans used to purchase the excess inventory
- increased insurance costs on the greater value of the inventory in stock

The natural reaction of many restaurateurs to excess inventory is to move it out. While that may solve your overstocking problem, it will reduce your return on investment. In your financial projections, you based your figures on using specific ingredients in dishes that would be sold at full retail price. If you opt to clear out excess inventory by reducing menu prices and offering specials and one-time-only meal discounts, you're ultimately taking money out of your own pocket.

Responding to spoilage and inventory excesses with overly cautious reordering is understandable. The problem there is that, when you reduce your reordering, you run the significant risk of creating a stock shortage. We didn't say this would be easy. You need to plan carefully, establish a realistic safety margin, and do your best to order only what you're sure you'll use to prepare your foods.

Tracking Inventory

A critical part of managing inventory is tracking it—that means knowing what you have on hand, what's on order, when it will arrive, and what you've sold. This information allows you to plan your purchases intelligently, quickly recognize fast-moving items that need to be reordered and identify slow-moving merchandise that should be marked down and moved out.

There are a variety of inventory-tracking methods you can use, from basic handwritten records to computerized bar code systems. The food-service business owners we talked to use simple systems, most on basic computer databases. Your accountant can help you develop a system that will work for your particular situation.

Controlling Bar Losses

Managing liquor inventory is one of the most challenging aspects of having a bar. Losses from spillage, theft, and honest mistakes can cost a single outlet thousands of dollars per week—dollars that fall straight to the bottom line in the form of lost profits.

One popular solution is a computerized inventory-auditing system. Bevinco, a Canadian-based company with franchises in the United States and about 30 other countries, provides this service using portable electronic scales and a notebook computer. "When I started the business, we conducted a study, and I was amazed to learn that the accepted loss level in alcoholic beverages in the restaurant and bar business is 20 percent," says Barry Driedger, Bevinco's founder. "When you look at the volume most places do—even the smaller bars and restaurants—that's a lot of money."

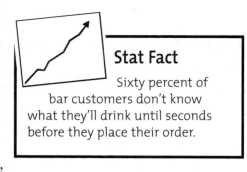

Stat Fact

Sixty percent of bar customers don't know what they'll drink until seconds before they place their order.

Driedger is quick to point out that bar losses aren't exclusively related to deliberate theft by employees. A significant amount of shrinkage can be traced to spills and carelessness in preparation, misdirected "good intentions" of bartenders who over-pour drinks for regular customers, and external fraud or theft. He also notes that although the primary reason for liquor-loss control is profitability, staff morale is likely to rise when control methods are implemented. "Most bars and restaurants have fairly large staffs, and it's usually only a small number of people who are causing the problem," he says. "The honest, hard-working people on the staff will appreciate having the dishonest people weeded out."

Bevinco's service starts with a baseline audit. After that, audits are conducted regularly—usually weekly or biweekly. All open liquor bottles, wine bottles, and beer kegs are weighed; other inventory is counted; sales and purchase figures are factored in; and the auditor is then able to generate a report identifying the source and volume of losses. With that information, a plan can be developed and implemented to correct the problem. Bevinco's audits typically range from $150 to $250, depending on the size of the inventory and the frequency of the audit. Although the Bevinco system is proprietary, if you want to audit yourself, you can purchase the necessary equipment through other companies.

There are a variety of liquor inventory management systems on the market, and the choices increase as technology advances. Check the Appendix of this book for resources, or search the internet for "liquor inventory management."

Critics of auditing systems say using them is like closing the proverbial barn door after the cow has escaped. An alternative is liquor control systems, which are designed to prevent rather than simply identify losses and which use various techniques to measure and track product use. If you're shopping for a liquor control system, consider these points:

- *Flexibility*. The bartenders should be able to move around comfortably while they're working and be able to pour more than one drink at a time.
- *Compatibility with other systems*. Be sure the liquor control system can communicate data to your cash register and inventory system.

- *Reliability.* Check the vendor's references carefully to evaluate the performance record of the system.
- *Training.* Be sure the vendor will provide thorough training on the system.
- *Warranty and ongoing support.* Find out the details of the warranty, and make sure the company will answer questions and respond to problems after the sale.

While technology can go a long way toward reducing bar area losses, it can't replace common sense. Here are some simple, easy-to-implement suggestions that can improve profits and customer service:

- *Restrict access to the bar.* Allow only bartenders behind the bar, and be sure that they're the only personnel making drinks.
- *Require drink purchases to be entered into the register before they're made.*
- *Watch back-door security.* Check in and put away deliveries promptly; never allow inventory to sit unsupervised in loading areas. Install an alarm on the back door that will alert you if an unauthorized person attempts to leave the facility.
- *Provide lockers for employees to store their personal belongings in*, and don't allow them to bring bags or containers into the bar or serving area.
- *Make people accountable for mistakes.* Require mistakes, such as mixing the wrong drink and causing spills, to be logged in and signed off on by the manager on duty. Such accountability increases awareness and leads to a reduction in these types of losses.
- *Cushion surfaces to reduce breakage.* Quality floor mats not only prevent slipping and ease back and leg stress on bartenders, they can also provide a cushion that reduces breakage if bottles or glasses are dropped.
- *Be sure spouts fit securely.* Sometimes spouts can loosen and leak, especially when used on odd-shaped bottles.
- *Check the ice.* Be sure the ice is free from debris that would cause the drink to be refused.
- *Provide incentives for loss reduction.* Come up with ways to reward employees for positive performance in this area.
- *Encourage employees to report theft.* Consider setting up a system where such reports can be made either anonymously or, at the very least, in strict confidence.
- *Hire carefully.* Screen prospective employees thoroughly. Conduct complete background checks, and contact references.

Structuring
Your Business

No doubt you're attracted to the food-service

business because you enjoy food preparation and service. And

while that's a big part of the business, there are plenty of other

mundane issues you'll have to address both in the startup phase

and in the long run.

Legal Structure

One of the first decisions you'll need to make about your new food-service business is what type of legal structure the company should have. This is an important decision, it can affect your financial liability, the amount of taxes you pay, and the degree of ultimate control you have over the company, as well as your ability to raise money, attract investors and, ultimately, sell the business. However, legal structure shouldn't be confused with operating structure. Attorney Robert S. Bernstein of Bernstein Law Firm PC in Pittsburgh explains the difference: "The legal structure is the ownership structure: who actually owns the company. The operating structure defines who makes management decisions and [who] runs the company."

A sole proprietorship is a business owned by the proprietor; a partnership is owned by the partners; and a corporation is owned by its shareholders. Sole proprietorships and partnerships can be operated however the owners choose. In a corporation, the shareholders typically elect directors, who in turn elect officers, who then employ other people to run the company and work there. But it's entirely possible for a corporation to have only one shareholder and to essentially function as a sole proprietorship. In any case, how you plan to operate the company shouldn't be a major factor in your choice of legal structures.

So what goes into choosing a legal structure? The first thing to consider, says Bernstein, is who's actually making the decision about the legal structure. If you're starting the company by yourself, you don't need to take anyone else's preferences into consideration. "But if there are multiple people involved, you need to consider how you're going to relate to each other in the business," he says. "You also need to consider the issue of asset protection and limiting your liability in the event things don't go well."

Something else to think about is your target customers and what their perception will be of your structure. While it's not necessarily true, Bernstein says, "There's a tendency to believe that the legal form of a business has some relationship to the sophistication of the owners, with the sole proprietorship as the least [sophisticated], and the corporation as the most sophisticated." So if your target market is going to be other businesses, it might enhance your image if you incorporate.

Stat Fact

More than 4 out of 10 food-and-drink establishments are sole proprietorships or partnerships.

Your image notwithstanding, the biggest advantage of forming a corporation is asset protection, which, says Bernstein, means ensuring that the assets you don't want to put into the business aren't liable for the business's debt. However, to take advantage of the protection a corporation offers, you must respect the corporation's identity. That means you must maintain the corporation as a separate entity, keeping your corporate and personal funds separate, even if you're the sole shareholder, and following your state's rules regarding holding annual meetings and other record-keeping requirements.

Is any one structure better than another? Not really. We found food-service businesses operating as sole proprietorships, partnerships, and corporations, and their owners made their choices based on what was best for their particular situation. Choose the form that's most appropriate for your particular needs.

Do you need an attorney to set up your business's legal structure? Again, no. Bernstein says there are plenty of good do-it-yourself books and kits on the market, and most of the state agencies that oversee corporations have guidelines you can use. Even so, it's always a good idea to have a lawyer at least look over your documents before you file them, just to make sure they're complete and will allow your business to function the way you want to.

Finally, remember that your choice of legal structure is not an irrevocable decision, although if you're going to make a switch, it's easier to go from the simpler forms to the more sophisticated ones than the other way around. Bernstein says the typical pattern is to start as a sole proprietor, then to switch to a corporation as the business grows. But if you need the asset protection of a corporation from the beginning, start out that way. Says Bernstein: "If you're going to the trouble to start a business, decide on a structure and put it all together, it's worth the extra effort to make sure it's really going to work."

Naming Your Company

One of the most important marketing tools you'll ever have is your company's name. A well-chosen name can work very hard for you; an ineffective name means you will have to work much harder at marketing your company.

There's no surefire formula for naming a food-service business. Names range from the name of the owner to the name of a place to the wildest name the owner could think of. You should pick a name in keeping with the theme of your restaurant so it's compatible with the food and atmosphere. A dramatic example of this is the Rainforest Cafe. The entire restaurant is designed to create the atmosphere of a jungle, complete with lush vegetation, animals, volcanoes, and sound effects. You probably won't go to such an extreme, but if your goal is a fine-dining restaurant, you don't want to name it something like Road Kill Cafe.

Your company name should also clearly identify what you do in a way that will appeal to your target market. If you're going to use your own name, add a description. For example, instead of just Angelo's, call your pizzeria Angelo's Pizza and Pasta. As you become known in the community, people will likely drop the description when they refer to you, but until that time, it will pay to avoid confusing the public.

The name should be short, catchy, and memorable—and it doesn't hurt to make it fun. It should also be easy to pronounce and spell. People who can't say your restaurant's name may patronize your business, but they probably won't tell anyone else about you.

> **Bright Idea**
>
> Once you've narrowed down your name search to three or four choices, test-market your ideas by asking a small group of people who fit the profile of your potential customers what they think of the names you're considering. Find out what kind of company the name makes them think of and if they'd feel comfortable patronizing a food-service business with that name. Get them to explain the reasoning behind their answers.

Although naming your food-service business is without a doubt a creative process, it helps to take a systematic approach. Once you've decided on two or three name possibilities, take the following steps:

- *Check the name for effectiveness and functionality*. Does it quickly and easily convey what you do? Is it easy to say and spell? Is it memorable in a positive way? Ask several of your friends and associates to serve as a focus group to help you evaluate the name's impact.

- *Search for potential conflicts in your local market*. Find out if any other local or regional food-service business serving your market area has a name so similar that yours might confuse the public.

- *Check for legal availability*. Exactly how you do this depends on the legal structure you choose. Typically, sole proprietorships and partnerships operating under a name other than that of the owner(s) are required by the county, city, or state to register their fictitious name. Even if it's not required, it's a good idea, because that means no one else can use that name. Your attorney can help you file the paperwork for your business's fictitious name, or your "doing business as" name. Corporations usually operate under their corporate name. But no matter which route you choose, you need to check with the appropriate regulatory agency to be sure the name you choose is available. Bakery owner Jim Amaral says one of his biggest mistakes was in not checking the availability of the name he initially chose for his company, Bodacious Breads. He used that name for two years and then had to change it when he was challenged by the trademark owner.

- *Check for use on the internet.* If someone else is already using your name as a domain site on the web, consider coming up with something else. Even if you have no intention of developing a website of your own, the fact that someone else is using it online could be confusing to your customers.

- *Check to see if the name conflicts with any name listed on your state's trademark register.* Your state department of commerce can either help you or direct you to the correct agency. You should also check with the trademark registry maintained by the U.S. Patent and Trademark Office (PTO). Visit the PTO's website at www.uspto.gov.

Once the name you've chosen passes these tests, you'll need to protect it by registering it with the appropriate state agency. Again, your state department of commerce can help you with this. If you expect to be doing business on a national level—for example, if you'll be handling mail orders or operating on the web—you should also register the name with the PTO.

Business Insurance

It takes a lot to start a business, even a small one, so protect your investment with adequate insurance. If you maintain your office at home—as many food-service business

If the Unthinkable Happens

You buy insurance hoping you'll never need it, but if you do, take the appropriate steps to make sure you get the full benefit from your coverage. Notify your agent or carrier immediately if you suffer a property loss or if something happens that could turn into a liability claim. In the case of a property claim, be prepared to provide the appropriate documentation and proof of loss.

In the case of potential liability, there doesn't have to be an actual loss before you get your insurance company involved. For example, if a customer slips and falls on your premises, even if he or she says there is no injury, get the person's name, address, and telephone number as well as contact information for any witnesses, and pass this information on to your insurance company. Don't wait until you're served with legal papers.

operators do—don't assume your homeowner's or renter's policy covers your business equipment. While many homeowner's policies cover some business equipment, not all do and the total amount covered is usually limited and may not be sufficient to protect you in the event of a loss. If you're located in a commercial facility, be prepared for your landlord to require proof of certain levels of liability insurance when you sign the lease. And in either case, you'll need coverage for your inventory, equipment, fixtures, and other valuables.

A smart approach to insurance is to find an agent who works with businesses similar to yours. The agent should be willing to help you analyze your needs, evaluate what risks you're willing to accept, and what risks you need to insure against, and work with you to keep your insurance costs down.

Once your business is up and running, consider business interruption insurance to replace lost revenue and cover related costs if you're ever unable to operate due to covered circumstances.

Professional Services

As a business owner, you may be the boss, but you can't be expected to know everything. You'll occasionally need to turn to other professionals for information and assistance. It's a good idea to establish a relationship with these people before you get into a crisis situation.

A pizzeria owner learned the value of quality professional advice the hard way. He was inadequately protected by the lease on his first store. When that lease expired, the landlord refused to renew it and then opened his own successful pizzeria in that location, capitalizing on all the hard work and marketing efforts of his tenant. A good commercial real estate attorney would have made sure the lease prevented the landlord from opening a competing operation.

To shop for a professional service provider, ask friends and associates for recommendations. You might also check with your local chamber of commerce or trade association for referrals. Find someone who understands your industry and specific business and who appears eager to work with you. Check out the person with the Better Business Bureau and the appropriate state licensing agency before committing yourself.

> **Smart Tip**
>
> When you purchase insurance on your equipment and inventory, ask what documentation the insurance company requires for filing a claim. That way, you'll be sure to maintain appropriate records, and the claims process will be easier if it's ever necessary.

As a food-service business owner, the professional service providers you're likely to need include:

- *Attorney.* You'll need a lawyer who understands and practices in the area of business law, who's honest, and who appreciates your patronage. In most parts of the United States, there's an abundance of lawyers willing to compete fiercely for the privilege of serving you. Interview several, and choose one you feel comfortable with. Be sure to clarify the fee schedule ahead of time, and get your agreement in writing. Keep in mind that good commercial lawyers don't come cheap. If you want good advice, you must be willing to pay for it. Your attorney should review all contracts, leases, letters of intent, and other legal documents before you sign them. They can also help you with collecting bad debts and establishing personnel policies and procedures. Of course, if you're unsure of the legal ramifications of any situation, call your attorney immediately.

- *Accountant.* Of all your outside advisors, your accountant is likely to have the greatest impact on the success or failure of your business. If you're forming a corporation, your accountant should counsel you on tax issues during startup. On an ongoing basis, your accountant can help you organize the statistical data concerning your business, assist in charting future actions based on past performance, and advise you on your overall financial strategy regarding purchasing, capital investment, and other matters related to your business goals. A good accountant will also serve as a tax advisor, making sure you're in compliance with all applicable regulations but also ensuring you don't overpay any taxes. Sam Mustafa, owner of Charleston Hospitality Group, says that one of his biggest mistakes was attempting to be his own accountant.

- *Insurance agent.* A good independent insurance agent can assist you with all aspects of your business insurance, from general liability to employee benefits, and probably even handle your personal policies as well. Look for an agent who works with a wide range of insurers and understands your particular business. This agent should be willing to explain the details of various types of coverage, consult with you to determine the most appropriate coverage, help you understand the degree of risk you're taking, work with you to develop risk-reduction programs, and assist in expediting claims.

- *Banker.* You'll need a business bank account and a relationship with a banker. Don't simply choose the bank that you've always done your personal banking with; it may not be the best bank for your business. You'll want to interview several bankers before making a decision on where to place your business funds. Once your account is opened, maintain a relationship with the banker.

Periodically sit down with the person and review your accounts and the services you use to make sure you're getting the package that's most appropriate for your situation. Ask for advice if you have financial questions or problems. When you need a loan or a bank reference to provide to creditors, the relationship you have established will work in your favor.

"Your banking relationship is critical," says Paul Mangiamele, president and CEO of Bennigan's. "Typically, you're not going to do one store, you're going to do several. If your restaurant starts making money, you'll want to replicate it and increase your market share. Your banker has to be your friend, your confidant."

- *Consultants.* The consulting industry is booming—and for good reason. Consultants can provide valuable, objective input on all aspects of your business. Consider hiring a general business consultant to evaluate your business plan, a marketing consultant to help you promote your new business, and a restaurant consultant to help you design your facility. As part of your marketing strategy, you may want to hire a consultant who specializes in social media, search engine optimization (SEO), and online reputation management (ORM). When you're ready to hire employees, an HR consultant may help you avoid some costly mistakes. Consulting fees vary widely, depending on the individual's experience, location, and field of expertise. If you can't afford to hire a consultant, consider contacting the business school at the nearest college or university and hiring an MBA student to help you.

- *Computer/IT expert.* Find someone to help you select a system and the appropriate software and who will be available to help you maintain, troubleshoot, and expand your system as necessary. Your point of sale (register) system should have 24/7 IT support. "Your register will always go down at the worst possible time, such as Friday night at 8 o'clock," says Mangiamele. "If you don't have someone to call, you're out of luck. That old cigar box becomes your cash register, and that's not a good way to go." If you're going to pursue internet sales, use a professional web page designer to set up and maintain your website. Just as you wouldn't serve sloppily prepared food, you shouldn't put up an unprofessional web page.

> ## Smart Tip
>
> Sit down with your insurance agent every year to review your insurance needs. As your company grows, your needs are sure to change. Also, insurance companies are always developing new products for the growing small-business market, and it's possible that one of these new policies will be appropriate for you.

Create Your Own Advisory Board

Not even the president of the United States is expected to know everything. That's why he surrounds himself with advisors—experts in particular areas—who provide knowledge and information to help him make decisions. Savvy small-business owners use a similar strategy.

When Maxine Turner decided to expand her Salt Lake City catering company, Cuisine Unlimited, to include a delicatessen, she made some serious mistakes, and nearly bankrupted her company. In the middle of her crisis, she realized that the way to get a handle on her own company was to get help from other business owners. She formed an advisory board of successful small-business owners, offering them nothing but good food at the meetings and her personal commitment to return the kindness by helping them in the future. "We met once a month, and the first meeting was about the biggest jolt I had ever had in my life," she recalls. At her request, her advisors were completely candid. She realized how much she was doing wrong that she thought she had been doing right and came up with a strategy to correct her problems. Today, she believes that if she had started her company with an advisory board in place, she would never have had the problems she did. "I think it's a great idea to have an advisory board before you open your doors, while you're still putting together your business plan," she says. And if you're seeking financing, having such a support network will likely weigh heavily in your favor with potential lenders.

You can assemble a team of volunteer advisors to meet with you periodically to offer advice and direction. Because this isn't an official or legal entity, you have a great deal of latitude in how you set it up. Advisory boards can be structured to help with the operation of your company as well as to keep you informed on various business, legal, and financial trends that may affect you. Use these tips to set up your board:

- *Structure a board that meets your needs.* Generally, you will want a legal advisor, an accountant, a marketing expert, an HR person, and perhaps a financial advisor. You may also want successful entrepreneurs from other industries who understand the basics of business and will view your operation with a fresh eye.

- *Ask the most successful people you can find, even if you don't know them well.* You'll be surprised how willing people are to help other businesses succeed.

- *Be clear about what you're trying to do.* Let your prospective advisors know what your goals are and that you don't expect them to take on an active management role or to assume any liability for your company or for the advice they offer.

- *Don't worry about compensation.* Advisory board members are rarely compensated with more than lunch or dinner—something you can easily provide. Of course, if a member of your board provides a direct service—for example, if an attorney reviews a contract or an accountant prepares a financial statement—then they should be paid at their normal rate. But that's not part of their job as an advisory board member. Keep in mind that even though you don't write them a check, your advisory board members will likely benefit in a variety of tangible and intangible ways. Being on your board will expose them to ideas and perspectives they may not otherwise have encountered and will also expand their own network of contacts.

- *Consider the group dynamics when holding meetings.* You may want to meet with all the members together or in small groups of one or two. It all depends on how the individuals relate to one another and what you need to accomplish.

- *Ask for honesty, and don't be offended or defensive when you get it.* Your pride might be hurt when someone points out something you're doing wrong, but the awareness will be beneficial in the long run.

- *Learn from failure as well as success.* Encourage board members to tell you about their mistakes so you can avoid making them yourself.

- *Respect the contribution your board members are making.* Let them know you appreciate how busy they are, and don't abuse or waste their time.

- *Make it fun.* Create a pleasant atmosphere. You are, after all, asking these people to donate their time.

- *Listen to every piece of advice.* Stop talking and listen. You don't have to follow every piece of advice, but you do need to hear it.

- *Provide feedback to the board.* Good or bad, let the board know what you did and what the results were.

13

Locating and Setting Up Your Business

Successful food-service businesses can occupy a wide array of facilities, from free-standing buildings constructed especially to house a specific operation to existing buildings converted to suit the particular operation. Train stations, retail stores, and even banks are among the numerous structures that have been successfully converted to food-service businesses.

With most restaurants, the owner begins by coming up with the concept, then determines the market, and finally finds a location. After determining the general location, the next step is to find a specific facility in the area. This is when you must decide whether you'll convert an existing structure, or build a new facility. Typically, converting will cost less than building. Even if you gut an entire building and install new fixtures, it will be less expensive than buying the vacant land, building the structure, and adding the necessary fixtures.

Of course, a little bit of creativity can go a long way toward saving startup capital. When Maxine Turner started Cuisine Unlimited in Salt Lake City, she was working out of a school cafeteria. She leased the space, provided lunches for the school, and used the kitchen to prepare foods for her corporate clients. That setup worked successfully for 10 years, until she decided to open a retail deli and moved her commercial kitchen there.

Depending on how much money you have to invest in your food-service business and the particular type of eatery you choose, you can spend anywhere from $40,000 to $1.75 million on a facility.

> ## Bright Idea
>
> If you're opening an independent operation in a food-service business with a lot of national competition, take a look at where the national chains are locating. They invest in a tremendous amount of market research. Study the characteristics of their sites, and then look for a location for your own business that's similar, perhaps even nearby, and offer a better product or service.

Retail Locations

Not every food-service operation needs to be in a retail location, but for those that depend on retail traffic, here are some factors to consider when deciding on a site:

- *Anticipated sales volume.* How will the location contribute to your sales volume? Consider the presence or potential presence of other food-service businesses that will compete with you, and be sure the market is strong enough to support both of you.

- *Accessibility to potential customers.* Consider how easy it will be for customers to get into your business. If vehicle traffic is often heavy, or if the speed limit nearby is more than 35 mph, drivers may have difficulty entering or leaving your site. Narrow entrances and exits, turns that are hard to negotiate, and parking lots that are always full can prevent would-be customers from patronizing your business.

If you're relying on strong pedestrian traffic, consider whether nearby businesses will generate foot traffic for you. Large department stores will draw shoppers who may then stop in your restaurant for a meal or snack, and shopping centers in busy office districts might attract pedestrian customers, particularly during weekday lunch hours. By contrast, a strip mall anchored by a supermarket may not be the best location, as grocery shoppers typically go directly to the store and back to their cars.

Consider the entrance to the site: Is it on the street level or an upper floor? Can it be reached from a main street, or is it difficult to find?

Analyze the site: Monitor foot and auto traffic patterns at different times of the day; see if those patterns fit the hours when you want to do business; visit the prospective site over several days to assess changes in the patterns.

- *The rent-paying capacity of your business.* The best locations will usually command the highest rents. If you've done a sales-and-profit projection for your first year of operation, you'll know approximately how much revenue you can expect to generate. Use that information to decide how much rent you can afford to pay.

- *Restrictive ordinances.* You may encounter unusually restrictive ordinances that make an otherwise strong site less than ideal, such as limitations on the hours of the day when trucks can legally load or unload. Cities and towns are composed of areas—from a few blocks to many acres in size—that are zoned only for commercial, industrial, or residential development. Each zone may have further restrictions. For example, a commercial zone may permit one type of business but not another, so check the zoning codes of any potential location before pursuing a specific site or spending a lot of time and money on a market survey.

- *Traffic density.* Modern site analysis distinguishes between automobile and pedestrian traffic. If only auto traffic were important, most businesses would be located near highways or main roads. With careful examination of foot traffic, you can determine the approximate sales potential of each pedestrian passing a given location. Two factors are especially important in this analysis: total pedestrian traffic during business hours and the percentage of it that's likely to patronize your food-service business.

To count pedestrian traffic, select a few half-hour periods during busy hours of the day. You should only count potential customers for your business; total numbers of passersby aren't the most significant factor. To determine whether people are potential customers or not, you need to know if they're dining out or picking up prepared food to take home. Why are they at the location at this time? To find out, conduct a brief interview. Ask them if they feel there's a

▲

And the Answer Is . . .

As you analyze the pedestrian traffic at a retail location you're considering, use this as a model for your interviews:

Begin by dressing professionally and carrying a clipboard on which you can make notes. Approach people courteously and say, "Excuse me, I'm considering opening a restaurant in this shopping center, and I'm trying to decide if this is a good location for my type of operation. May I have two minutes of your time to ask a few questions?"

If they refuse, thank them anyway, and move on to the next person. However, most people will agree. When they do, quickly ask your questions, and let them get on with their day. Make your survey simple. The following questions should give you an idea of what to ask:

- ❍ What's your primary purpose for being at this shopping center today?

- ❍ Which store or stores have you visited or will you visit?

- ❍ Do you think this shopping center needs a [name the specific type of food-service business you intend to open]?

- ❍ If a [name the specific type of food-service business you intend to open] opened in this location, would you patronize it?

need for a food-service business of the type you want to start at that location and if they would patronize the business if it existed.

Take your sample periods, and multiply the results out over a week, month, and quarter, and use those figures in your financial forecasts. Certainly this process involves some guesswork in your calculations, but if you're careful with your questions and honest in your analysis, you should get a reasonably accurate picture of what to expect.

- *Customer parking facilities.* The site should provide convenient, adequate parking as well as easy access for customers. Storefront parking is always better than a rear lot; people like to be able to see the parking lot before they turn off the main thoroughfare. The lot should be well-lit and secure, with adequate spaces for patrons with disabilities. Consider whether the parking area will need expansion, resurfacing, or striping—possibly at an additional cost. If you're looking at a free-standing location, think big and envision how you will accommodate the hordes of customers your restaurant will eventually attract. Generally speaking, you should have one parking spot for every three seats in your restaurant. If you do a substantial amount of takeout business, you may want to reserve two or three places near the entrance for takeout customers to park briefly when they pick up their orders.

If construction costs and acquiring land for parking are a problem, consider offering valet parking. Once reserved for elegant, fine-dining establishments, this service is becoming more common at casual-dining and even family-oriented operations. Check out nearby parking facilities and research the costs involved; then compare that to the cost of constructing and maintaining your own lot, and make a decision on what's most efficient and effective for your particular circumstances.

- *Proximity to other businesses.* Neighboring businesses may influence your store's volume, and their presence can work for you or against you. Studies of the natural clustering of businesses show that certain types of companies do well when located close to one another. For example, men's and women's apparel and variety stores are commonly located near department stores. Florists are often grouped with shoe stores and women's clothing stores. Restaurants, barbershops, and candy, tobacco, and jewelry stores are often found near theaters.

- *History of the site.* Find out the recent history of each site under consideration before you make a final selection. Who were the previous tenants, and why are they no longer there? There are sites—in malls and shopping centers as well as free-standing locations—that have been occupied by numerous business failures. The reasons for the failures may be completely unrelated to the success potential of your food-service operation, or they could mean your business will meet the same fate. You need to understand why previous tenants failed so you can avoid making the same mistakes.

- *Terms of the lease.* Be sure you understand all the details of the lease, because it's possible an excellent site may have unacceptable leasing terms. The time to negotiate terms is before you sign the lease; don't wait until you've moved in to try to change the terms.

- *The rent–advertising relationship.* You may need to account for up to six months of advertising and promotion expenditures in your working capital. Few businesses can succeed without any sales promotion, and the larger the sum you can afford for well-placed, well-targeted advertising and promotions, the greater your chances of success.

The amount you plan to spend on advertising may be closely related to your choice of site and the proposed rent. If you locate in a shopping center or mall that's supported by huge ad budgets and the presence of large, popular chain and department stores,

> **Bright Idea**
>
> Let your location complement your concept. If you're located on the water, have a great view; near a college, or in a locale known for something special, build on that natural advantage as you design your business.

you'll most likely generate revenue from the first day you open your doors—with no individual advertising at all. Of course, your rental expenses will be proportionately higher than those for an independent location.

- *Future development.* Check with the local planning board to see if anything is planned for the future that could affect your business, such as additional buildings nearby or road construction.

If you don't locate in an area that attracts high-foot traffic, you'll experience a slower growth rate, even if your business fronts a high-traffic street. Your real profits will come as you develop a clientele—and this will require advertising and promotion.

Additional Retail Options

One alternative to a traditional retail store is a cart or kiosk. Carts and kiosks are a great way to test your business before moving into a regular store, and in some cases, they could be a permanent part of your operating strategy. You may want to consider leasing mall space as a temporary tenant, which is a retailer that comes into a mall, sometimes in a store but often with a cart or kiosk, for a specified period, usually to capture holiday or seasonal sales.

> **Dollar Stretcher**
>
> To keep your overhead as low as possible, don't spend a lot of money on fancy fixtures and décor in your work, storage, and administration areas—places your customers never see.

If you have a retail store, such as a bakery or coffeehouse, a temporary cart at another location can generate immediate sales and serve as a marketing tool for your year-round location.

Renting cart or kiosk space usually costs significantly less than renting an in-line store, but rates vary dramatically depending on the location and season. Mall space in

Streetwise

The sunny side of the street is generally less desirable for retail operations than the shady side, especially in warm climates. Research shows rents to be higher on the shady side in high-priced shopping areas. Merchants acknowledge the sunny-side-of-the-street principle by installing expensive awnings to combat the sun and make customers more comfortable.

Marketing research has also demonstrated that the going-home side of the street is usually preferable to the going-to-work side. People have more time to stop at your food-service business on the way home than when they're rushing to work—unless, of course, you offer coffee and breakfast foods, in which case even the busiest person may take time to stop.

particular can be pricey, but these rates are always negotiable, especially in a slow economy. For example, a class C mall may charge as little as $400 a month for cart space during off-peak season, but a class A mall in December might charge $4,000 to $5,000 per month for the same cart space.

Carts can either be leased or purchased. New carts can be purchased for $3,000 to $5,000 and up, depending on how they're equipped. Monthly lease fees will typically run 8 to 12 percent of the new price. You can probably get a good deal on a used cart; just be sure it will suit your needs. If a used cart needs significant modifications to work for you, it may be better to buy new and get exactly what you need.

Though kiosks are often occupied by temporary tenants, they have a greater sense of permanency than carts. They typically offer more space and design flexibility. They're also more expensive: You can expect to pay $10,000 or more to purchase a new kiosk. As with carts, you may be able to lease a kiosk or find a used one to purchase for less money.

Carts and kiosks are available from a variety of sources. Check out manufacturers' and brokers' ads in retail trade publications, such as *Specialty Retail Report*; you can also contact the equipment suppliers listed in the Appendix. But before you invest in a cart or kiosk, decide where you're going to put it. Many malls have restrictions on the size and design of temporary tenant facilities, or they want all such fixtures to look alike.

Another alternative to a traditional facility is also one of the hottest food service trends: a food truck. Food trucks aren't new, but with more than 3 million of them

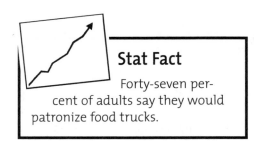

Stat Fact

Forty-seven per-
cent of adults say they would
patronize food trucks.

currently operating in the United States, it's clear that the mobile food industry is booming. Food trucks have a lower overhead than brick-and-mortar restaurants and can be moved if a location isn't generating enough business. The two basic types of food trucks are the mobile food preparation vehicle, where food is prepared as customers wait, and the industrial catering vehicle, which sells only prepackaged foods. You can expect to spend anywhere from $30,000 (for a used food truck) to $100,000 (for a new, fully-equipped truck) to get started in this segment of the food service business.

Pop-up restaurants are also increasing in popularity. A pop-up (also known as a supper club, closed door restaurant, or underground restaurant) is a temporary restaurant that operates from a private home or other non-traditional venue. Pop-ups are an option for restaurateurs who don't have the capital for a permanent installation and can be used to test a concept for a permanent restaurant, or provide exposure for young chefs, or to simply operate in a creative way. Marketing is typically done by word-of-mouth and social media, and some pop-ups bypass local zoning and health code regulations.

Holding Court

A food court is a congregation of 6 to 20 restaurants—usu-ally quick-service establishments—in one location. The primary attraction of the concept is the wide assortment of menus from which to choose. In addition, food courts are appealing due to their convenience, atmosphere, and value.

Food courts are often located in large shopping malls, but they're also found in office buildings, sports arenas, universities, and other places where large num-bers of people congregate. Food courts can serve as anchors for strip malls. Some food courts insist that all restaurant tenants operate from in-line stores. Others allow some to operate from kiosks or carts. Popular food court restaurants include those specializing in pizza and Italian food, Chinese food, ice cream, Mexican food, soups and salads, baked potatoes, and hamburgers and hot dogs.

Food court rents tend to be on the high end of retail locations. But even though most food courts are in heavy-traffic areas, that's no guarantee that you'll get enough business to justify the cost of the location. Do careful market research before signing a lease.

Signage

When you're ready to order signs for your food-service business, keep this in mind: A 1-inch letter can easily be seen from 10 feet away, 2-inch letters can be seen from 20 feet, and so on. A common mistake is creating a sign with letters so small that your customers can't easily read them.

It's also important to have a professional proofreader check your sign for errors. Don't spend a lot of money just to make a poor impression or waste money because you have to do it over to correct a mistake.

If you're going to put up banner-type signs outside, don't hang them with rope, nails, or hooks. Rope doesn't hold on a windy day, which means your sign will double as a sail and quickly become tattered. Instead, use bungee cords, which allow your sign to flex in the wind and retain its original shape.

Mail Order

Setting up a mail order operation makes the entire world your market. If you have food products that are appropriate for shipping, you can take orders over the phone, by mail, by fax, or on the internet, and send items virtually anywhere.

The All-Important Mailing List

You'll develop your customer base by mailing your catalog or brochure to people who fit your target market profile. How do you find these folks? The easiest way is by buying mailing lists. As you probably know from the amount of marketing mail you receive yourself, developing, maintaining, and selling mailing lists is big business. And the list companies can provide you with names and addresses of potential customers who meet your desired demographics.

Buying a list can be expensive, so take the time to do it right. Contact several list brokers before making a decision about which lists to buy. Find out what guarantees the companies offer. Ask how they acquire data and what techniques are in place to assure the accuracy and currency of the information. In today's mobile society, a list that is even one year old will likely contain a sizable percentage of names of people who have moved. Ask for the list broker's references, and check them before making a final selection.

Once you've found a good list broker, stick with him or her. A good broker is a valuable partner in developing a mail order business, because you'll always be trying new lists, even after you're established and profitable.

Your most valuable list will be your in-house list—the people who have become your customers. Build your list by asking people to sign a guest book or by collecting business cards for a drawing. You need to mail frequently to this list, and be creative in developing ideas for ways they can purchase your products. As this list grows, you'll find maintaining it is a complex, time-consuming, and critical task. Consider hiring an outside company to take over your database management.

> **Smart Tip**
> Whenever you try a new list, test the potential response by mailing to a small segment before you spend the money on mailing to the entire list.
>
> *Tip...*

Selling on the Internet

In addition to having a website to promote your food-service business, you may also want to sell specific products online. For example, one bakery in Louisiana offers Creole fruitcake on its website and ships the famous holiday treat and other baked goods—formerly available only through select retail outlets—worldwide.

For more information on setting up and running an online business, see Entrepreneur's *Start Your Own e-Business*.

Packing and Shipping Tips

Get your orders out the door and on their way as quickly as possible. People want immediate gratification, and the faster you deliver, the more orders you'll get. Package your products with extreme care, and be sure the exterior of the box can take a serious beating without damaging the contents. No matter how many "Fragile" and "Handle With Care" stamps you put on the outside, you can be sure that while it's in transit, the box will be shaken, turned upside down, tossed, dropped, and have things stacked on top of it. That's simply the nature of the shipping business.

Be Creative

Look for ways to add revenue without substantially increasing your overhead. For example, caterer Ann Crane only has to stock a few extra items to offer a gift basket service. She already has the food contents—fresh bakery items, fruit, cheeses, and crackers—and just keeps baskets and brightly colored seasonal ribbons on hand. For more information on gift baskets, see Entrepreneur's *Start Your Own Gift Basket Service and More*.

If you make a unique sauce or salad dressing, have it bottled and available for sale in your restaurant. If your employees wear printed T-shirts, make some extras available for purchase. If you have your logo on any items in your operation, make them available for purchase at a reasonable retail price—not only is that an extra revenue stream, it's advertising that doesn't cost you a thing.

Should You Buy an Existing Operation?

If you find the startup process a bit overwhelming, you may think taking over an existing food-service operation seems like a simple shortcut to getting your own business up and running. It can be, but you must proceed with extreme caution.

You can find various types of food-service businesses for sale advertised in trade publications, shopping center publications, and your local newspaper. You might also want to check with a business broker—they're listed in the online and offline Yellow Pages—to see what they have available.

Buyers frequently purchase food-service businesses "lock, stock, and barrel," including store fixtures, equipment, inventory, and supplies. Others negotiate for portions of these items, preferring to remain free to create their own inventory and image.

Be careful not to select a business that's already doomed, perhaps due to poor location or the unfavorable reputation of the former owner. Especially in the case of the latter, it's much easier to start with a clean slate than to try to clean up after someone else. Before buying an existing business, take the following steps:

- *Find out why the business is for sale.* Many entrepreneurs sell thriving businesses because they're ready to do something else or they want to retire. Others will try to sell a declining business in the hopes of cutting their business losses.

- *Do a thorough site analysis to determine if the location is suitable for your type of food-service business.* Has damaging competition moved in since the business originally opened?

> ### Bright Idea
> Want to offer delivery without having to buy or lease a vehicle and hire a driver? Set up an arrangement with an independent delivery service. Many communities have delivery services that focus on restaurant food. These services distribute menus from a variety of quick-service and midrange restaurants. The consumer places an order with the service, which sends a driver to the restaurant to pick up the food and deliver it to the customer for the menu price of the food plus a small service charge.

- *Examine the store's financial records for the past three years and for the current year to date.* Compare sales tax records with the owner's claims.
- *Sit in on the store's operation for a few days.* Observe daily business volume and clientele.
- *Evaluate the worth of existing store fixtures.* They must be in good condition and consistent with your plans for image and food products.
- *Determine the costs of remodeling and redecorating if you want to change the store's décor.* Will these costs negate the advantage of buying?

Be sure any business you're considering buying is worth the price. If you're going to make substantial changes, it may make more sense to start from scratch. But if you do decide to buy, include a noncompete clause in your contract so the seller can't go out and start a competing operation in your service area. And remember that no seller can guarantee that the customers they have when they sell you the business will stick around.

Franchise

Another alternative to starting from scratch is to purchase a franchise. Many people do well with this option, but there are significant risks.

Franchising is a way to market a product or service within a structure dictated by the franchisor. When you buy a franchise, you're entering into an agreement either to distribute products or to operate under a format identified with and structured by the parent company. One major advantage of franchising is that you have the opportunity to buy into a product or system that's established rather than having to create everything yourself. There is, of course, a price for this: In addition to your startup equipment and inventory, you'll have to pay a franchise fee. Also, most franchise companies collect ongoing royalties, usually a percentage of your gross sales. They do, however, provide you with ongoing support.

Franchises are regulated by the FTC and also by a number of states. There are many food-service franchises available, and it's likely that you'll be able to find one that meets your vision of the type of operation you want to open. Thoroughly research any franchise you're considering, and expect the franchisor to want to know a lot about you, too. After all, if you're going to be responsible for operating under the franchisor's name, they'll want to be sure you'll do it right.

The bottom line: Make sure you investigate any franchise or business opportunity carefully before you invest money.

Way to Grow!

Once your new operation is up and running, you may consider growth through franchising. If so, Paul Mangiamele, president and CEO of Bennigan's, says the first thing you need to do is "forget what you serve, because it's just another widget." What's important is that your operation is profitable and that it can be profitably duplicated. "If it doesn't make money, you're never going to franchise it."

Another important consideration is what will differentiate you from other franchisors. "Franchising has never been more viable," Mangiamele says. "There are 3,000 franchised systems growing out there—not just in food service, but any type of business. What's going to [make you stand out in] the clutter? If you've got a good business model, good unit economics and can show a solid return on investment, and your system is replicable in whatever part of the country you want to expand to, you've got a winning combination."

Is Two Better Than One?

One of the hottest trends in the food-service industry is dual-branding, or dual-concepting. The basic idea is to pair two and sometimes more restaurants that offer complementary menu items, which maximizes the use of the facility and increases customer satisfaction. Such pairings can also help companies deal with seasonal fluctuations and provide a vehicle for menu expansion. For example, frozen-treat companies and quick-service chains have benefited from this trend. The Florida-based Miami Subs Corp. (which has since been acquired by Nathan's Famous) was one of the first restaurant chains to experiment with dual-branding. In the late 1980s, the company was searching for a new strategy to boost sales and to strengthen some of the weaker dayparts (an industry term that refers to various meal cycles that occur throughout the day). Rather than investing time and capital into menu research and development, the chain decided to add a familiar product customers enjoyed but could not previously purchase at Miami Subs: Baskin-Robbins ice cream and frozen yogurt. Baskin-Robbins filled the afternoon and early-evening dayparts that account for Miami Subs' downtime, and the dual-brand arrangement dovetailed with the frozen-treat chain's expansion plans.

▲

Dynamic Duos

Increasingly, convenience stores and gas stations are incorporating various food-service businesses into their operations, often by partnering with a franchise or leasing space to an independent restaurateur. A configuration worth considering for a pizzeria, deli/sandwich shop, or limited-menu restaurant is known as a bump-out. Similar to a porch or sunroom on a house, a bump-out is an extension of the existing floor space so the restaurant is adjacent to, rather than housed within, the convenience store or gas station.

Such partnering creates a win-win situation because the restaurant and the store can benefit from each other's traffic and combine marketing efforts. The bump-out configuration gives the restaurant greater visibility and more of its own identity, even though it's under the same roof as the convenience store or gas station.

So if dual-branding is good, does that mean multibranding is better? The popularity of food courts would indicate that consumers will not only accept but enthusiastically embrace the idea.

While its benefits are numerous, dual-branding does have its risks. Here are some guidelines to keep in mind before you join forces with another company:

- *Make sure you're ready for the expansion.* Be sure the base operation is solid enough to function on its own before taking on a partner. Adding another concept to an already-foundering operation can cause both to fail.

- *Complement, don't compete.* Look for a partner that won't undercut your existing sales. You want to dual-brand with a product line that won't force customers to choose. If you're selling burgers, you can dual-brand with a line of vegetarian items or desserts. But if you're selling ice cream, don't dual-brand with a frozen yogurt company.

- *Seek comparable quality.* Any dual-branding partner should offer the same quality that you do.

- *Consider company culture.* The corporate culture of any dual-branding partner must be compatible with your own for the relationship to work.

14

Human Resources

One of the biggest challenges businesses in all industries face is a lack of qualified labor. As the food-service industry in general continues to grow and thrive, the demand for workers who have both the abilities and the desire to work in this business is also increasing. Finding qualified workers (even in

Stat Fact

Approximately 12.8 million people are employed in the restaurant industry in the United States. The restaurant industry is expected to add 1.3 million positions over the next decade.

areas with high unemployment) and rising labor costs are two key concerns for food-service business owners.

Guests will remember—and talk about— poor service long after they've forgotten how good the food was. That's why human resources management must be a top priority.

Stefano LaCommare treats the employees of Stefano's Trattoria like family, and they reciprocate with respect for him, the business, and the customers. He cooks for them every day and believes those free meals pay off in performance and loyalty. Not only is his turnover rate much lower than the industry average, customers appreciate his employees' knowledge of and enthusiasm for the food he serves. In addition to a strong training program, he has created a comprehensive employee handbook that clearly states the requirements of each job, what is expected of each employee, and the policies workers must follow. The result is happy employees who value their jobs and care about their customers.

According to research conducted by the National Restaurant Association, the typical person working in a food-service occupation has no higher than a high school degree (62 percent), is female (54 percent), under 30 years of age (54 percent), single (67 percent), living in a household with relatives (80 percent), and living in a household with two or more wage earners (78 percent). The typical supervisor is female (56 percent) and between the ages of 25 and 44 (43 percent). The typical food-service manager is male (55 percent) and between 25 and 44 years old (48 percent).

The typical food-service employee has less tenure than the average employed person in the United States. Food-service employees were with their current employer a median of 1.4 years, compared with 4 years for all employed persons.

The first step in developing a comprehensive HR program is to decide exactly what you want someone to do. The job description doesn't have to be as formal as one you might expect from a large corporation, but it needs to clearly outline the person's duties and responsibilities. It should also list any special skills or other required credentials, such as a valid driver's license and clean driving record for someone who's going to make deliveries for you.

Next, you need to establish a pay scale. In previous chapters, we've indicated the pay ranges for many of the positions you're going to need to fill. You should do some research on your own to find out what the pay rates are in your area. You'll want to establish a minimum and maximum rate for each position. Remember that you'll pay more even at the start for better qualified and more experienced workers. Of course, the pay scale will be affected by whether the position is one that regularly receives tips.

You'll need a job application form. You can get a basic form at most office supply stores, or you can create your own. Have your attorney review the form you'll be using to ensure it complies with the most current employment laws.

Every prospective employee should fill out an application—even if it's someone you already know, and even if that person has submitted a detailed resume. A resume isn't a signed, sworn statement acknowledging that you can fire the person if he or she lies about his or her background; the application, which includes a truth affidavit, is. The application will also help you verify the applicants' resumes, so you should compare the two, and make sure the information is consistent.

Now you're ready to start looking for candidates.

Look in the Right Places

Picture the ideal candidate in your mind. Is this person likely to be unemployed and reading "help wanted" ads? It's possible, but you'll probably improve your chances for a successful hire if you're more creative in your searching techniques than simply placing an ad in your local paper or posting the opening on an online job site.

Sources for prospective employees include vendors, customers, and professional associations. Check with nearby colleges and perhaps even high schools for part-time help. Put the word out among your social contacts as well—you never know who might know the perfect person for your food-service business.

Roughly 80 percent of food-service business operators say that the most common resources for hourly employees are walk-in inquiries, word of mouth, and newspaper ads, according to a National Restaurant Association survey. Restaurants with average check amounts of $25 or higher are more likely to recruit hourly employees from vocational schools, while operators of establishments with average check amounts of $8 or less are more likely to use signage in their businesses to attract employees.

Consider using a temporary help or an employment agency to fill some open positions. Many small businesses shy away from agencies because they think they can't afford the fee—but if the agency handles the advertising, initial screening, and background checks, the fee may be worth paying.

Use caution if you decide to hire friends and relatives. Many personal

Stat Fact
The restaurant industry provides work for nearly 10 percent of those employed in the United States.

relationships aren't strong enough to survive an employee-employer relationship. Small-business owners in all industries tell of nightmarish experiences when a friend or relative refused to accept direction or otherwise abused a personal relationship in the course of business. The key to success as an employer is making it clear from the

Stat Fact
Approximately 9 out of 10 salaried employees in table-service restaurants started out as hourly employees in the restaurant industry.

start that you're the one in charge. You don't need to act like a dictator, of course. Be diplomatic, but set the ground rules in advance, and stick to them.

Recruiting Young People

According to the National Restaurant Association, about half of today's restaurant employees are under age 25, but fewer young people are participating in the labor force. Fifty-nine percent of 16- to 24-year-olds were in the labor force in 2008, a drop of nearly 10 percent over the last 20 years.

Too often, young people see food-service jobs as a way to work toward their "real" career without realizing the tremendous potential and varied opportunities the industry offers. The solution is a combination of awareness and educational programs that will introduce high school and middle school students to hospitality careers and provide them with training that will allow them to move smoothly from school to the workplace. Across the country, restaurateurs and educators are joining forces to attract and train young people for food-service careers.

Hiring Seniors

Changing demographics and the lifting of the Social Security earnings cap have strengthened the senior labor pool and provided restaurants of all kinds with an excellent source of staffing. According to the National Restaurant Association, older Americans are a key resource for restaurateurs. Adults age 65 and older reached a labor force participation rate of 16.7 percent in 2008, nearly a 40-year high, and the number of individuals age 65 and older in the workforce is expected to grow 80 percent in the next decade. Seniors tend to provide a higher level of customer service than their younger counterparts and often have experience that will help with the overall management of your operation. Also, seniors—whether they're first-time jobholders or are returning to work after retirement—are more likely to stay with you than the worker who's just beginning a career. Another benefit of hiring seniors is that many have their health insurance and retirement plans in place, which saves you the cost of providing those benefits.

Most older workers can handle the demands of just about all front-of-the-house jobs and many back-of-the-house positions, as well. As much as possible accommodate whatever physical limitations senior employees have. If you notice a physical deterioration, communicate your concerns before it becomes a serious problem, and work with the employee to make adjustments in their duties if appropriate. Focus on specific performance issues to avoid the possibility of an age discrimination charge.

If it becomes necessary to terminate a senior worker because of a declining physical condition, try to maintain the relationship. You might, for example, offer dinner on the house once a week. It won't cost you much, but it keeps the worker feeling like a part of the team and provides you with continued access to his or her knowledge base.

Second Chances

Should you hire workers with criminal backgrounds? It's a judgment call that you'll need to make after you've considered all the facts. Sam Mustafa, owner of Charleston Hospitality Group, hired an ex-con to work in his first restaurant in Illinois. Mustafa put him in charge of the kitchen, where he flourished. They worked together for years before the he left to start his own business.

He has since hired a number of employees with criminal records—though not all with the same degree of success. "I am a big believer in second chances, simply because I feel like I have been given many of them myself," he says. "Everyone deserves a second chance. I have hired many people that may not have looked right on paper, but I saw something in them—I could see they were coachable."

Hire Education

Foreign-born workers account for an increasing percentage of the restaurant work force. Under the Immigration Reform and Control Act of 1986, you may only hire people who may legally work in the United States, which means citizens and nationals of the United States and aliens authorized to work in the United States. As an employer, you must verify the identity and employment eligibility of everyone you hire. You must complete and retain the Employment Eligibility Verification Form (I-9) on file for at least three years, or one year after employment ends, whichever is longer.

▲

Evaluating Applicants

What kinds of people make good employees for food-service businesses? It depends on what you want them to do. If you're hiring a delivery person, you need someone with a good driving record who knows the city. If you're hiring someone to help with administrative tasks, you need someone who is computer literate and who can learn your systems. If you're hiring someone to wait tables, he or she needs to be friendly, people-oriented, and able to handle the physical demands of the job. Bartenders need to know how to make drinks, cooks need to know how to cook, and managers need to know how to manage. What's really important is that the people you hire are committed to giving you their best effort while they're working so that your customers receive the best service.

When you actually begin the hiring process, don't be surprised if you're as nervous at the prospect of interviewing potential employees as they are about being interviewed. After all, they may need a job, but the future of your company is at stake.

It's a good idea to prepare your interview questions in advance. Develop open-ended questions that encourage the candidates to talk. In addition to knowing what they've done, you want to find out how they did it. Ask each candidate for a particular position the same set of questions, and make notes as each responds so you can make an accurate assessment and comparison later.

When the interview is over, let the candidate know what to expect. Is it going to take you several weeks to interview other candidates, check references, and make a decision? Will you want the top candidates to return for a second interview? Will you call the candidate, or should he or she call you? This is not only a good business practice; it's also common courtesy.

Always check former employers' and personal references. For legal reasons many companies restrict the information they'll verify, but you may be surprised at what you can find out. You should at least confirm that the applicant told the truth about dates and positions held. Personal references are likely to give you some additional insight into the general character and personality of the candidate; this will help you decide if they'll fit into your operation.

Be sure to document every step of the interview and reference-checking process. Even small companies are finding themselves targets of employment discrimination suits; good records are your best defense if it happens to you.

Bright Idea

Post the duties of all positions so new people can quickly see what they are supposed to do each day and also have a clear picture as to how their positions interact with others.

Once They're on Board

The hiring process is only the beginning of the challenge of having employees. The next thing you need to do is train them.

Many small businesses conduct their "training" just by throwing someone into the job. That's not fair to the employee, and it's certainly not good for your business. If you think you can't afford to spend time on training, think again: Can you afford not to adequately train your employees? Do you really want them preparing food or interacting with your customers when you haven't told them how you want things done?

In an ideal world, employees could be hired already knowing everything they need to know. But this isn't an ideal world, so if you want the job done right, you have to teach your people how to do it. Bakery owner Jim Amaral says he looks for people with food-service experience because they're used to being on their feet in a fast-paced environment, but he expects to have to train people in the art of sourdough bread making. "Because we do so much training, we really look for people who we think are going to be around for a couple of years or more," he says.

Virtually all table-service restaurant operators provide employees with some sort of on-the-job training, with about 90 percent providing ongoing training and 80 percent offering formal job training.

Whether done in a formal classroom setting or on the job, effective training begins with a clear goal and a plan for reaching it. Training will fall into one of three major categories: orientation, which includes explaining company policies and procedures; job skills, which focuses on how to do specific tasks; and ongoing development, which enhances the basic job skills and grooms employees for future challenges and opportunities. The following tips will help maximize your training efforts.

- *Find out how people learn best.* Delivering training is not a one-size-fits-all proposition. People absorb and process information differently, and your training method needs to be compatible with their individual preferences. Some people can read a manual, others prefer a verbal explanation, and still others need to see a demonstration. In a group-training situation your best strategy is to use a combination of methods. When you're working one-on-one, tailor your delivery to fit the needs of the person you're training.

  Figuring out how employees learn best can be as simple as asking them. But some people may not be able to

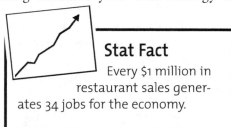

Stat Fact
Every $1 million in restaurant sales generates 34 jobs for the economy.

tell you how they learn best because they don't know themselves. In those cases, experiment with various training styles, and see what works for the specific employee.

- *Use simulation and role-playing to train, practice, and reinforce.* One of the most effective training techniques is simulation, which involves showing an employee how to do something, then allowing him or her to practice it in a safe, controlled environment. If the task includes interpersonal skills, let the employee role-play with a co-worker to practice what he or she should say and do in various situations.

- *Be a strong role model.* Don't expect more from your employees than you're willing to do yourself. You're a good role model when you do things the way they should be done, all the time. Don't take shortcuts you don't want your employees to take or behave in any way that you don't want them to behave. On the other hand, don't assume that simply doing things the right way is enough to teach others how to do things. Role modeling is not a substitute for training; it reinforces training. If you only use role modeling but never train, employees aren't likely to get the message.

- *Look for training opportunities.* Once you get beyond basic orientation and job skills training, you'll need to be constantly on the lookout for opportunities to enhance the skills and performance levels of your people.

- *Make it real.* Whenever possible, use real-life situations to train—but avoid letting customers know they've become a training exercise for employees.

- *Anticipate questions.* Don't assume that employees know what to ask. In a new situation, people often don't understand enough to formulate questions. Anticipate their questions and answer them in advance.

- *Ask for feedback.* Finally, encourage employees to let you know how you're doing as a trainer. Just as you evaluate their performance, convince them that it's OK to tell you the truth. Ask them what they thought of the training and your techniques, and use that information to improve your own skills.

Bright Idea

Use other restaurants as a training tool. Ask your employees to share tips and techniques from their own dining-out experiences. And have your workers periodically mystery shop the competition with activities such as calling for reservations and information, just to see how such requests are handled.

Smart Tip

Training employees— even part-time, temporary help—in your way of doing things is important. These people represent your company, and they need to know how to maintain the image and standards you've worked hard to establish.

Stat Fact

Each dollar spent in restaurants generates 82 cents in household earnings throughout the economy.

Employee Benefits

The actual wages you pay may be only part of your employees' total compensation. While many small companies don't offer a formal benefits program, more and more business owners have recognized that benefits—particularly in the area of health and life insurance—are important when it comes to attracting and retaining quality employees.

Typical benefit packages include group insurance (your employees may pay all or a portion of their premiums), paid holidays, and vacations. The issue of health insurance is volatile; be proactive at staying current on any legislation that could affect you and what you must provide your workers. You can build employee loyalty by seeking additional benefits that may be somewhat unusual—and they don't have to cost much. For example, if you're in a retail location, talk to other business owners in your shopping center to see if they're interested in providing reciprocal employee discounts. You'll not only provide your own employees with a benefit, but you may also get some new customers out of the arrangement.

Beyond tangible benefits, look for ways to provide positive working conditions. "We're not just about making bread; we're about creating a good work environment where people feel like they're making some progress in their own lives in terms of developing skills and becoming better people," says Amaral. "We don't just look at the financial bottom line, we look at what the employees are doing and the value being added for the employees and the customers." Amaral's bakery provides a strong

Got It Covered

In most states, if you have three or more employees, you are required by law to carry workers' compensation insurance. This coverage pays medical expenses and replaces a portion of the employee's wages if he or she is injured on the job. Even if you have only one or two employees, you may want to consider investing in this coverage to protect both your staff and you in case of an accident.

Details and requirements vary by state, so contact your state's insurance office or your own insurance agent for information so you're sure you're in compliance.

benefits package that includes health insurance, paid vacations, and holidays. He also pays employees for doing volunteer work at their regular hourly rate for up to three hours a month.

Caterer Ann Crane sends her full-time staffers to seminars to help sharpen their skills. She also provides extras, such as the time she bought tickets to Disneyland for the staff and their families. And periodically, she brings lunch in from another restaurant—since staff members cook their own lunches every day, ordering out is a treat.

Same-Sex Marriages and Domestic Partnership Benefits

One of the hottest political topics these days is the issue of same-sex marriages. While many people are quick to offer an opinion on the subject, what isn't clear is the impact of a state allowing same-sex marriages in the areas of employment and employee benefits.

At the present, federal law, which dominates the area of employee benefits, does not recognize same-sex marriage. This means employers don't need to treat same-sex spouses in the same manner as opposite-sex spouses for purposes of benefits governed by the Employee Retirement Income Security Act (ERISA).

However, there are areas in which state law and the recognition of same-sex marriage may have an impact. For example, an employer generally may extend benefits to same-sex spouses, even where not required by law.

Your best strategy is to understand the issues related to same-sex marriage and employee benefits and to decide on an overall approach to dealing with the issue. Be sure this approach is clearly defined in your policies and consistently applied. Review and revise your benefit plans and employment practices as necessary.

Child Labor Issues

Teenagers make up a significant portion of the food-service industry's labor force, and it's important that you understand the child labor laws that apply to your particular operation. The Fair Labor Standards Act has set four provisions designed to protect the educational opportunities of youths and prohibit their employment in jobs and under conditions that are detrimental to their health and well-being.

The minimum age for most nonfarm workers is 16; however, 14- and 15-year-olds may be employed outside of school hours in certain occupations under certain conditions. At any age, youths may work for their parents in their solely owned nonfarm businesses (except in mining, manufacturing, or other occupation declared hazardous by the Secretary of Labor). This means your minor children can work in your food-service business if you're the sole owner, as long as they're not violating other age-related laws, such as serving alcohol.

The basic age-related guidelines of the Fair Labor Standards Act are:

- Youths 18 years or older may perform any job for an unlimited number of hours.

- Youths aged 16 and 17 may perform any job for an unlimited number of hours that's not declared hazardous by the Secretary of Labor.

- Youths aged 14 and 15 may work outside school hours in nonmanufacturing, nonmining, nonhazardous jobs under the following conditions: no more than three hours on a school day, 18 hours in a school week, eight hours on a non-school day, or 40 hours in a nonschool week. In addition, they may not begin work before 7 A.M. or work after 7 P.M., except from June 1 through Labor Day, when evening work hours are extended until 9 P.M.

- Youths aged 14 and 15 who are enrolled in an approved Work Experience and Career Exploration Program (WECEP) may be employed up to 23 hours during school weeks and three hours on school days, including during school hours.

Department of Labor regulations require employers to keep records of the date of birth of employees under age 19, their daily starting and quitting times, daily and weekly hours worked, and their occupation. Protect yourself from unintentional violation of the child labor provisions by keeping an employment or age certificate on file for each youth employed to show that they're of the required minimum age for the job.

Keep in mind that in addition to the federal statutes, most states also have child labor laws. Check with your own state labor department to see what regulations apply to your business. When both federal and state laws apply, the law setting the higher standards must be observed.

Minimum Wage

The Fair Labor Standards Act also establishes minimum wage, overtime pay, and record-keeping standards. The act requires employers of covered employees who aren't otherwise exempt to pay these employees a minimum wage. Youths under 20 years old

▲

You Deserve a Break

No matter how much you enjoy your work, you need an occasional break from it. This is a challenge for small-business owners, but it's critical. You need to be able to get away from your operation occasionally, not only for vacations, but for business reasons, such as attending conferences and trade shows. Also, you need a plan in place in case of illness, accidents, or other emergencies. Be sure your staff is well-trained and committed to maintaining your service levels when you aren't there.

may be paid a youth minimum wage that's lower than the standard minimum wage during the first 90 consecutive calendar days of employment. Employers may not displace any employee to hire someone else at the youth minimum wage. Because minimum wage laws change, be sure to check with your state labor board or the Department of Labor Wage and Hour Division for the current minimum wage amounts.

Under federal law, employers of tipped employees, which are defined as employees who customarily and regularly receive more than $30 a month in tips, may consider those tips part of their employees' wages but must pay a direct wage of at least $2.13 per hour if they claim a tip credit. Certain other conditions must also be met. States may establish minimum wages that are higher than the federal rate. Check with your accountant or the appropriate agency to be sure you're in compliance.

The act permits the employment of certain individuals at wage rates below the statutory minimum wage, but they must be working under certificates issued by the Department of Labor. Those individuals include student learners (vocational education students), full-time students in retail or service establishments, and individuals whose earning or productive capacity is impaired by a physical or mental disability, including those related to age or injury.

Tips and Taxes

Tips received by your employees are generally subject to withholding. Your employees must report to you all cash tips they've received by the 10th of the month after the month in which the tips are received. This report should include tips employees receive directly in cash as well as tips you paid from charge receipts. Also include the tips employees receive from other employees and through tip-splitting.

Employees should report their tips on IRS Form 4070, Employee's Report of Tips to Employer, or on form 4070-A, Employee's Daily Record of Tips, or on a similar statement. The statement must be signed by the employee and include the employee's name, address, and Social Security number; your name and address; the month or period the report covers; and the total tips received. No report is required when tips are less than $20 a month.

As an employer, you must collect income tax, employee Social Security tax, and employee Medicare tax on employees' tips. You can collect these taxes from wages or from other funds the employee makes available. You are also responsible for paying employer Social Security tax on wages and tips.

You must file Form 941 to report tip withholding. Your accountant can help you set up a system to be sure you comply with IRS reporting and payment requirements.

Certain establishments must report allocated tips under certain circumstances. The IRS requires that large food and beverage establishments, which are defined as providing "food or beverages for consumption on the premises, where tipping is customary and where there are normally more than 10 employees on a typical business day during the preceding year," report allocated tips (which can be calculated by hours worked, gross receipts, or good-faith agreement). But you don't withhold income, Social Security, or Medicare taxes on allocated tips. Check with your accountant or the IRS for more information.

When You Suspect an Employee of Stealing

Employee theft can seriously impact your bottom line as well as the morale of other employees who may be aware of what's going on. When you become aware of actual or suspected employee theft, you need to act quickly—but carefully—to resolve the situation.

"Treat the complaint as valid until it's established otherwise, and treat the accused as innocent until proven guilty," says Michael P. O'Brien, a labor and employment attorney with Jones Waldo Holbrook & McDonough PC in Salt Lake City. "Also, treat the matter confidentially to the greatest extent possible." In today's litigious world, protecting the privacy of a suspect is essential; failing to do so can leave you vulnerable if that individual decides to sue later—regardless of whether the person was actually guilty.

The first step is to conduct a thorough investigation, including a review of all relevant documents, such as personnel files, time sheets, performance evaluations of the people involved, inventory and delivery records, and applicable financial records. If your security system includes video surveillance, you'll want to review the tapes. You may also want to interview witnesses and others who may have knowledge of

Stat Fact

Approximately 94 percent of table-service operators provide advancement opportunities, and roughly 92 percent offer flexible work schedules.

the situation. Of course, you should also interview the accused—without making an accusation. When conducting interviews, be very clear that the issue under investigation is not to be discussed with unconcerned parties. "If a witness can't be trusted, think carefully about involving that person [in the investigation] in order to avoid possible defamation problems," says O'Brien.

Regardless of how much you trust a particular witness, avoid disclosing information unnecessarily, and don't ask questions that indicate the direction of your inquiry. Document every step of the investigation, and maintain those records in a secure place separate from your personnel records. Don't make details of an investigation part of an employee's personnel file unless and until the results are in and misconduct has been proved.

If your investigation confirms misconduct, take immediate and appropriate disciplinary action consistent with your general policies. "The worst thing you can do is nothing," O'Brien says. "You need to take some sort of disciplinary action against the individual you've concluded has done an inappropriate act." Certainly you'll want to consider the severity, frequency, and pervasiveness of the conduct—for example, occasionally overpouring drinks for regular customers is certainly less severe than skimming cash out of the register—but whatever remedy you apply must end the offensive behavior. Keep in mind that whatever you do may eventually wind up in court, so maintain good records and be sure you can always justify your actions.

You must also decide whether to involve law enforcement. Weigh the potential for negative publicity against the potential good, which could include restitution and the fact that the perpetrator may receive some much-needed rehabilitation.

Regulatory Issues

Because of the significant impact food-service businesses can have on the health and safety of their patrons, these establishments are subject to a wide range of regulatory requirements, which vary by city and state. You're responsible for knowing what regulations apply to your operation and for complying with them. Don't try to bend or break the regulations; if you get caught, you'll be subject to civil and perhaps even criminal liability, along with the potential of negative publicity that could put you out of business.

In addition to enforcing health and safety regulations, many agencies offer resources to help new and existing restaurateurs stay in compliance. Some will conduct what they call a "helpful inspection," where they'll let you know what you need to do without citing you for violations. Check with your local health department and licensing agencies to find out how they can help you avoid problems.

Licenses and Permits

Most cities and counties require food-service business operators to obtain various licenses and permits. Requirements vary by municipality, so do your own research to make sure your business fully complies with local regulations.

Business License

City business license departments operate as tax-collecting bureaus and don't perform any public service. You simply pay a fee to operate your business in that city. Some cities also claim a percentage of your gross sales.

The planning or zoning department will process your license application and check to make sure applicable zoning laws allow the proposed use and that there are enough parking spaces to meet the code.

Health Department Permit

To purvey and distribute food, you'll need a food establishment permit from your state or county health department. All food-service operations, including temporary food-service establishments and mobile units such as carts, must obtain this permit before beginning operation. The health department will inspect your facility before issuing your initial permit and will perform inspections on an ongoing basis as long as you're in business.

Health inspectors will want to make sure all areas of your operation meet legal standards. They'll be concerned with food storage, food preparation, food display, employee health and cleanliness, the design and installation

> ### Smart Tip
> *Tip...*
>
> While you're still in the planning stages, contact your local health department for information about its requirements. It'll be happy to give you the information you need so you'll qualify for all the necessary permits.

of equipment, the cleaning and storage of equipment and utensils, sanitary facilities, and the construction and maintenance of the facility. The type of food your restaurant specializes in isn't an issue; what is important is how you store and prepare that food. Your local or state health department can provide you with guidelines.

Liquor and Beer-and-Wine Licenses

Most states require you to obtain one type of license to serve beer and wine and another to serve hard liquor. A liquor license is more difficult to obtain than a beer-and-wine license. In some areas, no new liquor licenses are being issued at all, which means you can only obtain one by buying it from an existing license holder.

One advantage of buying an existing restaurant is that if it serves liquor, you may be able to acquire the license as part of the deal. Typically, you'll have to file an application with the state beverage control board, then post notice on the premises of your intent to serve liquor.

In some states, the beverage control board requires holders of liquor licenses to keep all purchase records for a specific number of years, during which time they're subject to inspection by the control board and/or the IRS.

Under most circumstances, it's easier to obtain a license to serve beer and wine than a hard-liquor license. Beer-and-wine licenses are usually issued for a one-year period and are easy to renew if you haven't committed any offenses, such as selling alcohol to minors. The government section of your telephone directory will have the number for the nearest beverage control agency, which can provide you with information.

Fire Department Permit

Your fire department may require you to obtain a permit if your business will use any flammable materials or if your premises will be open to the public. In some cities, you must secure a permit before you open for business. Other jurisdictions don't require permits. Instead, they schedule periodic inspections to see that your facility meets the regulations. Restaurants, theaters, clubs, bars, retirement homes, day-care centers, and schools are subject to especially close and frequent scrutiny by the fire department.

Sign Permit

Many municipalities have sign ordinances that restrict the size, location, and sometimes the lighting and type of sign you can use in front of your business. Landlords may also impose their own restrictions. You'll likely find sign restrictions most stringent in malls and upscale shopping areas. Avoid costly mistakes by checking regulations and securing the written approval of your landlord before you invest in a sign.

County Permit

County governments often require the same types of permits and licenses as cities. These permits apply to commercial enterprises located outside city limits.

State Licenses

Many states require persons engaged in certain occupations, such as hairdressers, contractors, medical-care providers, teachers, child-care providers, and others, to hold licenses or occupational permits. Food-service employees generally aren't required to hold licenses, but to make sure you're complying, check with your state government for a complete list of occupations that do require licensing.

> **Beware!**
> Regardless of what the laws say about your liability, just about anyone can sue anyone else in civil court for just about any reason. And although you may win the verdict in a lawsuit where the plaintiff had insufficient grounds, fighting a lawsuit is expensive and time-consuming. Your best strategy is to avoid situations that could result in any potential liability.

Zoning Laws

In most cases, if you locate your food-service business in a structure that was previously used for commercial purposes, zoning regulations won't be a problem. However, if you intend to construct a new facility, use an existing building for a different purpose, or do extensive remodeling, you should check local building and zoning codes. If zoning regulations don't allow for the operation of the type of food-service business you want to open, you may file for a zoning variance, a conditional-use permit, or a zone change.

Music Licenses

If you plan to play music in your restaurant—whether you hire a live performer or play on-hold music on your telephone—you'll need to obtain the appropriate licenses. Federal copyright laws require that any business that plays copyrighted music pay a fee. Fees are collected by the American Society of Composers, Authors and Publishers; Broadcast Music Inc.; and SESAC Inc. (formerly the Society of European Stage Authors and Composers; see the Appendix for contact information).

U.S. copyright law requires you to obtain permission from and negotiate a fee with the composer and publisher of a musical piece before you can reproduce or perform the material. Since contacting each composer and publisher is impossible, especially if the composer is deceased, the previously listed organizations work on behalf of their members. They require business owners who play music in their establishments to obtain licenses through them instead of directly from the composers and publishers. The fees for these licenses are used to pay composers and publishers royalties for the performance of their material. By going through these performance rights organizations, you'll pay a general fee that will cover the performance of all their members' songs. You must obtain a license from each of these organizations because they represent different artists. If you play copyrighted music without having a license to do so, the appropriate agency could levy a $5,000 to $20,000 fine.

The organizations base their fees on a number of factors, including the seating capacity in your establishment, the number of days or evenings each week you play music, whether you charge patrons for admission, and whether the music is performed live or by mechanical means.

The Legalities of Liquor Vending

Most food-service businesses find that serving alcoholic beverages improves their profit margins and offsets the costs associated with some of the less profitable aspects of the business. Over the past decade or so, however, there has been a marked increase in sociopolitical pressure and legal trouble facing businesses that sell alcoholic beverages. Some are calling this the "new temperance era" and "a time of neoprohibitionism." On both the state and federal levels, legislators, public health officials, and special-interest groups are warning against alcohol abuse and bringing to light the fatalities and injuries caused by drunk driving. The effect on those who serve liquor, regardless of their personal beliefs, has been profound.

As a part of this movement, old statutes are being dusted off and new laws promulgated to place pressure on not just the alcohol abuser but also the supplier. It has always been incumbent on the owners of liquor-vending establishments to observe state liquor laws or face criminal penalties. However, these days, businesses selling liquor also face the threat of increased popular and legal support for those filing civil suits against liquor vendors.

It used to be that the average bartender or liquor-store owner just had to worry about getting caught serving minors or those who were obviously already intoxicated. Proprietors would buy special liquor liability insurance for coverage in the event of a lawsuit from a drunken patron. Lately, the liquor vendor has become potentially liable financially when a third party is injured.

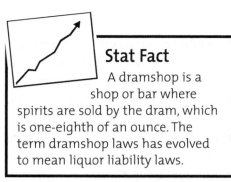

Simply stated, dramshop laws and other types of third-party liability work this way: If you, the server of alcoholic beverages, act irresponsibly and over-serve a patron and that patron is later involved in an automobile crash, then the individual server, as well as the establishment, can be held financially liable for the death or injury of not only an innocent third party but of the intoxicated patron as well.

Laws regarding liquor liability vary by state and can change quickly. Your state's liquor board or alcoholic beverage commission should be able to tell you what the current laws are in your state.

Whether your state exposes you to high or low risks of liability, or whether your type of establishment puts you in jeopardy of civil suits, you must be aware of and take precautions against legal action. Progressive owners and managers minimize the risk of criminal charges and civil litigation.

One step is learning to perceive intoxication and cutting off customers as soon as it becomes necessary. Most liquor vendors (and drinkers) are familiar with the warning signs, but all sellers and servers should be acquainted with them. Among the more common indicators are staggering, slurred speech, impaired thinking, heavy eyelids, silence, talking too much or too loudly, tearfulness, hostility, acting out, nausea or vomiting, sudden mood changes, physical imbalance, and forcing verbal or physical confrontations.

Steps You Can Take

Most liquor vendors could use some reform to protect customers and themselves from accidents that can turn into lawsuits. The general idea is to control the quantity of alcohol consumed by individual patrons and the ways in which drinking is encouraged. Though it may appear counterproductive for a liquor vendor to restrict the sale of alcoholic beverages, the trouble caused by not doing so will cost more in the long run than any negligible decrease in liquor sales.

Here's one way to think of the situation: For every drunk you throw out of your place, consider how many customers are made more relaxed by his or her absence and are likely to return.

Preventive measures employed by many liquor vendors include:

Bright Idea
Consider a program that offers free nonalcoholic beverages to the designated driver in groups of patrons. Your investment will be minimal, but the impact on your potential liability, as well as the marketing benefit, will be significant.

- *Not serving minors.* Drunk driving is a primary killer of teenagers in this country. Observe the legal drinking age, and check ID on any patron who appears to be under 30. Everyone on your staff, whether their duties include serving alcohol or not, should know the minimum drinking age in your state and which state laws apply regarding proof of age and other alcohol service issues. Check with your state's liquor board or alcoholic beverage commission to find out what programs are available to help you train your staff and stay in legal compliance.

- *Dealing with intoxicated patrons.* Develop and implement consistent, diplomatic procedures for denying alcohol to customers who arrive drunk or who become so, and for making last calls. Each employee, from the busperson to the manager, should be familiar with these procedures and the philosophy behind them.

- *Bar layout.* Your bar cannot become so crowded that bartenders can't keep track of whom and how much they have served. You can't allow customers in inconspicuous areas of your establishment to drink all night without being monitored at least casually. Adding bartenders and servers or changing the layout of your bar can help you avoid this situation.

- *Controlling the flow.* Free pouring (as opposed to measuring) drinks isn't economical, makes it difficult to control inventory, and hampers your servers' abilities to monitor alcohol consumption. Also, a free-pour bar may be in a difficult spot if you must legally account for the quantity of alcohol consumed by a particular customer. Consider cutting back on the happy-hour specials and closing time for two-for-one or all-you-can-drink specials. Instead, promote your nonalcoholic bar drinks. Your bartender can create these beverages inexpensively, with an even greater profit margin than for alcoholic beverages. Try putting more emphasis on food items, and encourage the safe consumption of alcohol by selling snacks or providing complimentary hors d'oeuvres so people aren't drinking on an empty stomach.

- *Alternative transportation.* Serving liquor responsibly may include ensuring that inebriated customers get home safely. Some establishments will provide complimentary taxi service or call a cab for intoxicated customers. Many bars and restaurants band together to provide carpool service. Cab companies and community organizations may be willing to help provide transportation for free or at a nominal cost.

Despite your best precautions, any time alcohol and people mix in your establishment, you'll have the potential for danger to the public and liability to you. An important step in self-protection is becoming familiar with the liquor liability laws in your state and purchasing adequate insurance. Your lawyer or insurer should be able to inform you of the relevant state laws and evaluate your risk.

For more information about bar operations, check out Entrepreneur's *Start Your Own Bar/Club*.

Sanitation

Sanitation is crucial to a successful food-service operation, not only for health and safety reasons but also for image reasons. Your storage area, kitchen preparation area, serving areas, waiting area, lounge, restrooms, and dining area should be clean and in good repair from floor to ceiling.

Set standards for all employees and reinforce them with charts, labels, and placards in areas where the staff will be reminded of sanitation issues. (Certain sanitation-related signs are required by law. Your health department can inform you of the necessary requirements.) The National Restaurant Association produces a wide range of training materials that deal with various aspects of sanitation. Contact the association (listed in the Appendix) for more information.

You or your manager should perform thorough sanitation inspections at least once every six months. This inspection should focus on the storage of food; employees' personal hygiene; the cleanliness of all equipment and utensils; all floors, walls, and ceilings; lighting; ventilation; the dishwashing facility; water, sewage, and plumbing; restrooms; garbage and refuse disposal; insect and animal control; and linens.

Proper food storage is critical. A single case of food poisoning can put a restaurant out of business. Nothing should be placed directly on the floor, whether it's food in dry storage or frozen or refrigerated food. Use pallets, racks, or anything else that will raise your inventory off the floor. This makes it easier to clean the floors and protects the food from vermin and from being splashed by chemicals or dirty water.

To keep food free from contamination, place it in an area where you can maintain the proper temperature: Keep hot food hot and cold food cold. Cover all refrigerated food. Don't leave anything out longer than necessary during the preparation period.

Whether you serve fruits and vegetables raw or cooked, wash them all thoroughly. Use proper utensils and plastic gloves when appropriate during preparation so human contact with food is kept to a minimum.

Your employees' personal hygiene is also important. Employees with cuts, abrasions,

> **Smart Tip**
>
> Too many incidences of food contamination that lead to illness can be traced to workers failing to wash their hands after using the restroom. Stress to all employees who handle or serve food the importance of thorough hand washing.

dirty fingernails, any type of skin disease, or a communicable disease should certainly not be involved in preparing or serving food. Employees involved in food preparation or serving should have clean uniforms, and clean hair, hands, and fingernails. Employees with long hair should either wear a hairnet or at least pull their hair back away from their faces to prevent hairs from falling into the food.

Emphasize to the dishwasher and all of your servers that pots, pans, preparation utensils, plates, silverware, glassware, and serving utensils should be spotless before

Preventive Medicine

The possibility that someone could get sick from eating food you served is a food-service business owner's worst nightmare. First, there's the fact that you—however unintentionally—caused someone to suffer. Then there's the potential liability, in terms of both paying direct medical costs and additional punitive damages. Finally, there's the bottom-line damage, because when word gets out—and it will—your business will suffer, and sales can plummet.

Preventing food-borne illnesses begins with awareness. Everyone in your operation needs to understand how to prevent problems and the consequences of failing to do so. It's not enough just to tell workers that salads need to be kept at a certain temperature and that they need to wash their hands thoroughly after using the restroom. Your employees need to know what can happen if they fail to follow these health and safety regulations.

The National Restaurant Association (NRA) offers a number of training programs and educational materials, such as signs and posters, that can help you maintain an operation that's safe for both your employees and your customers.

You might also consider providing inoculations for employees. For example, many restaurants in high-risk areas require employees to be vaccinated against hepatitis A (contact your local health department for information on whether your restaurant is located in a high-risk area). Exposure can result when an infected person uses the restroom, doesn't wash his or her hands, then handles food that others will eat. It can also be waterborne and spread through bodily fluids such as saliva and blood. While seldom fatal, the virus can cause diarrhea, nausea, cramping, fatigue, and jaundice. The cost of the vaccine is about $90 per person, but it may be available for less through the NRA or some local public health programs.

they're used. It's a good idea to specifically check cups and glasses for lipstick that may not get removed in the dishwashing process. All production equipment should be checked and cleaned regularly by your cooks. Maintain proper hot water temperatures, and make sure your water source is safe.

Your floors, walls, and ceilings should be cleaned regularly. Check them to make sure that all surfaces are smooth and free of dust, grease, and cobwebs. Set up a service contract with a local exterminator to ensure that your facility is free of insects and rodents. Clean drains often. Rubber mats should be easy to move for cleaning.

Don't neglect your garbage area. All trash containers should be leak-proof and nonabsorbent and have tight-fitting covers. Wash your containers thoroughly inside and out when you empty them.

Equipment

For most food-service businesses, the focus is on the food preparation and service equipment. For your office, as we've said in previous chapters, chances are a small desk, a chair, a couple of locking filing cabinets, and a few bookshelves for catalogs and pricing guides will be sufficient in the beginning. Your office furnishings should be comfortable and efficient, but don't worry about how they look. Your customers aren't going to see your office, so don't waste money in this area that could be more effectively spent on the front of the house. Speaking of the front of the house, keep the following information in mind when purchasing major equipment for your food-service business.

Major Equipment

While each of the food-service operations discussed in this guide has specific equipment requirements, there are many items that are basic to just about any type of food-service business. Food-service equipment dealers are often good sources for finding out what you need and what particular piece of equipment will do it best. A good salesperson will also function as a consultant, helping you make wise decisions. After all, if you're satisfied, you're likely to come back when you need more equipment— and you'll refer others. However, you still need to be cautious when accepting advice and guidance from a salesperson. Get several opinions and price quotes before making a final decision.

Careful and thoughtful equipment selection will mean a cost-effective and productive operation over the long run. Don't buy based on price alone. You can cut down on labor costs by purchasing equipment that's fully automatic and self-cleaning, even though it may cost more upfront. Install as much modern, energy-efficient equipment as possible. That way, when gas and electricity costs rise, your energy-saving equipment will help keep your utility bills reasonable.

Buy from a well-known manufacturer who has reliable equipment and a network of repair facilities. Look for standard lines of equipment that are both versatile and mobile. Avoid custom-designed lines whenever possible. Standard equipment is generally lower priced and less expensive to install. It's also easier and less expensive to replace at the end of its service life.

Most food-service operations will need a walk-in refrigerator/freezer for primary food storage at the rear of the facility near the receiving door. You'll also need a smaller reach-in refrigerator/freezer in your production area to keep the food supplies you need that day or for that meal period fresh and easily accessible.

Your receiving area should also include a scale to verify weights of deliveries, a breakdown table, at least one dolly or hand

> **Dollar Stretcher**
>
> Shopping for used equipment? Don't overlook new-equipment suppliers. They frequently have trade-ins or repossessions that they're willing to sell at a discount of 75 percent or more.

To Lease or Not to Lease?

If your initial equipment investment will be significant, you may want to consider leasing rather than purchasing. Leasing is an excellent alternative when startup capital is limited. You should also check with your tax advisor about the tax advantages of leasing.

The disadvantage to leasing is that if you have a tax-deductible lease, you don't build equity in your equipment and therefore don't build up your balance sheet. A financial statement showing a strong net worth is important to any business. In addition, the total cost of leasing over a period of years is going to be higher than if the same items were purchased. Consult with your accountant to make the best choice based on your tax status and cash situation.

truck, dry shelving, and shelving for the walk-in refrigerator/freezer. You may find wheeled carts a convenient tool for managing your inventory.

Buying Used Equipment

Heavy-duty restaurant hardware doesn't wear out quickly, so why buy brand-new when "seasoned," used merchandise can be as good or even better? You can buy secondhand equipment for a fraction of what it would cost new. And there's plenty available from other food-service businesses that have failed, merged, or grown to the point where they require larger or more modern equipment.

Since Ann Crane bought her catering company, she's been expanding at a healthy pace. When she needed additional gear to support her growing business, she says, "I couldn't afford to go out and buy all new equipment. The only thing I bought new was my walk-in refrigerator and the overhead hood for the cooking line. Everything else was used."

Caterer Maxine Turner buys used equipment. She used to go to auctions but got burned a few times when she bought equipment that wasn't as good as she thought. Now she only buys at auction if

Dollar Stretcher

Just about any type of secondhand business equipment can be purchased for a fraction of its original retail cost. Check the classified section of your local newspaper. Careful shopping for used items can save you hundreds of dollars.

she knows whom she's working with and is familiar with the equipment being sold. She also learned how to work with equipment dealers, particularly new-equipment dealers who sell used items that have come in through trade-ins.

Buying used equipment is normally a good cost-cutting measure, but there are some pitfalls. Consider that some major equipment has a useful lifetime of only 10 years. If you buy a used walk-in refrigerator/freezer that's near the end of its useful life, you run the risk of repeated breakdowns, resulting in costly maintenance and food spoilage. Also, newer equipment is generally going to be more cost-efficient to operate.

> **Beware!**
> Resist the temptation to fritter away time on your computer under the guise of working. The abundance of easy-to-use software on the market today gives us fun ways to turn out impressive documents, tempting you and your employees to add artwork, color, and even motion to your materials. While a certain amount of creativity can help your competitive position, take care that it doesn't get out of control and become a serious time waster.

Before buying a piece of used equipment, perform a cost analysis of the item you're considering over its expected lifetime versus that of a comparable new item. When you factor in maintenance and operating costs, it's possible new equipment may actually be less expensive in the long run.

Look for standard lines of equipment that are both versatile and mobile so you won't have to duplicate hardware. Try to avoid custom-designed lines. Standard equipment is generally less expensive to buy, install, and replace. Also, try to install as much energy-efficient equipment as possible, as long as it's affordable.

When shopping for used equipment, carefully check it for wear, and buy only from reputable dealers. Judicious shopping may turn up some excellent bargains. Check the online or offline classified section of your local newspaper as well as other resources such as www.craigslist.com for a wide range of used furniture and equipment for sale. Also look under the "Business Opportunities" classification because businesses that are being liquidated or sold may have fixtures or equipment for sale at substantial savings.

Basic Office Equipment

Many entrepreneurs find a trip to the local office supply store more exciting than any mall. It's easy to get carried away when you're surrounded by an abundance of clever gadgets, all designed to make your working life easier and more fun. But if, like most new business owners, you're starting on a budget, discipline yourself and buy only what you need. Consider these primary basic items:

- *Computer and printer*. A computer can help you manage complex bookkeeping and inventory control tasks, maintain customer records, and produce marketing materials. A computer is a valuable management and marketing tool, and an essential element for developing a strong and profitable business—especially in today's technology-dependent world. Computer and printer technology is advancing rapidly; an office supply dealer can help you decide what type of computer and printer you'll need based on what type of work you'll be doing.

- *Software*. Think of software as your computer's "brain," the instructions that tell your computer how to accomplish the functions you need. There are a myriad of programs on the market that will handle your accounting, inventory, customer-information management, word processing, and other administrative requirements. Software can be a significant investment, though, so do a careful analysis of your own needs, and then study the market and examine a variety of products before making a final decision. Many new computers come bundled with software, so be sure you know what you have before buying additional software.

> **⚠ Beware!**
> Although multifunction devices—such as a copier/printer/fax machine or a fax/telephone/answering machine—may be cost- and space-efficient, you risk losing all these functions simultaneously if the equipment fails. Also, weigh your anticipated volume against the machine's efficiency rating and cost to operate, and compare that with stand-alone items before making a decision. However, these machines are more reliable than ever before, so one might work for your business.

- *Internet access*. High-speed internet access is essential for an efficient business operation. Your choices will typically include a high-speed telephone line, cable service, or satellite, although not all these options will be available in every area. Prices will vary depending on the service you need. Shop around for the best service and price package.

  Beware of extremely low prices, as-is deals, and closeouts when it comes to purchasing computer equipment. Deals like these often hide problems you wouldn't want, even for free.

- *Photocopier*. A photocopier is a fixture of the modern office, but whether you need one will depend on the specific type of food-service operation you're starting. Chances are a deli or pizzeria can do without a copier, but a wholesale bakery or a catering service will likely find one useful. You may find that a multi-purpose printer/scanner/copier/fax machine will meet your needs, or you can get a basic, no-frills personal copier for less than $400 in just about any office supply store. More elaborate models increase proportionately in price. If you anticipate a heavy volume, you should consider leasing.

- *Fax machine.* For most food-service businesses, fax capability is essential. You'll want to fax orders to your suppliers, and you may want to receive faxed orders from your customers. You can either use an online fax service or buy a stand-alone machine. For most food-service operations, a stand-alone machine on a dedicated telephone line is a wise investment. Expect to pay around $200 for a high-quality fax machine or $400 for a multifunctional device. When assessing the cost of a fax machine, don't just consider the cost of the machine itself, also take into account how much the cartridges cost and how often you'll need to change them.

- *Postage scale.* Unless all your mail is identical, a postage scale is a valuable investment. An accurate scale takes the guesswork out of applying postage and will quickly pay for itself. The U.S. Postal Service estimates accurate weighing can save customers up to 20 percent on mailings. It's a good idea to weigh every piece of mail to eliminate the risk of items being returned for insufficient postage or overpaying when you're unsure of the weight. If you send out an average of 12 to 24 items per day, consider a digital scale, which generally costs $50 to $200. If you send more than 24 items per day or use priority or expedited services frequently, invest in an electronic computing scale, which weighs the item and then calculates the rate via the carrier of your choice, making it easy for you to make comparisons. Programmable electronic scales cost $80 to $250.

- *Postage meter.* A postage meter allows you to pay for postage in advance and print the exact amount on the mailing piece when it is used. Many postage meters can print in increments of 1/10th of a cent, which can add up to big savings for bulk-mail users. Meters also provide a "big company" professional image and are more convenient than stamps. Postage meters are leased, not sold, with rates starting at about $20 to $30 per month. They require a license, which is available from your local post office. Only four manufacturers are licensed by the U.S. Postal Service to build and lease postage meters. Your local post office can provide you with contact information. An alternative to a postage meter is to print your postage online. Visit the USPS website at www.usps.gov, or check out private

> ## Smart Tip
> *Tip...*
>
> If you're going to accept orders via fax, be sure the fax machine is visible and that someone checks it at least every five minutes. You don't want someone arriving to pick up a faxed order that you haven't even started to prepare.

companies, such as www.stamps.com for more information.

- *Paper shredder.* In response to both a growing concern for privacy and the need to recycle and conserve space in landfills, shredders are increasingly common in homes and offices. They allow you to efficiently destroy incoming unsolicited direct mail, as well as sensitive internal documents. Shredded paper can be compacted much more than paper tossed in a wastebasket, and it can also be used as packing material. Light-duty shredders start at about $30, and heavier-capacity shredders run $150 to $500 and up.

> **Bright Idea**
>
> Postage stamps come in a variety of sizes, designs, and themes, and can add an element of color, whimsy, and thoughtfulness to your mail. Some people prefer stamps because they look personal; others prefer metered mail because it looks "corporate." Here's a suggestion: Use metered mail for invoices, statements, and other "official" business, and use stamps for thank-you notes and marketing correspondence that could use a personal touch.

Telecommunications

The ability to communicate quickly with your customers and suppliers is essential to any business, but especially for a food-service business, where customers often have last-minute needs and questions.

Advancing technology gives you a wide range of telecommunications options. Most telephone companies have created departments dedicated to helping small and home-based businesses. Contact your local service provider and ask to speak with someone who can review your needs and help you put together a service and equipment package that will work for you. Specific elements to keep in mind include:

- *Telephone.* You should start with two telephone lines. As you grow and your call volume increases, you may want to add more lines.

   The telephone itself can be a tremendous productivity tool, and most of the models on the market today are rich in features you'll find useful, such as automatic redial, which redials the last number called at regular intervals until the call is completed; programmable memory, for storing frequently called numbers; and a speakerphone function, for hands-free use. You may also want call forwarding, which allows you to forward calls to another number when you're not at your desk, and call waiting, which signals that another call is coming in while you're on the phone. These services are typically available through your telephone company for a monthly fee.

If you're going to be spending a great deal of time on the phone, perhaps doing marketing or handling customer service, consider purchasing a headset for comfort and efficiency. Another option is a cordless phone, which lets you move around freely while talking. However, these units vary widely in price and quality,

> **Bright Idea**
> Be sure the announcement on your answering machine or voice mail includes your business name, location, hours of operation, website address, and fax number. If a caller wants just that basic information, he or she won't have to call back when you're open to get it.

so research them thoroughly before making a purchase. As a rule of thumb, you should have one business phone line for every five employees.

- *Answering machine/voice mail.* Because your business phone should never go unanswered, you will need some sort of reliable answering device to take calls when you can't do it yourself. Whether to buy an answering machine (which costs $40 to $150 for a model that's suitable for a business) or use a voice-mail service provided by your telephone company is a choice you must make depending on your personal choice, work style preferences, and needs.

- *Cell phone.* Cell phones are standard business equipment these days. In addition to your own phone, you may want to provide your delivery personnel or catering crews with company phones. If you choose to give your employees cell phones, work out a policy regulating their use.

- *Toll-free number.* If you're targeting a customer base outside your local calling area, you'll want to provide a toll-free number so they can reach you without having to make a long-distance call. Most long-distance service providers offer toll-free numbers, and they have a wide range of service and price packages. Shop around to find the best deal. Though an increasing number of consumers have phone packages that do not charge for long-distance calls, toll-free numbers still have a marketing appeal that is worth considering.

- *Website.* An internet presence is essential for any business. For a restaurant, a website allows customers to check your menu and prices, look up locations and operating hours, make reservations, and even place orders online. Invest in a professionally designed website, and keep it up-to-date.

> **Stat Fact**
> According to the Pew Research Center, more than half of adults use the internet when looking for information on local restaurants, bars, and clubs.

Get With the Program

The birth of online communications has been one of the most significant technological breakthroughs in history. The ability to link millions (and potentially billions) of computers allows individuals and businesses to communicate in ways never before possible and gain access to unlimited information.

You can use online services for research about your specific type of food-service operation or to find out more about small business and entrepreneurship in general. Most professional associations, equipment manufacturers, and other industry suppliers have websites that provide a wealth of information about how they can help you. Take the time to visit these sites, and study the information they contain. You can also network online with food-service business owners across the country and around the world through electronic mailing lists, message boards, chat rooms, blogs, and social/professional networking sites.

It's worth your time to get comfortable with online researching and networking. Being so will give you a distinct advantage over those who are not.

Other Equipment

In addition to the basics just mentioned, there are other items you may need, depending on your particular operation. They include:

- *Cash register*. For a retail operation, you need a way to track sales, collect money, and make change. You can do this with something as simple as a divided cash drawer and a printing calculator, or you can purchase a sophisticated, state-of-the-art point-of-sale system that's networked with your computer. This type of register is ideally suited for a multiregister operation, with a bar and main dining area, or a multiunit chain. Of course, a high-end register will cost somewhere between $1,000 and $4,000 per terminal and may not be a practical investment for a startup operation. A preferable option is an electronic cash register (ECR), which ranges in price from $200 to $2,500 and can be purchased outright, leased, or acquired under a lease-to-purchase agreement. Many ECRs offer such options as payment records to designate whether a customer paid by cash, check, or credit card; department price groupings; sign-in keys to help managers monitor cashiers; and product price groupings for tracking inventory more effectively. To free capital in the early stages of your business, check on a lease-to-purchase arrangement, which will run about $100 to $150 per month, or consider leasing a mechanical cash register in the early stages, and make your purchasing decision later. You may be able to justify the investment in an ECR because it can perform several bookkeeping functions, and track inventory and customer preferences. A word of caution: Many business owners believe any cash register is a highly visible invitation to thieves, so you should consider security options not only for your cash receipts but also for the safety of your employees and customers.

- *Credit and debit card processing equipment.* This could range from a simple imprint machine to an online terminal. Consult with several merchant status providers to determine the most appropriate and cost-effective equipment for your business.

Security

Small merchandise, office equipment, and cash attract burglars and shoplifters. Not only do you need to protect your inventory and equipment with alarms and lighting and by selecting your employees carefully, but you also need to ensure your personal safety as well as that of your staff.

Begin by investigating your area's crime history to determine what kind of measures you'll need to take (this is something you'll want to look into before you choose a

---

Meals on Wheels

If you plan to offer delivery services, you'll need a company vehicle. The type and style you need depends on the food-service business you have and exactly what you're delivering. A pizzeria, for example, can have employees use their own personal cars to make deliveries. But a wholesale bakery or a catering service will likely need commercial vehicles with greater capacity than that of the typical passenger car. And, of course, if you're interested in starting a food truck or other type of mobile operation, an appropriate vehicle is essential.

Whether you lease or buy depends on exactly what you need, your cash flow, and your tax situation. Do a needs analysis, research the costs of buying both new and used vehicles, check out lease deals, and consult with your tax advisor before making a final decision.

location for your business). To learn whether your proposed or existing location has a high crime rate, check with the local police department's community-relations division or with a crime prevention officer. Most will gladly provide free information on safeguarding your business and may even visit your site to discuss specific crime prevention strategies. Many also offer training seminars for small retailers and their employees on workplace safety and crime prevention.

Common techniques that merchants use to enhance security and reduce shoplifting include installing mirrors, alarms, and video cameras. Technology is rapidly bringing down the cost of these items, and installing them may earn you the fringe benefit of discounts on your insurance. You can also increase the effectiveness of your security system by posting signs in your store window and discreetly around the store announcing the presence of the equipment.

17

Marketing

Every business needs a marketing plan, and your food-service business is no exception. But even as you consider various marketing vehicles, keep this in mind: Research conducted by the National Restaurant Association (NRA) reveals that word of mouth is still the best method of advertising. More than four out of five consumers are likely to choose a table-service restaurant they

▲

haven't patronized before on the basis of a recommendation from a family member or friend. So make the foundation of your marketing program an absolutely dazzling dining experience that customers will want to talk about and repeat. Freddy's Frozen Custard owner Scott Redler says, "I truly believe people are going to try you, and if you take care of them when they come in the door, that's your best marketing. It has proven to be true for us."

Ask every new customer how they found out about you, and make a note of this information so you know how well your various marketing efforts are working. You can then decide to increase certain programs and eliminate those that aren't working.

As you develop your marketing plan, be aware that there are issues and ideas specific to various types of food-service businesses that you should know about. A key question for restaurant owners is this: Do your marketing materials—menus, signs, table tents, ads, and other items—send an accurate message about who you are and what you do? Or are they confusing and misleading?

Marketing is the process of communicating with your existing and prospective customers. A key component of successful restaurant marketing is being sure your message is consistent with what you really are about. Certainly a fine-dining establishment isn't going to put its menus in clear vinyl sleeves and illustrate them with photographs of children enjoying burgers and fries. But the same restaurateur who chuckles at the absurdity of that image may well be guilty of a variety of other more subtle marketing sins.

For example, if senior citizens are a key segment of your market, do your menus and signs consider the physical changes, such as declining vision, that come with age? If you're trying to attract families, are your photographs and illustrations contemporary and relative to your market? Does each element of your marketing package—from décor to menu selections to printed materials—reflect a consistent marketing message? Have you taken societal changes into account when designing your marketing materials? It's possible that what worked well for you a few years ago may have a negative impact on your business today.

The first step in creating a complete marketing package is to know your market, and it's not enough to gather demographic information only once. Markets change and food-service businesses that don't change their marketing strategies with population shifts are missing out on a lot of opportunities.

Next, step back and take a look at each element in your facility. Everything from the parking lot to the interior décor to the printed items contributes to your marketing message—and each should be an accurate reflection of what that message is.

It's not enough for each marketing component to be relevant to the audience. Rather, the elements must create a sense of continuity. Colors and textures should blend comfortably. Your printed materials should have enough common elements so there's no question that they represent the same restaurant.

Keep Up with the Trends

Staying in step with market trends is standard business advice. Restaurants can do this in various subtle ways. Certainly an increasing number of diners are looking for healthy, low-fat fare, but you can take advantage of trends that go beyond food selection.

Many people are concerned about the environment. You can let them know you share their feelings by using recycled stock for all your printed items. Include a small line of type that says, "Because we care about the environment, this menu [or whatever] has been printed on recycled paper." Expressing support for a particular charity is a popular business trend; choose one that's consistent with your image and not controversial.

To appeal to parents, a family restaurant may want to provide crayons, coloring books, balloons, or toys for children. If you choose to do this, be sure each item carries your logo and basic marketing message and has been chosen with safety in mind.

Other notable trends include wireless internet access; electrical outlets at or near every table to provide power for laptops and other electronic devices; ornate menus; thank-you gifts, such as golf tees and key chains; signature dishes; loyalty programs; and an increasing amount of direct interaction between customers and chefs.

Make Your Grand Opening Truly Grand

You should plan to open for business a few weeks before your grand opening. This "soft opening" gives you a chance to get things arranged properly in your facility and train your employees. At the time of your soft opening, you should have your business sign(s) up and most, or all, of your inventory in stock. Customers will wander in, and if they're pleased with your business, they'll start spreading the word. As both a soft-opening exercise and a marketing technique, one pizzeria distributed coupons for free pizzas in its target delivery area, explaining on the coupon that the restaurant was in the soft-opening phase and that the coupons were good for a specific day and time only.

Use every possible method available to attract customers during your grand opening. Have daily drawings for door prizes such as free meals or a free dessert with a meal purchase. Keep liberal supplies of promotional fliers (perhaps with coupons for discounts on first purchases), business cards, gift certificates, and specialty advertising items in the restaurant. Complimentary coffee, refreshments, and food samples will add to the excitement. You might even consider throwing a party and inviting local dignitaries and celebrities. Whatever you do, open your food-service business with a splash.

Look for Marketing Opportunities

Marketing opportunities are often where you least expect them, and it pays to pay attention. Maxine Turner saw her deli business decrease sharply when the road in front of her building was under construction one summer. "It was very hot, so we put out a flier to all of the businesses here in our own complex and all around us, targeting all the people who came into our deli but who were frustrated because the construction made it difficult for them to get here," she recalls. "We did a 'beat the heat, beat the construction, bring a friend and have lunch on us' campaign. It was a two-for-one promotion—just a reminder that we were there and serving the community. Our business increased by 30 percent immediately, and it was amazing to see how many people came in without the two-for-one card."

Turner also pays close attention to what's going on in the offices around her store. "If someone is moving in, we send them a little complimentary lunch to introduce ourselves and to welcome them to our business community," she says. "We try to do anything we can to put our name in front of people."

You can look for ways to tie other events into a visit to your restaurant. For example, you could offer a dinner-and-a-show package, with a multicourse dinner and tickets to a play. If you're not located near a theater, add transportation—typically in a small bus or van—from your restaurant to the theater and back.

Going Social

One of the most effective and affordable ways to promote a food-service business is through social media. "We entered the Facebook world early on and continue to be amazed at this extremely cost-effective method of communicating directly with guests," say Scott Redler. "One person in our office is the 'voice' of Freddy's on

> **Bright Idea**
>
> Check your paper's business section for announcements of staff appointments and promotions at local companies. Send a congratulatory letter to the people listed and include a coupon for a free drink or dessert.

Facebook. She responds directly to friends who post messages to us. We launched a fan club that allows guests to sign up for email alerts and special offers."

Don't limit yourself to one social media platform; explore all of them and pay attention to trends and new opportunities. The social media landscape is evolving at a mind-boggling pace; get someone on your team—either an employee or a consultant—whose job it is to stay current on the latest trends and make them work for you. Sam Mustafa, owner of Charleston Hospitality Group, uses various social media platforms to promote special meals and events, as well as to offer discounts.

Social-media networking is important. Redler says, "We are constantly expanding our understanding of social media and the advantages of programs [that allow people to broadcast their location to their friends]. You can't make up for poor food quality or bad operations with social media, but you can use it to enhance the loyalty of your guests."

Public Relations and Promotions

An easy way to promote your food-service business is to give away gift certificates, such as for dinner for two, coffee and bagels for 10, or a free pizza. Call local radio stations that reach the demographics of your target market and ask to speak to their promotions manager. Offer to provide gift certificates or coupons to use as prizes for on-air contests and promotions. Your company name and location will probably be announced several times on the air during the contest, providing you with valuable free exposure, and it's always possible that the winner will become a paying customer.

You can also donate coupons and gift certificates to be used as door prizes at professional meetings or for nonprofit organizations to use as raffle prizes. Just be sure every coupon or gift certificate clearly identifies your business name, location, hours of operation, and any restrictions on the prize.

Make being active in the community part of your overall marketing strategy. Sometimes you have to leave your store to bring people in, so get out and be visible, and people will follow you back to your business.

Some promotional methods to try include:

- *Gift certificates.* Gift certificates are convenient for gift giving, especially around holidays. Current customers may give gift certificates to friends or relatives who have never tried your restaurant. Employers may give gift

> **Beware!**
> If someone says they can design a menu, ad, or some other marketing piece without visiting your restaurant, don't hire him or her. Anyone you hire to assist with your marketing materials should spend time in your restaurant so he or she knows what you're trying to do.

▲

Remember the Tourists

More than two-thirds of table-service restaurant operators say that tourists are important to their business. At table-service restaurants with average check sizes of $25 or more, an estimated 40 percent of revenue comes from tourists. Where the check sizes are less than $25, spending by travelers and visitors accounts for about 15 to 30 percent. According to the Travel Industry Association of America, approximately half of all travelers dine out when they travel and say that dining out is the most popular activity they have planned after they arrive at their destination. Be sure to consider this lucrative market in your marketing plan.

certificates as employee incentives. Many people will gladly try a new eating establishment for a free meal. If you give them good food and service, they'll happily return as paying customers. Be sure your gift certificates include your address, hours of operation, and website address.

- *Sponsorships.* By sponsoring a local event or sports team, you can put your restaurant's name in front of a whole new group of customers. Your name will appear on ads promoting the event or on team members' uniforms. This constant exposure will keep your name in customers' minds. Because people are typically drawn to establishments they are familiar with, you may attract customers who have never visited your restaurant but feel familiar with it due to the exposure from your sponsorship.

- *Discount coupon books.* Many communities have companies that produce coupon books for participating businesses that schools and nonprofit organizations sell as fundraisers. As with gift certificates, many people will try a new establishment if they know they're getting a significant discount, and they'll return as full-paying customers if you give them good food and service.

- *Frequent dining clubs.* Reward your regular customers with free food. For example, you can issue a card with 12 spaces so you can mark off each visit. When the customer has purchased 12 entrées, give him or her a free entrée.

- *Menu promotions.* By offering regular lunch or dinner specials, you can appeal to those who are on a limited budget or who just like saving money. You can also offer early-bird specials (dinner at discounted prices, usually from 4 to 6 P.M.), or two-for-one specials during certain periods. These promotions not only attract customers but can also help you reduce your inventory of overstocked items.

- *Announce your specials*. If you serve special dishes that are not on your regular menu, let your customers know when they will be available. Stefano LaCommare, owner of Stefano's Trattoria, used to keep a list of people a staff person would call when he prepared their favorite items. That became very labor intensive (it could take three hours for someone to call everyone who wanted to know when LaCommare was preparing his famous meatloaf parmesan), so he switched to doing the notification by email and Facebook. Other social media platforms can work for this purpose as well.

- *Contests*. The most common restaurant contest involves placing a fishbowl (or other glass container) near the cash register where patrons can drop their business card for a drawing for a free lunch or dinner. The winners may bring along friends when they come in for their free meal. Also, the cards give you a list of customers to use for direct-mail and email campaigns. Of course, you should get permission before adding someone to your email marketing list. You could, for example, send an email that says, "Thank you for entering our weekly free lunch contest. We're sorry you didn't win this time, but we hope you'll come back and try again. To receive periodic email alerts about special events and other happenings at our restaurant, click here to confirm your subscription to our mailing list."

Plan for Community Involvement

Your community-relations activities are an important part of your overall marketing campaign, and they should be carefully planned. In a recent NRA survey, restaurant owners said they received an average of 75 requests for help each year from community groups or nonprofits and chose to donate time or money to about 35 projects. The respondents said the most important reason for participating in these activities was to give back to the community; about half cited boosting their restaurant's image and two out of five said aiding in the recruitment of new employees were "very important" reasons for being involved in civic efforts.

Be sure the organization or event you agree to sponsor is compatible with your image and won't offend prospective customers. Avoid political and controversial issues

▲

Crazy for Coupons

Coupons are among the most popular marketing tools food-service businesses use. You can include coupons with any print media or direct-mail advertisements you produce. Direct-mail advertising uses computer-selected mailing lists and blanket mailings to entire zip codes to distribute fliers, coupon mailers, and other advertisements. Special mailing rates make this a highly effective, low-cost medium.

If you use coupons, track them carefully, and make sure they're having the impact you want—which is to introduce your operation to people who will come back and pay the full price. Many restaurateurs have found that coupons often attract customers who only come in when they have a coupon.

Stefano LaCommare says his food is good and fairly priced, and he has a loyal following along with plenty of word-of-mouth advertising, so he doesn't use coupons. The one time he tried coupons, more than 99 percent of the people who redeemed them were already regular customers who would have paid full price anyway.

If people don't come in unless they can get a few dollars off their meal, you may be charging too much to begin with. Consider your particular style of food-service operation, what's customary (pizza coupons are common; coupons for fine-dining establishments are unusual), and what you want to accomplish with the coupon, and then try this marketing technique.

and events; you can support those privately, but it's better to stay neutral when it comes to your business.

Include the amount of your cash, food, or other donations in your annual financial forecasts, and don't feel bad if you have to say no to a worthwhile cause because you've reached your budget limit.

Be Media Savvy

When your name is mentioned in the newspaper and on local radio and TV broadcasts, it means one of two things: Either you have done something wrong and gotten caught, or you have a strong, positive relationship with the local media. Assuming that you're going to work hard to avoid the former, here are some tips for achieving the latter:

- *Build a media list.* Find out the names of local journalists who might include you in a story, including food and business editors and reporters at your local newspaper, as well as the feature editors and reporters at TV stations. Make a list of these people, and then call them and find out how they would like to receive information from you. Be brief and professional. Simply say, "I have a [description] business, and I'd like to send you periodic news releases. How do you prefer to receive that information?" Typically, they'll want it by regular mail, email, or fax.

- *Make your news releases newsworthy.* Avoid news releases that are obvious bids for self-promotion. Your releases should have a news "hook." The person reading the release should have a clear answer to the question, "So what?" You can tie your releases to a national event or a holiday to provide a local connection.

- *Be available as a local expert.* Let your media contacts know you can be counted on as a local expert. For example, if a national wholesale food supplier has a problem with contaminated products, offer to be a resource for a feature on what local food-service operations can do to protect the health and safety of their customers.

A Guaranteed Gamble

Let your customers gamble for a free meal. Keep a set of dice by the cash register, and put up a few signs that read:

WIN A FREE MEAL TODAY!
Roll the dice and win!

Two sixes—your meal is free!	Two threes—take 33% off
Two fives—take 55% off	Two twos—take 22% off
Two fours—take 44% off	Two ones—take 11% off

If you calculate the odds, the total discounts work out to an average of 1.2 percent on each order, but the contest produces excitement. When someone wins a free meal, your cost is minimal, but the word-of-mouth advertising is priceless. Besides, the winner is likely to come in with at least one friend to claim his or her prize.

- *Take media calls immediately and return them promptly.* Reporters are usually on tight deadlines. When they call, they need to talk to you right away. If you're not available, they'll find someone who is—and that's whom they'll call next time.

- *Only give away compliments.* If a reporter does a particularly good story, either about your operation or the industry in general, write the person a brief note letting him or her know you appreciate his or her work. But never send gifts or food; most reporters aren't allowed to accept them, and you'll only create an awkward situation.

> ### Bright Idea
>
> Take professional photos of yourself, your operation, and even some of your food so you have them available to provide to publications that may write articles about your establishment. That way, you can control the quality and image that goes into print. Also, many local publications are on limited budgets and can't afford to send out a photographer but will use photos you provide.

Trade Shows

In addition to attending trade shows to find merchandise and learn more about running your business, consider exhibiting in trade shows to market your business. Local trade shows can provide a tremendous amount of exposure at an affordable cost.

There are two types of shows—consumer (which focus on home and garden and other consumer themes) and business-to-business (where exhibitors market their products and services to other companies). Both can work for a food-service business.

"When you go to a show, you're tapping into an audience that's typically outside your network," says trade show consultant Allen Konopacki. "The other important thing is that the individuals who are going to shows are usually driven by a need. In

Trade Secrets

Trade shows and conventions are valuable business tools, whether you're attending them to shop and learn or exhibiting to get more business. For more information on how to get more out of trade shows and to find show schedules, visit Incomm Research Center, www.tradeshowresearch.com, and Trade Show News Network, www.tsnn.com.

Time for a Makeover

Maintaining a consistent marketing message is an ongoing effort. In the craziness of dealing with deliveries that don't arrive on time, cooks who don't show up, and servers who drop trays of food on their way out of the kitchen, it's easy to overlook a messy parking lot or a faded poster. It's important to schedule a regular checkup of your facility. At least once a year, step back and look at your restaurant through the eyes of someone who has never eaten there.

Answer these questions during your annual image overhaul:

- What are the most recent demographic trends of your trading area?
- What is the profile of your target market?
- Is your parking lot clean, easily accessible, well-marked, and well-lit for safety and comfort?
- Are your exterior signs in good condition and easy to read?
- Is your waste disposal equipment visible, and, if so, how does the area look and smell?
- Is your flooring clean and in good condition?
- Are your restrooms clean and functioning properly?
- Do your restrooms provide adequate accommodations for your target market—such as diaper-changing stations, lighted vanities, telephones, and vending machines with personal products?
- Are your menus clean, attractive, readable, and designed for your target market?
- Do all your promotional materials—including banners, in-house signs, table tents, menu inserts, and other items—clearly identify your restaurant and share a common theme?
- Do the photographs on your walls, your menu boards, and your carryout menus accurately reflect what you're offering?
- Do your posters and signs look fresh, new, and appealing?
- Are your ads easily recognizable with art and copy that appeal to your target market?
- Is the information on your website current and complete and the overall look up-to-date?

ercent of the people who go to a show are looking to make some kind of a
n a purchase in the near future."

out about shows in your area, call your local chamber of commerce or
...uon center and ask for a calendar. You can also check out Tradeshow Week's
Tradeshow Directory, which should be available in your public library, or do an
internet search. (See the "Trade Secrets" sidebar on page 232.)

When you have identified a potential show, contact the sponsors for details. Find out
who will attend—show sponsors should be able to estimate the total number of attendees
and give you their demographics so you can tell if they fit your target market profile.

Give as much thought to the setup of your show booth as you did to the design of
your facility. Your exhibit doesn't need to be elaborate or expensive, but it does need
to be professional and inviting. Avoid trying to cram so much into your booth that it
looks cluttered. If possible and appropriate, bring food samples, but be sure they can
be properly stored at correct temperatures to avoid the risk of contamination.

Your signage should focus on what you do for clients and then include your
company name. For example, if you operate a coffeehouse, the prominent words on
your booth signage might be "Great Coffee and Entertainment," followed by your
establishment's name.

Samples Sell

Provide diners with samples of menu items to encourage them to
order those items. One restaurant sends servers into the bar area with platters of
bite-size bits of main dishes. This allows people waiting at the bar for tables to
have a chance to sample several entrées ahead of time. Another restaurant owner
places small portions of desserts on the table when patrons are seated (they get
to eat dessert first—and last!). Tasting a bit of a delicious dessert at the beginning
of the meal seems to whet customers' appetites for a full-size portion afterward.

If you purchase your food products wholesale, help your customers promote
certain items with a sampling program. Baker Jim Amaral sends his employees
to new wholesale accounts to conduct a sampling promotion. Generally, two or
three times during the first month a new retailer is carrying his bread, Amaral
sends his own people into the store to pass out samples. "We know we've got a
good product," he says. "If we get it into people's hands and mouths in a no-risk
situation, we'll see a return in sales."

Even though the show sponsors may provide a table for you, don't put one across the front of your exhibit space. Doing so creates a visual and psychological barrier and will discourage visitors from coming in.

Be sure not to leave your booth unattended during exhibit hours. For one thing, it's a security risk: During a busy show, it would be easy for someone to walk off with valuable merchandise. More important, you could miss a tremendous sales opportunity.

Consider offering some sort of giveaway item such as a pen, mug, or notepad imprinted with your company name. But, cautions Konopacki, don't display these items openly, as that will only crowd your booth with "trade show tourists" who aren't really prospective customers. Instead, store them discreetly out of sight, and present them individually as appropriate. You should also have a stock of brochures, business cards, and perhaps discount coupons available.

Financial Management

There are two key things you need to think about in terms of money: How much do you need to start and operate your business, and how much can you expect to take in? Doing this analysis is often difficult for small-business owners who would rather be in the trenches getting the work done than bound to a desk dealing with tiresome numbers. But force yourself to do it anyway.

One of the primary indicators of the overall health of your business is its financial status, and it's important that you monitor your financial progress closely. The only way you can do this is to keep good records. There are a number of excellent computer accounting programs on the market, or you can handle the process manually. You might also want to ask your accountant for assistance with getting your system set up. The key is to do it from the beginning and to keep your records current and accurate throughout the life of your company.

Keeping good records helps generate the financial statements that tell you exactly where you stand and what you need to do next. The key financial statements you need to understand and use regularly are:

- *Profit and loss (P&L) statement.* Also called the income statement, a P&L illustrates how much your company is making or losing over a designated period—monthly, quarterly, or annually—by subtracting expenses from revenues to arrive at a net result, which is either a profit or a loss.

- *Balance sheet.* This statement shows your assets, liabilities, and capital at a specific point. A balance sheet is typically generated monthly, quarterly, or annually after the books are closed.

- *Cash-flow statement.* The cash-flow statement is a summary of the operating, investing, and financing activities of your business as they relate to the inflow and outflow of cash. As with the P&L statement, a cash-flow statement is prepared to reflect a specific accounting period, such as monthly, quarterly, or annually.

Successful food-service business owners review these reports regularly, at least monthly, so they always know where they stand and can quickly correct minor difficulties before they become major financial problems. If you wait until November to figure out whether you made a profit last February, you won't be in business long.

Sources of Startup Funds

How much money you need to start depends on the type of business, the facility, how much equipment you need, whether you buy new or used, your inventory, marketing, and necessary operating capital (the amount of cash you need on hand to carry you until your business starts generating cash). It's easy to spend hundreds of thousands of dollars starting a restaurant, but it's not essential. For instance, when Borealis Breads owner Jim Amaral started his first bakery in Maine, he rented a space that had been a commercial bakery and came complete with mixers, benches, ovens, and other equipment. He was able to start with just $10,000 he borrowed from family and friends and used that primarily for inventory.

Regardless of how much you need, you'll need some cash to start your food-service business. Here are some suggestions of where to go to raise your startup funds:

Beware!

When applying for credit, don't even think about inflating your financial statements to cover a lack of references. This is a felony, and it's easily detected by most credit managers.

- *Your own resources.* Do a thorough inventory of your assets. People generally have more assets than they realize, including savings and retirement accounts, equity in real estate, recreational equipment, vehicles, collections, and other investments. You may also opt to sell assets for cash, or use them as collateral for a loan. Also, look at your personal line of credit. Many a successful business has been started with credit cards.

- *Family and friends.* The logical next step after gathering your own resources is to approach friends and relatives who believe in you and want to help you succeed. Be cautious with these arrangements; no matter how close you are with the person, present yourself professionally, put everything in writing, and be sure the individual you approach can afford to take the risk of investing in your business.

- *Partners.* Using the "strength in numbers" principle, look around for someone who may want to team up with you in your venture. You may choose someone who has financial resources and wants to work side by side with you in the business. Or you may find someone who has money to invest but no interest in doing the actual work. Be sure to create a written partnership agreement that clearly defines your respective responsibilities and obligations. And choose your partners carefully—especially when it comes to family members.

- *Government programs.* Take advantage of the abundance of local, state, and federal programs designed to support small businesses. Make your first stop the Small Business Administration (SBA), but be sure to investigate other programs. Women, minorities, and veterans should check out special financing programs designed to help them get into business. The business section of your local library is a good place to begin your research.

Regardless of which sources of financing you go after, you should know that you'll still need to put up some of your own cash to get your business started. Most investors will want to see that you're willing to risk your own money along with theirs before they'll feel comfortable helping to fund your venture. When Scott Redler opened his

▲

first Timberline Steakhouse & Grill in Wichita, Kansas, he put up $24,000 of his own money and raised the rest through investors. He says the cash he invested was, to him,

Cold, Hard Cash

If you think finding startup funds is difficult, be prepared: Finding money to fund expansion after you're up and running can be even more challenging.

The real difficulty will come when you're trying to make the first expansion. That's a time when your personal resources are most likely stretched to the limit, and most of your assets are already pledged as collateral. But if you can hang in there and continue building a profitable operation, you'll get to the point where funds are readily available.

But just because lenders want you to borrow from them doesn't mean you should. There's always a price to money. Sometimes it's simply the interest you'll have to pay; sometimes it's something else. For example, you may find someone who wants to invest in your business, but the money will come with strings attached, such as the person wanting to take an active role in managing the operation, even though you don't agree on his strategies and methods. His daughter may have just graduated from culinary school, or maybe his wife has always wanted to run a bakery, and suddenly you end up with employees you didn't bargain for and are having trouble working with.

If someone expresses an interest in investing in your business, find out what his or her motives are. Is the person looking for a job for his or her spouse or kids? Is he or she looking for a place to bring friends to eat for free? Or does he or she simply see a good investment opportunity?

When Brian Neel opened his first Melting Pot Restaurant, he found an investor who was willing to put up the money while Neel did the work. "He contributed the money, and I contributed the sweat," Neel recalls. "We opened a new unit about every other year. After about 10 or 12 years, I was able to buy him out. We're still great friends, but he was never a restaurant guy, he was a real estate guy, and this was just an investment for him. He always said that when I was ready to buy him out, he would make me a good deal. And he did."

Don't automatically reject an investor, but don't be too quick to say yes, either. Be sure you know what you're getting into if you decide to take the money.

"a very significant amount of money. I also walked away from a job as a senior vice president of a local restaurant company, and everyone knew at that point, this guy has experience, he's risking a lot, he's giving up that salary. And if it doesn't work, he's going to be out as much as anybody else."

Billing

If you're extending credit to your customers—and it's likely you will if you have corporate accounts, especially if you start a bakery or go into the catering business—you need to establish and follow sound billing procedures.

Coordinate your billing system with your customers' payable procedures. Candidly ask what you can do to ensure prompt payment. That may include confirming the correct billing address and finding out what documentation may be required to help the customer determine the validity of the invoice. Keep in mind that many large companies pay certain types of invoices on certain days of the month. Find out if your customers do that, and schedule your invoices to arrive in time for the nearest payment cycle.

Most computer bookkeeping software programs include basic invoice templates. If you design your own invoices and statements, be sure they're clear and easy to understand. Detail each item, and indicate the amount due in bold with the words "Please pay" in front of the total. A confusing invoice may be set aside for later clarification, and your payment will be delayed.

> **Smart Tip** Tip...
>
> If possible, bill on delivery. That's when the appreciation of your work is the highest. When customers are thinking about you in a positive way, they're more likely to process your invoice faster.

Finally, use your invoices as marketing tools. Print reminders of upcoming specials or new products on them. Add a flier or brochure to the envelope. Even though the invoice is going to an existing customer, you never know where your brochures will end up.

Setting Credit Policies

When you extend credit to a customer, you're essentially providing them with an interest-free loan. You wouldn't expect someone to lend you money without getting information from you about where you live and work and your ability to repay the loan. It

▲

just makes sense to get this information from someone to whom you're lending money.

Reputable companies won't object to providing you with credit information or even paying a deposit on large orders. If you don't feel comfortable asking for at least part of the money upfront, just think how uncomfortable you'll feel if you deliver an expensive order and don't get paid at all.

> **Bright Idea**
>
> Consider putting an ATM in your facility. Your customers will appreciate the convenience of a safe place to get cash, and the machine can also generate income for you in the form of transaction surcharges.

The business owners we talked to all agreed they felt awkward asking for deposits—until they got burned the first time.

Extending credit involves some risk, but the advantages of judiciously granted credit far outweigh the potential losses. Extending credit promotes customer loyalty. People will call you before a competitor because they already have an account set up, so it's easy for them. Customers also often spend money more easily when they don't have to pay cash. Finally, if you ever decide to sell your business, it will have a greater value because you can show steady accounts.

Typically, you'll only extend credit to commercial accounts. Individuals will likely pay with cash (or by check) at the time of purchase, or they'll use a credit card. You need to decide how much risk you're willing to take by setting limits on how much credit you'll extend to each account.

Your credit policy should include a clear collection strategy. Don't ignore overdue bills. The older a bill gets, the less likely it will ever be paid. Be prepared to take action on past-due accounts as soon as they become late.

Red Flags

Just because a customer passed your first credit check with flying colors doesn't mean you should never re-evaluate his or her credit status—in fact, you should do it on a regular basis.

Tell customers when you initially grant them credit that you have a policy of periodically reviewing accounts. That way, when you do another check it won't be a surprise. Remember, things can change very quickly in the business world, and a company that's on sound financial footing this year may be quite wobbly next year.

An annual re-evaluation of all customers who have open accounts is a good idea. But if you start to see trouble in the interim, don't wait to take action. Another time to re-evaluate your customers' credit is when they request an increase in their credit line.

The Tax Man Cometh

Businesses are required to pay a wide range of taxes, and food-service business owners are no exception. Keep good records so you can offset your local, state, and federal income taxes with the expenses of operating your company. If you sell retail, you'll probably be required by your state to charge and collect sales tax. If you have employees, you'll be responsible for payroll taxes. If you operate as a corporation, you'll have to pay payroll taxes for yourself; as a sole proprietor, you'll pay self-employment tax. Then there are property taxes, taxes on your equipment and inventory, fees and taxes to maintain your corporate status, your business license fee (which is really a tax), and other lesser-known taxes. Take the time to review all your tax liabilities with your accountant.

Some key trouble signs are a slowdown in payments, increased returns, and difficulty getting answers to your payment inquiries. Even a sharp increase in ordering could signal trouble: Companies concerned that they may lose their credit privileges may try to stock up while they can. Pay attention to what your customers are doing. A major change in their customer base or product line is something you may want to monitor.

Take the same approach to a credit review as you would to a new credit application. Most of the time, you can use what you have on file to conduct the check. But if you're concerned for any reason, you may want to ask the customer for updated information.

Most customers will understand routine credit reviews and accept them as a sound business practice. A customer who objects may well have something to hide—and that's something you need to know.

Accepting Credit and Debit Cards

Unless you're exclusively a wholesale operation, you'll need to be able to accept

> **Smart Tip** *Tip...*
>
> When you take an order from a customer on open credit, be sure to check his or her account status. If the account is past due or the balance is unusually high, you may want to negotiate different terms before increasing the amount owed.

credit and debit cards. It's much easier now to get merchant status than it has been in the past. In fact, these days, merchant status providers are competing aggressively for your business.

To get a credit card merchant account, start with your own bank. Also check with various professional associations that offer merchant status as a member benefit. Shop around; this is a competitive industry, and it's worth taking the time to get the best deal.

Bright Idea

On your menu, include a statement describing the methods of payment (cash, specific credit cards, checks) you accept. That way, customers won't be surprised or embarrassed when they reach the cashier and try to pay with a method you don't accept.

Accepting Checks

Because losses for retailers from bad checks amount to more than $1 billion annually, many restaurants don't accept checks.

If you choose to accept checks, look for several key items. First, make sure the check is drawn on a local bank. Second, check the date for accuracy. Third, don't accept a check that's undated, postdated, or more than 30 days old. Fourth, be sure the written amount and numerical amount agree.

Post your check-cashing procedures in a highly visible place. Most customers are aware of the bad-check problem and are willing to follow your rules. If your customers don't know what your rules are until they reach the cash register, however, you may annoy them when, for example, you ask for two forms of identification before accepting a check.

Your main reason for asking for identification is so you can locate the customer in case you have a problem with the check. The most valid and valuable piece of identification is a driver's license. In most states, this will include the driver's picture, signature, and address. If the signature, address, and name agree with what's printed on the check, you're probably safe. If the information doesn't agree, ask which is accurate and record that information on the check.

You can get insurance against bad checks. Typically, a check-reporting service charges a fee for check verification, usually 1.5 to 2 percent of the face value of the check plus 30 to 50 cents per transaction, depending on the volume of checks you send through the system. If you called in a $60 check, for example, the service could cost you $1.70. If you weigh that charge against the possibility of losing the entire $60, the service has merit.

If you don't use a check verification system, you should ask for identification, such as a check guarantee card, a bank card, or oth... Retail merchants' associations often provide lists of stolen dr... credit cards. If you're dealing with a customer you don't know... the list. You might want to look into the latest in point-of-... which can significantly speed up the amount of time it takes to a... a customer.

Dealing with Your Own Creditors

Most business startup advice focuses on dealing with your customers, but you're also going to become a customer for your suppliers. That means you'll have to pay for what you buy. Find out in advance what your suppliers' credit policies are. Most will accept credit cards but won't put you on an open account until they've had a

> **Dollar Stretcher**
> Ask suppliers if payment terms can be part of your price negotiation. For example, can you get a discount for paying cash in advance?

chance to run a credit check on you. If you open an account with a supplier, be sure you understand their terms and preserve your credit standing by paying on time. Typically, you'll have 30 days to pay, but many companies offer a discount if you pay early.

Hold the Line on Costs

When you think about how to improve your bottom-line profit, your first thought is probably to increase sales. An equally important and often easier route to greater profitability comes from reducing costs. David Cohen, president of Expense Reduction Group Inc. in Boca Raton, Florida, offers this illustration: Your restaurant generates $1 million a year in sales at a net profit margin of 10 percent. If you reduce expenses by $5,000, you'll have accomplished the same bottom-line result as you would have if you had increased sales by $50,000. Cohen asks, "What's easier—finding $50,000 worth of new business or trimming costs by $5,000?"

The first step in a cost-reduction program is to identify the purchases that represent the greatest opportunity for savings. Typically, Cohen says, these are the items that are purchased repetitively in sizable quantities.

un a vendor report to identify the larger suppliers and to see whether there is correlation in product purchases from one supplier to another," Cohen advises. Though many business owners believe using multiple sources for the same item keeps vendors honest, he disagrees. "If you're buying the same product from more than one supplier, consolidating those purchases with a single source will give you the opportunity to take advantage of quantity discounts and also earn you more negotiating strength with the vendor you choose."

Keep seasonal price fluctuations and availability in mind. A restaurant owner in North Carolina buys seafood in bulk when prices are down and freezes it for later use. She also buys dry goods in bulk and stores them.

If you're buying multiple products from a single source, consider whether you'd be better off getting some of those purchases from a specialty vendor, which may offer better pricing. Cohen says segregating specific paper products and purchasing

Cost Cutters

Try these tips to reduce costs and increase profits while still providing a quality dining experience for your customers:

○ *Reduce portions.* Americans have become accustomed to "super-sized" portions, but you can serve less food for the same price. Consider buying smaller plates so customers won't notice that portions are smaller.

○ *Cut back on pricey ingredients.* Consider shifting to recipes that call for less expensive ingredients—chicken rather than beef, or pasta rather than chicken.

○ *Use everything.* Learn how to use every last piece of food. The meat and vegetables for a dish that didn't sell might make a great special soup. Chili can disguise leftover ground beef. Homemade croutons are a great way to use stale bread.

○ *Buy less expensive paper napkins, toilet paper, take-out containers, and bags.* Shop around for your paper goods to get the best prices on quality that's acceptable, even if it isn't top-of-the-line.

○ *Train servers to promote the items that generate the highest profit margins.* These may not necessarily be the highest-priced or fanciest dishes.

> ⚠ **Beware!**
> Including fliers or brochures with your invoices is a great marketing tool, but remember that adding an insert may cause the envelope to require extra postage. Getting out the marketing message is probably well worth the extra few cents in mailing costs. Just be sure you check the total weight before you mail so your invoices aren't returned to you for insufficient postage—or worse, delivered "postage due."

them at lower prices from specialty paper companies is a good example of how this can work.

Be sure the products you buy are the most appropriate and cost-effective items for your needs. It's often worthwhile to spend more money for a higher-quality cleaning or paper product if it does a better job or lasts longer. You may spend more per unit but less overall.

Regardless of how good your vendor relationships are, Cohen recommends an annual review of your overall purchasing process. "Put your major product purchases out for bid every year," he says. "Let two or three companies, plus your current vendor, bid on your business. If your current vendor is giving you good service and pricing, they should have nothing to fear. If they're treating you fairly, stay with them—don't change for the sake of change. But if they've gotten greedy or careless, they're going to get caught." The idea is to build loyalty but keep vendors on their toes. The best way to keep vendors from becoming complacent about your business is to not be complacent yourself.

Set an internal system to stay on top of rebates and manufacturer promotions. A lot of items have rebates with deadlines that are easy to overlook. Also, manufacturers might have end-of-year surpluses that will let you pick up a little extra quantity at a substantial savings.

Throughout the year, look to your vendors for co-op promotional support, which means that you share the cost of a promotion. If you're going to run a special of some sort, you can generally get co-op funds through a price reduction on the item, rebates, or even free products.

Once you reach an agreement on a purchase, follow up to make sure your invoices actually reflect the stipulated terms and that the arithmetic is accurate. Beyond the actual dollars involved, check the product itself. Weigh what's sold by weight; count what's sold by unit.

Be aware of the details of your contracts. Some business owners automatically renew when a contract is up, but this isn't always smart. You should review the terms, and consider renegotiating before the contract ends. Many have escalator clauses that increase prices after a certain amount of time, and this is a point for serious negotiation.

Shopping for Vendors

The process of putting purchases out for bid is not complicated, but it does take some thought. Use a written request for proposal (RFP) or request for quote (RFQ) that clearly defines your parameters. The RFP forces you to document your criteria and address all your needs, while allowing you to make a more accurate comparison of vendors, because everyone is responding to the same information. Formalizing your purchasing process in this manner also strengthens your own negotiating position because it lets vendors know you understand and are committed to using professional procurement procedures.

Evaluate each vendor on quality, service, and price. Look at the product itself, as well as the supplementary services and support the company provides. Confirm that the vendor has the resources to meet your needs from both a production and delivery standpoint. Remember, a great product at a good price doesn't mean anything if the vendor can't produce enough of it or is unable to get it to you on time.

Verify the company's claims before making a purchase commitment. Ask for references, and do a credit check on the vendor—just as the vendor will probably do on you. Product and service claims can be verified through references. You can confirm the company's reputation and financial stability by calling the Better Business Bureau, appropriate licensing agencies, trade associations, or D&B.

A credit check will tell you how well the supplier you're going to be using pays its vendors. This is important because it could ultimately affect you. If your vendor isn't paying its own suppliers, it may have trouble getting raw materials, and that may delay delivery on your order. Or it may simply go out of business without any advance notice, leaving you in the lurch.

Know Your Negotiating Points

As you negotiate your vendor agreements, consider the cost of the item itself, the quantity discounts, add-ons such as freight and insurance, and the payment terms. To determine the true value of a quantity discount, calculate how long you can expect to have the material on hand and what your cost of carrying that inventory is. Quantity discounts are often available if you make a long-term purchase commitment, which may also allow you to lock in prices on volatile commodities.

In many cases, payment terms are an important consideration. Some vendors offer substantial discounts for early payment. Others will extend what amounts to an interest-free, short-term loan by offering lengthier terms.

Freight is an excellent and often overlooked negotiating point. If you're paying the freight charges, you should select the carrier and negotiate the rates. If the vendor is delivering on its own trucks, you can negotiate the delivery fee as part of your overall price.

Every element of the sale is open for negotiation. At all stages of the process, leave room for some give and take. For example, if you're asking for a lower price or more liberal payment terms, can you agree to a more relaxed delivery schedule?

Finalize the Deal in Writing

Contracts are an excellent way to make sure both you and the vendor are clear on the details of the sale. This is not "just a formality" that can be brushed aside. Read all agreements and support documents carefully, and consider having them reviewed by an attorney. Make sure everything that's important to you is in writing. Remember, if it's not part of the contract, it's not part of the deal—no matter what the salesperson says. And if it's in the contract, it's probably enforceable.

Any contract the vendor writes is naturally going to favor the vendor, but you don't have to agree to all the boilerplate terms. In addition, you can demand the inclusion of details that are appropriate to your specific situation. Here's some advice on contracts:

- *Make standard provisions apply to both parties.* If, for example, the contract exempts the supplier from specific liabilities, request that the language be revised to exempt you, too.

- *Use precise language.* It's difficult to enforce vague language, so be specific. A clause that states the vendor isn't responsible for failures due to causes "beyond the vendor's control" leaves a lot of room for interpretation. More precise language forces a greater level of accountability.

- *Include a "vendor default" provision.* The vendor's contract probably describes the circumstances under which you would be considered in default. Include the same protection for yourself.

- *Be wary of supplier reps who have to get contract changes approved by "corporate" or some other higher authority.* This is a negotiating technique that generally works against the customer. Insist that the vendor make available personnel who have the authority to negotiate.

David Cohen of Expense Reduction Group Inc. advises including an escape clause. "If you're not pleased with the quality and service levels, you want a way to get out of the contract," he says. "You also need to know if there are any other circumstances that could release either party from the agreement and what the liability is." In any case, don't substitute an escape clause for thorough and careful vendor selection.

Tales from the Trenches

By now, you should know how to get started and have a good idea of what to do—and not do—in your own food-service business. But nothing teaches as well as the voice of experience. So we asked established food-service business operators to tell us what has contributed to their success and what they think causes some companies to fail. Here are their stories.

▲

Start with a Job

The best preparation for starting your own restaurant is to first work in someone else's establishment. While you should certainly read books and take courses, you should also plan to work in a restaurant for at least a couple of years, doing as many jobs as possible. Pay attention to people who are doing different jobs in the restaurant as well, so you can understand the various positions. Think of it as getting paid to learn.

Scott Redler, owner of Freddy's Frozen Custard, agrees. "Before you open your own restaurant," he says, "you need to work for a good operator for a couple of years."

But just because you worked in a McDonald's doesn't mean you're ready to open a fine-dining restaurant. You need to work in a restaurant that's similar to the one you plan to start, says Paul Mangiamele, president and CEO of Bennigan's. "Work in different positions, in the front of the house, back of the house, bartending, hosting, serving, cooking," he says. "Know every single aspect of the operation, because when you're an owner, the buck really does stop with you. No matter what comes up, you need to be able to jump in and handle it because it's your business."

Do Basic Market Research

When Jim Amaral decided to start Borealis Breads, a wholesale bakery specializing in sourdough bread, no one else was doing anything similar in Maine. To find out if there was a market for the breads he wanted to bake, he called restaurants and retailers, explained his idea, and asked if they'd be interested in buying his breads. "I came up with about 15 accounts that said they would be interested," he says. And that was enough to get him started.

Test Your Real Market

When you're test marketing, be sure you conduct your tests on sample groups that represent the market you plan to target. And remember that many people will compliment free food because they think it's the polite thing to do. So ask questions that will get you information you can work with. It's not enough for people to say they like something. Find out why they like it, if there's anything they don't like, if there's anything they would change, and if they'd be willing to buy it.

Find Your Market Niche; Stay Focused

Jim Amaral says one of the key things he's done that has contributed to his success is find a market niche that no other baker occupies. "We've positioned ourselves as having a unique product. We don't have a lot of competitors, and that has allowed us to maintain fairly high wholesale prices."

One of the best ways to survive in this industry is to become an expert in your area, so don't go too far from your core business. If you do, you might become indistinguishable and get lost in a cluttered marketplace.

Don't Let Customers Leave Hungry or Unhappy

Even the best restaurant will have the occasional dissatisfied customer. Stefano LaCommare's policy is that no one leaves Stefano's Trattoria hungry. If someone isn't satisfied with a dish, he determines if the issue is personal taste or a problem with the preparation. In either case, he replaces the meal.

In his Melting Pot restaurants, Brian Neel takes the approach that the customer is always right—even when they're not. "Even if we know the customer's perspective is not entirely correct, we do our best to be understanding, and do what it takes to make them happy," he says. But it's not just what you do, it's how you do it. "A manager or the owner sees the customer immediately. We don't leave it in the hands of a staff person to try to resolve the situation." Sometimes an apology is all that's needed;

Site Keeping

Renew the domain name for your website before it expires, or you risk someone else buying it. Stefano LaCommare learned this lesson the hard way, when he failed to renew stefanostrattoria.com. The URL was purchased by someone else, and LaCommare had to change his restaurant's web address to www.stefanos-trattoria.com—a time-consuming, expensive process that included changing the address on menus and other marketing materials, as well as having to notify all his business associates of his staff's new email addresses. Worst of all is that customers accustomed to looking for Stefano's Trattoria online at that address found something totally different. Protect this important part of your marketing identity by making a note on your calendar two to four weeks before your domain name expires so you can be sure it's renewed on time. Though many domain name registration services offer automatic renewal plans, it's still a good idea to keep track of this yourself in case your registration service drops the ball or another service tries to trick you into transferring your registration.

---

sometimes a free item will take care of it. Or, Neel says, "If it's a really bad experience, we'll comp a check and invite them back to dinner again on us. The most important thing is that they feel that you're sympathetic to their concerns and that you are very sincere in dealing with them."

Make Your Food Consistent

Once you've developed recipes that you're confident in and you know your customers enjoy, be consistent with them. It might be fun for you to add a different spice or try something new, but a customer who's expecting a dish to taste the way it has in the past is going to be disappointed if his expectations aren't met.

Make sure everyone who cooks understands this. Stefano LaCommare recalls hiring a chef who had a hard time with this concept. LaCommare was pleasant but clear and firm about how things were going to be. "I said, 'This is my kitchen. My way. My style. I'm not saying you don't know how to cook. But if you want to work here, you do it my way.'"

Recognize the Lifetime Value of a Customer

If your average check per person is $25 and it's reasonable to expect that a repeat customer could visit your operation 25 times a year, that guest is worth $625 a year to you, or more than $3,000 over five years. And if that person brings in a friend, his value has increased. So look at the lifetime value of each guest, says Paul Mangiamele. "Treat them like the total value they represent, not a single transaction. Deliver the experience so they'll feel a connection and spread the word. And they'll bring in 10 other guests that are worth $5,000 to $10,000. That's how you build not only a restaurant; that's how you build a chain."

Choose Your Partners Carefully

Because of the financial investment most food-service businesses require, many people opt to form partnerships to raise the capital. Be cautious, however, if these partners are friends or family members. Going into business with a friend or family member can change the relationship. Don't assume that just because you like someone, you can run a business together. Draw up a detailed partnership agreement and be sure you're clear on your mutual goals and working styles.

Similarly, be careful when you hire friends and family to work for you. Draw a clear line between your professional and personal relationships, and understand that you may be risking the relationship if the job doesn't work out.

Build Relationships with Your Suppliers

Create a bond with your suppliers so when you're in a bind, they're willing to do something extra to help you out. Be loyal to them; don't make unreasonable demands, pay your bills on time, and respect everyone on their staff—including the delivery drivers.

"Your distributors are your life blood," says Mangiamele. "They're going to make sure you're aware of specials, discounts, and purchasing opportunities."

Get It in Writing

If you're in the catering or wholesale food business, never assume you have an order until you have a signed contract or purchase order. Caterer Ann Crane recalls making a bid on an upscale party. It was a new client, and she had taken her art director and florist with her to meet with the person—and they all left with the impression that they had the job. But the client was accepting bids from three other caterers. The lesson is clear: Don't take anything for granted. Find out whom you're competing against and when you can expect a final decision. And don't buy any supplies or materials until you have a signed contract and a deposit.

Give Back to the Community

Jim Amaral encourages his employees to do volunteer work in the community by paying them for up to three hours of volunteer work (at their regular pay rate) each month.

Ann Crane is a strong believer in giving back to the community and serves on a variety of nonprofit boards. She says it opens her up to being asked to provide food at a discount, but it also exposes her to potential customers. "One of the more positive things that has come from volunteering is when I have underwritten a party for a nonprofit organization, the people who attend are the same people I want to taste my food, and the word-of-mouth benefit from that has been substantial."

Stefano LaCommare says he will usually buy ads in school yearbooks and similar publications, though not for any advertising benefit but to help the students.

Listen to Your Customers

Customers are happy to tell you what they want, so give them opportunities to provide feedback. Use comment cards in your restaurant, a feedback system on your website and Facebook page, and any other way you can think of.

▲

"We place a lot of emphasis on guest-driven decisions," says Scott Redler. "We recently replaced our standard ice machines with 'chewable' ice machines after guests requested chewable ice. Although it was hard to justify the new equipment on a spreadsheet, we believe it makes financial sense in the long run because it increases the loyalty of our guests."

Keep Customer Requests in Perspective

Providing outstanding customer service is certainly a worthwhile goal, but you won't be able to meet every single customer request. Trying to do so will stretch your resources to an unmanageable point. For example, if a few people want you to extend your hours, you have to be able to generate enough business to cover the additional overhead and make a profit, or it's not worth doing. If a few customers ask for certain products, be sure the overall demand is strong enough to make purchasing those items worthwhile. One coffeehouse operator says a few people have asked her to carry goat's milk, but in her market, to do so wouldn't be profitable. However, years ago, when customers began asking for skim milk, she realized that the market was strong enough to justify adjusting her inventory.

Provide Employees with Feedback and Recognition

Employees need to know how they're doing—both good and bad—and that their contributions are appreciated. "Our employees know they're coming to a job where a certain level of professionalism is expected, and in return, they are treated as professionals," says Amaral. Good managers provide regular verbal feedback, both for a job well done and when improvement is necessary. "We also do a lot of off-the-cuff stuff," Amaral says. "If somebody has done a really good job at something, we might give them a gift certificate to go out to dinner or something like that. We also have company events where we all go bowling or sailing."

Crane says she makes it a point to pass along customer compliments immediately. When a customer calls to praise a staff member, she immediately contacts that staff person and relays the comments. When customers write positive letters, they're also shared with staffers.

It's often just a matter of treating your employees the way you'd like to be treated. View employees as another market you have to please. In addition to supplying individual feedback, it helps to give your staff the opportunity to discuss problems and possible solutions as a group. Even after a situation has been resolved, you can use the circumstances as a training tool, letting employees talk about how a better resolution could have been achieved and what can be done to prevent a recurrence of a problem.

Sam Mustafa, owner of Charleston Hospitality Group, says he coaches his employees so they will take pride and a sense of ownership in running the restaurant. "I always remind them that what we do today affects us tomorrow," he says.

Stay Open to New Ideas

Sam Mustafa had owned his various restaurants as separate entities until he took a vacation cruise. He was impressed with how the cruise line offered several different types of restaurants with different cuisines in close proximity—all operated by the cruise ship. That inspired him to build an all-inclusive company that could offer a complete package of dining and entertainment services with enough variety to appeal to virtually any market segment.

No Negatives

A basic rule of salesmanship is never to ask a question the prospect can answer with "no." Turn this technique into a policy for your restaurant by never saying no to your customers. Train your staff to always respond in the positive. Even if customers are asking for something they can't get, don't say, "I can't do that." Instead, tell them what you can do. For example, let's say you stock Pepsi products and a customer asks for a Coke. Don't say, "We don't carry Coke" (or worse, serve a Pepsi without confirming it's acceptable). Instead say, "Is Pepsi okay?" or "May I bring you a Pepsi instead?"

Get in with an Out

In addition to your startup plan, you need an exit plan. Know how you're going to eventually get out of this business—whether you need to get out because things are going badly, you want to retire, or for any other reason. For example, if you have to close the operation because of a lack of business, how will you handle that process? Or, if your restaurant is a rousing success, would you entertain an offer from someone to buy it? If you're 40 when you start your restaurant, will you still want to be running it 25 years later?

Appendix
Restaurant Resources

They say you can never be too rich or too thin. While those points could be argued, we believe you can never have too many resources. Therefore, we present for your consideration a wealth of sources for you to check into, check out, and harness for your own personal information blitz.

These sources are tidbits, ideas to get you started on your research. They are by no means the only sources out there, and they should not be taken as the "Ultimate Answer." We have done our research, but businesses tend to move, change, fold, and expand. As we have repeatedly stressed, do your homework. Get out and start investigating.

Associations

International Dairy-Deli-Bakery Association, 636 Science Dr., Madison, WI 53711-1073, (608) 310-5000, www.iddba.org

International Guild of Hospitality and Restaurant Managers, www.hospitalityguild.com

National Academy Foundation, 218 West 40th St., 5th Floor, New York, NY 10018, (212) 635-2400, fax: (212) 635-2409, www.naf.org

National Association of Catering Executives, 9891 Broken Land Pkwy., #301, Columbia, MD 21046, (410) 290-5410, fax: (410) 290-5460, www.nace.net

National Association of Pizzeria Operators, 908 S. Eighth St., #200, Louisville, KY 40203, (800) 489-8324, www.napo.com

National Barbecue Association, 455 S. 4th St., Suite 650, Louisville, KY 40202 (888) 909-2121, www.nbbqa.org

National Coffee Association of U.S.A., 45 Broadway, Suite 1140, New York, NY 10006, (212) 766-4007, www.ncausa.org

National Pasta Association, 750 National Press Building, 529 14th St. NW, Washington, DC 20045, (202) 637-5888, www.ilovepasta.org

National Restaurant Association, 1200 17th St. NW, Washington, DC 20036-3097, (800) 424-5156, (202) 331-5900, www.restaurant.org

National Restaurant Association Educational Foundation, 175 W. Jackson Blvd., #1500, Chicago, IL 60604-2702, (800) 765-2122, www.nraef.org

Specialty Coffee Association of America, 330 Golden Shore, #50, Long Beach, CA 90802, (562) 624-4100, www.scaa.org

Consultants and Other Experts

Robert S. Bernstein, Esq., Bernstein Law Firm P.C., #2200 Gulf Tower, Pittsburgh, PA 15219, (412) 456-8100, www.bernsteinlaw.com

David Cohen, President, Expense Reduction Group Inc., 945 Clint Moore Rd., Boca Raton, FL 33487, (561) 852-1099, www.expensereductiongroupinc.com

Allen Konopacki, Ph.D., Trade show consultant, Incomm Research Center, 5574 N. Northwest Hwy., Chicago, IL 60630, (312) 642-9377, www.tradeshowresearch.com

The NPD Group Inc., Market research and consulting, 900 West Shore Rd., Port Washington, NY 11050, (866) 444-1411, www.npd.com

Michael P. O'Brien, Esq., Jones Waldo Holbrook & McDonough PC, 170 S. Main St., #1500, Salt Lake City, UT 84101-1644, (801) 521-3200, www.joneswaldo.com

Credit Card and Check Verification Services

American Express Merchant Services, (888) 829-7302, www.americanexpress.com

Discover Card Merchant Services, (800) 347-6673, www.discovernetwork.com

MasterCard, (800) 627-8372, www.mastercard.com

Telecheck, www.Firstdata.com

Visa, (800) VISA-911 (847-2911), www.visa.com

Equipment Services

AccuBar—G4 Technologies Corporation, Liquor inventory management systems, 7000 S. Potomac St., #150, Centennial, CO 80112, (800) 806-3922, www.accubar.com

Alcohol Controls Inc., 1023 Havenridge Ln. NE, Atlanta, GA 30319-2692, (800) 285-BEER (2337), www.alcoholcontrols.com

All A Cart Manufacturing Inc., Custom-designed and manufactured carts, kiosks, and other custom vending vehicles, 1450 Universal Rd., Columbus, OH 43207, (800) 695-CART (2278), (614) 443-5544, www.allacart.com

Bakers Pride Oven Co., Pizza ovens, commercial baking equipment, 30 Pine St., New Rochelle, NY 10801, (800) 431-2745, (914) 576-0200, www.bakerspride.com

Bevinco Liquor Inventory Systems, 505 Consumers Rd., #510, Toronto, ON, Canada M2J 4V6, (888) 238-4626, (416) 490-6266, www.bevinco.com

Bunn Commercial Products, Coffee-making equipment, 1400 Stevenson Dr., Springfield, IL 62703, (800) 637-8606, www.bunn.com

CBL, Carts, kiosks, and RMUs, P.O. Box 404, Medford, MA 02155, (617) 292-6499, www.cblpushcarts.com

Consolidated Plastics Co. Inc., Commercial matting, bags, and other plastic items, 4700 Prosper Dr., Stow, OH 44224, (800) 362-1000, fax: (800) 858-5001, www. consolidatedplastics.com

DMX Music, Music services, sound, and video systems, 1703 West Fifth St., Suite 600, Austin, TX 78703, (512) 380-8500, www.dmx.com

Fetco Corp., Beverage service equipment, 600 Rose Rd., Lake Zurich, IL 60047, (800) FETCO-99, (847) 719-3000, www.fetco.com

Globe Food Equipment Co., Food slicers, processors, mixers, and scales, 2153 Dryden Rd., Dayton, OH 45439, (800) 347-5423, (937) 299-5493, www. globeslicers.com

Grindmaster-Cecilware Corp., Beverage systems, coffeemakers, espresso machines, tea equipment, and grinders, 4003 Collins Ln., Louisville, KY 40245, (800) 695-4500, (502) 425-4776, www.grindmaster.com

Hollowick Inc., Liquid candle lamps, lamp fuel, wax candles, P.O. Box 305, Manlius, NY 13104, (800) 367-3015, (315) 682-2163, www.hollowick.com

Liquor Control Solutions, Liquor inventory management systems, 40 New Brunswick Ave., Hopelawn, NJ 08861, (866) 803-3000, (732) 442-8608, www. lcpos.com

Mainstreet Menu Systems, Menu systems, point-of-purchase displays, and visual merchandising systems, 1375 N. Barker Rd., Brookfield, WI 53045, (800) 782-6222, (262) 782-6000, www.mainstreetmenus.com

Manitowoc Co., Ice and beverage systems, 1200 Intervale Dr., Salem, VA 24153, (800) 334-4875, (812) 246-1000, www.manitowocbeverage.com

Plymold Seating, Food-service furniture, 615 Centennial Dr., Kenyon, MN 55946, (800) 759-6653, (507) 789-5111, www.plymold.com

Rapids Wholesale Equipment Co., Restaurant and bar equipment; commercial food-service supplies, 6201 S. Gateway Dr., Marion, IA 52302, (800) 472-7431, (319) 447-1670, www.rapidswholesale.com

Renato Ovens Inc., Display-cooking equipment, including brick ovens and rotisseries, 3612 Dividend Dr., Garland, TX 75042, (866) 575-6316, www.renatos. com

Restaurant Equipment World, Restaurant equipment and supplies, 2413 N. Forsyth Rd., Orlando, FL 32807, (800) 821-9153, (407) 679-9004, www. restaurantequipment.net

Sicom Systems Inc., PC point-of-sale equipment, 4434 Progress Meadow Dr., Doylestown, PA 18902, (800) 547-4266, www.sicom.com

The Trane Company, Heating, ventilation, and air-conditioning equipment, 1001 Hamilton Dr., Holland, OH 43528-8210, (419) 491-2280, www.trane.com

Franchises and Business Opportunities

Atlanta Bread Co. International Inc., Upscale bakery and cafe, 1200 Wilson Way, Suite 100, Smyrna, GA 30082, (770) 432-0933, www.atlantabread.com

Bagger Dave's Legendary Burger Tavern, Full-service family restaurant, 27680 Franklin Rd., Southfield, MI 48034, (248) 223-9160, ext. 106, www.baggerdaves.com

Cousins Subs, N83 W13400 Leon Rd., Menomonee Falls, WI 53051, (800) 238-9736, (262) 253-7700, www.cousinssubs.com

Firehouse Subs, 3410 Kori Rd., Jacksonville, FL 32257, (800) 388-FIRE (3473), www.firehousesubs.com

Freddy's Frozen Custard & Steakburgers, 1445 N. Rock Rd., #210, Wichita, KS 67206, (316) 260-8282, www.freddysfrozencustard.com

Fresh To Order, Casual fine dining, 8460 Holcomb Bridge Rd., Suite 200, Alpharetta, GA 30022, (770) 594-8644, www.fresh2order.com

Highway 55 Burgers Shakes & Fries, Classic American diner, 102 Commercial Ave., Mount Olive, NC 28365, (919) 635-0902, www.hwy55burgers.com

Hungry Howie's Pizza, Pizza, sub sandwiches, chicken wings, 30300 Stephenson Hwy., Suite 200, Madison Heights, MI 48071, (248) 414-3300, www.hungryhowies.com/franchising

Juice It Up!, Smoothie and juice bar, 17915 Sky Park Circle, Suite J, Irvine, CA 92614, (949) 475-0146, www.juiceitup.com

Manchu Wok, Quick-service Chinese restaurant, (800) 361-8864, ext. 112, www.manchuwok.com

McAlister's Deli, Quick-casual restaurant featuring deli-style foods, 731 South Pear Orchard Rd., Suite 51, Ridgeland, MS 39157, (888) 855-DELI (3354), www.mcalistersdeli.com

Milio's Sandwiches, Sub sandwiches, 901 Deming Way, Suite 202, Madison, WI 53717, (608) 662-3000, www.milios.com

Newk's Express Café, Fast casual restaurant, 2660 Ridgewood Rd., Suite 100, Jackson, MS 39216, (601) 982-1160, www.newkscafe.com

Panchero's Mexican Grill, Quick service Mexican, 2475 Coral Court, Suite B, Coralville, IA 52241, (319) 545-6565, www.pancheros.com/franchise

Penn Station East Coast Subs, Sub sandwiches, 1226 US Highway 50, Milford, OH 45150, (513) 474-5957, www.penn-station.com/franchise

Salsarita's Franchising, LLC, Mexican cantina, 2908 Oak Lake Blvd., Suite 205, Charlotte, NC 28208, (704) 540-9447, www.salsaritas.com

Submarina California Subs, Sub sandwiches, 300 Rancheros Dr., Suite 120, San Marcos, CA 92069, (760) 471-3377, www.submarina.com

Tasti D-Lite, Soft-serve frozen dessert, 341 Cool Springs Blvd., Suite 100, Franklin, TN 37067, (615) 550-3110, www.tastiopportunity.com

Yogurtland, Self-serve frozen yogurt, 1911 East Wright Circle, Anaheim, CA 92806, (714) 939-7737, www.yogurt-land.com

YO!Sushi, Casual Asian and Japanese food, 95 Farringdon Rd., London EC1R 3BT United Kingdom, +44 (0)20 7841 0700 (UK), (877) YO-SUSHI (USA), www.yosushi.com

Internet Resources

Coffee Forums, www.coffeeforums.com

Coffee Science Source, (website created by the National Coffee Association), www.coffeescience.org

Coffee Universe, www.coffeeuniverse.com

FastCasual, www.FastCasual.com

Monkey Dish (website created by Restaurant Business), www.restaurantbiz.com

Open Table, www.Opentable.com

Restaurant Report, www.restaurantreport.com

Restaurant Startup & Growth, www.rsgmag.com

Salary.com, on-demand data and software related to employee compensation, www.salary.com

Inventory and Supply Sources

Campbell's Foodservice, (800)TRYSOUP (879-7687), www.campbellfoodservice.com

Georgia-Pacific Professional, Dispensing systems, paper goods, and more, 133 Peachtree St. NE, Atlanta, GA 30303, (866) 435-5647, www.gppro.com

Great American Stock, Food photography, 1375 N. Barker Rd., Brookfield, WI 53045, (800) 624-5834, www.greatamericanstock.com

McCain Foods USA, French fries, appetizers, vegetables, and more, 2275 Cabot Dr., Lisle, IL 60532, (800) 938-7799, www.mccainusa.com

Neighbors Coffee, Specialty coffees, gourmet hot chocolate, instant cappuccino mixes, and gourmet teas, 3105 E. Reno, Oklahoma City, OK 73117, (800) 299-9016, (405) 236-3932, www.neighborscoffee.com

Rich Products Corp., Food products, including meats, desserts, toppings, rolls, and breads, 1 Robert Rich Way, Buffalo, NY 14213, (716) 878-8000, www.richs.com

Sweet Street Desserts, Frozen gourmet desserts, 722 Hiesters Ln., Reading, PA 19605, (610) 921-8113, www.sweetstreet.com

SYSCO Corp., National distributor of food-service products, including food, beverages, and supplies, 24500 Highway 290, Cypress, TX 77429, (281) 584-1390, www.sysco.com

Magazines, Books, and Publications

Baking Management magazine, (312) 840-8449, www.Baking-management.com

Beverage World, www.beverageworld.com

Complete Idiot's Guide to Starting a Restaurant, Howard Cannon, Alpha Books

Fresh Cup magazine, 2627 N.E. Martin Luther King Jr. Blvd., Suite 203, Portland, OR 97212, (800) 868-5866, (503) 236-2587, www.freshcup.com

Menu: Pricing & Strategy, Jack E. Miller and David V. Pavesic, Wiley

Modern Baking, The professional baker's online magazine, 330 N. Wabash, Suite 2300, Chicago, IL 60611, (508) 771-3500, www.modern-baking.com

Nation's Restaurant News, www.nrn.com

The New Restaurant Entrepreneur: An Inside Look at Restaurant Deal-Making and Other Tales from the Culinary Trenches, Dearborn Trade Publishing

Penton Media, publications include *Restaurant Hospitality*, 249 W. 17th St., New York, NY 10011, (212) 204-4200, www.penton.com

Pizza Today, 908 S. Eighth St., #200, Louisville, KY 40203, (800) 489-8324, (502) 736-9500, www.pizzatoday.com

QSR: The Magazine of Quick Service Restaurant Success, 4905 Pine Cone Dr., #2, Durham, NC 27727, (800) 662-4834, ext. 120, (919) 489-1916, www.qsrmagazine.com

The Restaurant Business Start-up Guide, Paul Daniels, Venture Marketing

Restaurant Management, www.rmgtmagazine.com

Restaurant Success by the Numbers: A Money-Guy's Guide to Opening the Next Hot Spot, Roger Fields, Ten Speed Press

Restaurants and Institutions, Reed Business Information, (800) 323-4958, www.rimag.com

Running a Restaurant For Dummies, Michael Garvey, Andrew G. Dismore, Health H. Dismore, For Dummies

Special Events magazine, 17383 W. Sunset Blvd, Suite A220, Pacific Palisades, CA 90272, (800) 543-4116, (310) 230-7160, www.specialevents.com

Specialty Retail Report, 195 Hanover St., Hanover, MA 02339, (800) 936-6297, (781) 312-1055, www.specialtyretail.com

Start Your Own Food Truck Business, Entrepreneur Press and Rich Mintzer

Trademark: Legal Care for Your Business and Product Name, Stephen Elias, Nolo Press, (800) 992-6656

Music Licensing Agencies

American Society of Composers Authors and Publishers (ASCAP), (800) 95-ASCAP, www.ascap.com

Broadcast Music Inc., www.bmi.com

SESAC Inc., 55 Music Square East, Nashville, TN 37203, (615) 320-0055, www.sesac.com

Successful Food Service Business Owners

Borealis Breads, Jim Amaral, P.O. Box 1800, Wells, ME 04090-1800, (207) 641-8800, www.borealisbreads.com

Charleston Hospitality Group, LLC, Sam Mustafa, 209 Meeting St., Charleston, SC 29401, (866) 969-6690, www.Charlestonhospitalitygroup.com

Cuisine Unlimited, Maxine Turner, 4641 S. Cherry St., Salt Lake City, UT 84123, (801) 268-2332, www.cuisineunlimited.com

Freddy's Frozen Custard & Steakburgers, Scott Redler, 1445 N. Rock Rd., #210, Wichita, KS 67206, (316) 260-8282, www.freddysfrozencustard.com

Kenny's Great Pies, Kenny Burts, 5200 Highlands Parkway SE, Smyrna, GA 30082, (707) 333-0043, www.kennysusa.com

The Melting Pot, Brian Neel, www.meltingpot.com

Meyerhof's & Cuisine M, Ann Crane, 17805 Sky Park Cir., Ste. B, Irvine, CA 92614, (949) 261-6178, www.meyerhofs.com

Stefano's Trattoria, Stefano LaCommare, 1425 Tuskawilla Rd., Winter Springs, FL 32708, (407) 659-0101, www.stefanos-trattoria.com

Glossary

Arabica beans: a kind of coffee bean that produces superior-quality coffees that possess the greatest flavor and aromatic characteristics

BAC: blood alcohol content

Barista: a master espresso maker; a barista is an expert in both coffees and brewing

Breakdown table: a utility table in the receiving area of a food-service facility used to open, inspect, and sort incoming shipments of food and supplies

Bump-out: a term describing the addition of a food-service area to a gas station or convenience store in a configuration that resembles a sunroom or porch on a house

Comp sheet: a form on which bartenders record drinks that are given away

Comps: free food or drinks authorized by management

Corrosion-resistant materials: materials that maintain their original surface characteristics under prolonged influence of the food with which they are in contact, the normal use of cleaning compounds and bactericidal solutions, and other conditions

▲

Cross contamination: occurs when bacteria, chemicals, etc., from one product are allowed to come into contact with another product

Cupping: a process professional coffee-bean tasters use to determine the quality, acidity, and aroma of beans for selection in their blends; the process involves steeping the coffee beans, as with tea leaves, then smelling and tasting the brew at different temperatures as it cools

Curb sign: a sign placed outside a business for the posting of specials, menus, or artwork

Dayparts: a restaurant-industry term that refers to various meal cycles that occur throughout the day; typically breakfast, lunch, dinner, and early evening

Dramshop laws: statutes that impose a special liability on those in the business of producing, distributing, and selling or serving alcoholic beverages to the public

Dual-branding: when two or more brand-name operations are located in the same retail space, working cooperatively; also called dual-concepting

Food-contact surfaces: surfaces of equipment and utensils with which food normally comes into contact and surfaces from which food may drain, drip, or splash back onto surfaces normally in contact with food

Free pour: pouring alcohol without a measuring device

Front of the house: the parts of a restaurant the customer visits, including the customer service area, bar, and dining room

HVAC: an acronym for heating, ventilation, and air conditioning

Kitchenware: all multiuse utensils other than tableware

Meat jobber: a distributor that specializes in portion-controlled meat supplies for restaurants

Mystery shopper: someone who visits a restaurant as a customer in order to evaluate its performance

Online reputation management (ORM): the practice of monitoring the internet reputation of a person, brand, or business and taking appropriate action to deal with negative mentions

Pass station: the area of a restaurant where food is passed from the kitchen to the wait staff

Peel: a long-handled, shovel-like implement used by bakers to move bread, pizza, and other items around in (or out of) an oven

Robusta beans: supermarket-grade coffee beans that can be grown in any tropical or subtropical climate and are cultivated for their ease of production as opposed to their taste

Safe materials: articles (including metal, plastic, and ceramic utensils; dishes; food storage containers; pots and pans) manufactured from or composed of materials that aren't expected to affect, directly or indirectly, the characteristics of any food

Search engine optimization (SEO): the process of improving the visibility of a website or web page in search engines via unpaid or organic results

Shrinkage: a term for inventory losses

Single-service articles: any tableware, carryout utensils, or other items designed for one-time use

Smallware: includes small kitchen and bar appliances, glassware, tableware, and flatware

Table turns: how many times a table is used to serve a new customer

Tableware: eating, drinking, and serving utensils for table use such as flatware (forks, knives, and spoons), bowls, cups, serving dishes, and plates

Utensil: any item used in the storage, preparation, conveyance, or serving of food

Index

▲